AVERSIVE INTERPERSONAL BEHAVIORS

THE PLENUM SERIES IN SOCIAL/CLINICAL PSYCHOLOGY

Series Editors: C. R. Snyder

University of Kansas
Lawrence, Kansas

Current Volumes in the Series:

AGGRESSION
Biological, Developmental, and Social Perspectives
Edited by Seymour Feshbach and Jolanta Zagrodzka

AVERSIVE INTERPERSONAL BEHAVIORS
Edited by Robin M. Kowalski

COERCION AND AGGRESSIVE COMMUNITY TREATMENT
A New Frontier in Mental Health Law
Edited by Deborah L. Dennis and John Monahan

EFFICACY, AGENCY, AND SELF-ESTEEM
Edited by Michael H. Kernis

PATHOLOGICAL SELF-CRITICISM
Assessment and Treatment
Raymond M. Bergner

PROCRASTINATION AND TASK AVOIDANCE
Theory, Research, and Treatment
Joseph R. Ferrari, Judith L. Johnson, and William G. McCown

THE PSYCHOLOGY OF VANDALISM
Arnold P. Goldstein

SELF-EFFICACY, ADAPTATION, AND ADJUSTMENT
Theory, Research, and Application
Edited by James E. Maddux

SOCIAL COGNITIVE PSYCHOLOGY
History and Current Domains
David F. Barone, James E. Maddux, and C. R. Snyder

SOURCEBOOK OF SOCIAL SUPPORT AND PERSONALITY
Edited by Gregory R. Pierce, Brian Lakey, Irwin G. Sarason, and Barbara R. Sarason

---

A Continuation Order Plan is available for this series. A continuation order will bring delivery of each new volume immediately upon publication. Volumes are billed only upon actual shipment. For further information please contact the publisher.

AVERSIVE INTERPERSONAL BEHAVIORS

EDITED BY

ROBIN M. KOWALSKI
Western Carolina University
Cullowhee, North Carolina

PLENUM PRESS • NEW YORK AND LONDON

Library of Congress Cataloging-in-Publication Data

Aversive interpersonal behaviors / edited by Robin M. Kowalski.
p. cm. -- (The Plenum series in social/clinical psychology)
Includes bibliographical references and index.
ISBN 0-306-45611-7
1. Interpersonal relations. 2. Social interaction.
3. Interpersonal conflict. 4. Personality. I. Kowalski, Robin M.
II. Series.
HM132.A95 1997
302--dc21 97-23743
CIP

ISBN 0-306-45611-7

A Division of Plenum Publishing Corporation
233 Spring Street, New York, N. Y. 10013

http://www.plenum.com

10 9 8 7 6 5 4 3 2 1

Printed in the United States of America

To my niece, Sarah Bagwell King

CONTRIBUTORS

ANITA P. BARBEE, Department of Psychology, University of Louisville, Louisville, Kentucky 40223

ROY F. BAUMEISTER, Department of Psychology, Case Western Reserve University, Cleveland, Ohio 44106-7123

RICHARD BEDNARSKI, Department of Psychology, Wake Forest University, Winston-Salem, North Carolina 27109

MICHAEL R. CUNNINGHAM, Department of Psychology, University of Louisville, Louisville, Kentucky 40223

PERRI B. DRUEN, Department of Psychology, University of Louisville, Louisville, Kentucky 40223

TIMOTHY DUNCAN, Department of Psychology, Wake Forest University, Winston-Salem, North Carolina 27109

JANET R. ERICKSON, Department of Psychology, Western Carolina University, Cullowhee, North Carolina 28723

LAURA R. GREEN, Department of Psychology, Florida Atlantic University, Boca Raton, Florida 33431

DUDLEY HAMMON, Department of Psychology, Wake Forest University, Winston-Salem, North Carolina 27109

ROBIN M. KOWALSKI, Department of Psychology, Western Carolina University, Cullowhee, North Carolina 28723

MARK R. LEARY, Department of Psychology, Wake Forest University, Winston-Salem, North Carolina 27109

ROWLAND S. MILLER, Department of Psychology and Philosophy, Sam Houston State University, Huntsville, Texas 77341-2447

DEBORAH R. RICHARDSON, Department of Psychology, Florida Atlantic University, Boca Raton, Florida 33431

WILLIAM F. SHARKEY, University of Hawaii at Manoa, 2560 Campus Rd., George Hall 326, Honolulu, Hawaii 96822

KRISTIN L. SOMMER, Department of Psychology, Case Western Reserve University, Cleveland, Ohio 44106-7123

KIPLING D. WILLIAMS, School of Psychology, University of New South Wales, Sydney, NSW 2052 Australia

PREFACE

Our dealings with other people are an inevitable, important, and rewarding part of everyday life. This is most true, of course, of our more intimate friendships and romantic relationships, but our interactions with acquaintances and even strangers also help to weave the fabric of our social lives. Yet, despite the fact that we are, by nature, social creatures and derive innumerable pleasures and benefits from interacting with other people, our social encounters are often awkward, distressing, and downright unpleasant. The flair and fascination that surrounds relationships as they are just beginning fades all too quickly as people perform annoying behaviors, hurt our feelings, embarrass us in front of others, and/or deprive us of interpersonal needs by excluding us. Behaviors that we once thought were cute and endearing at some point strike us as silly, mean, and aversive.

Until recently the study of aversive interpersonal behaviors was virtually ignored, superceded by a focus on the positive characteristics of interpersonal interactions. The irony behind this focus on the positive is that, when asked to evaluate the quality of their friendships and romantic relationships, people typically rely on the frequency of negative interpersonal exchanges as opposed to positive interactions. People's memory for aversive interpersonal interactions far exceeds their memory for favorable interpersonal exchanges.

The purpose of this book is to examine the less rosy side of interpersonal relationships. As will be shown, however, this does not mean that the reader will be confronted with a completely dark, bleak look at human relationships. Rather, he or she will discover the many facets of aversive interpersonal exchanges, including their role in enhancing the quality of relationships.

Several people were instrumental in the completion of this book. Because of the difficulty inherent in editing one's own chapters, I would like to thank Mark Leary for his editorial assistance with my part of the book. He also merits recognition for being always supportive and ever ready to bounce ideas around with me. Tom Britt is responsible for the book finally being completed by supporting and encouraging me during the "aversive" times, particularly as the project drew increasingly close to its deadline. Thanks also go to Anne Simons, Ellen Houston, Cindy Snyder, Rose Pritchett, and Benjamin Davis for all of the brainstorming sessions over the past year. Finally, I would like to thank Eliot Werner, Executive Editor at Plenum, and Rick Snyder, Editor of the Social/Clinical series of which this book is a part, for their help with this book.

ROBIN M. KOWALSKI

CONTENTS

Chapter 3

Making Someone Feel Guilty: Causes, Strategies, and Consequences

Kristin L. Sommer and Roy F. Baumeister

Chapter 4

Why Would Anyone Want to Intentionally Embarrass Me?

William F. Sharkey

Chapter 5

Complaining: What's All the Fuss About?

Robin M. Kowalski and Janet R. Erickson

CHAPTER 1

THE UNDERBELLY OF SOCIAL INTERACTION

AVERSIVE INTERPERSONAL BEHAVIORS

ROBIN M. KOWALSKI

I recently read about a contest to determine who had the most creative vanity license plate. The inscription on the winning license plate was "AXN28D+." For those who, like myself, are less than skilled at decoding some of these tags, the plate translates into "Accentuate the Positive." Although certainly a valuable guide for living life, this phrase also reflects the approach that social and behavioral researchers have taken in their investigations of social interactions and relationships. Rather than focusing on the broad spectrum of human behavior, emphasizing both the positive and negative facets of personal relationships, scientists studying personal relationships have tended to "accentuate the positive."

With a few exceptions, the topics investigated in social psychology and related fields would lead one to believe that relationships are perfect, people are typically kind to one another, hurt feelings are rarely experienced, and no one ever engages in behaviors that others might find the least bit annoying. Unfortunately, this slanted research focus on the positive side of human interaction does not mirror real life. In fact, relation-

---

ROBIN M. KOWALSKI • Department of Psychology, Western Carolina University, Cullowhee, North Carolina 28723. kowalski@wcuvax1.wcu.edu

Aversive Interpersonal Behaviors, edited by Kowalski
Plenum Press, New York, 1997

ships are seldom perfect, people are often cruel to one another, hurt feelings are experienced, and people frequently engage in behaviors that others find irritating.

Perhaps because of the negative connotations surrounding these less than positive behaviors, researchers have, until recently, shied away from examining the dark side (Cupach & Spitzberg, 1994) or underbelly of interpersonal relationships. Granted, they have studied negative emotions, such as shame and guilt (Tangney & Fischer, 1995), but rarely investigated interpersonal causes of these emotions. They have examined how people respond to others' helpfulness and good will but devoted little attention to the ways we respond when others are disagreeable or mean to us. They have examined negative feelings arising from interpersonal concerns, such as loneliness (Peplau & Perlman, 1982) and social anxiety (Leary & Kowalski, 1995), but have infrequently focused on people purposefully causing other individuals to feel bad. They have also examined the role of positive relationship variables, such as social support and attachment, in handling aversive events such as breast cancer (Bolger, Foster, Vinokur, & Ng, 1996), but, again, have neglected the aversive interpersonal exchanges that characterize all relationships at one time or another and that undermine people's ability to cope.

THE COURSE OF RELATIONSHIPS AND RELATIONSHIP RESEARCH

We should not be too critical of researchers devoting scant attention to the negative side of interpersonal relationships. Indeed, the study of interpersonal relationships began in earnest only three decades ago.

A comparison of the history of relationship research and the time course of relationships suggests that research on personal relationships has followed a trajectory much like relationships themselves. Let's look at relationships first. Through their affiliations with others, people are attracted to certain individuals and not to others. Based on the patterns of attraction that emerge, personal relationships, both platonic and romantic, develop. As time passes, and the relationship deepens, two people may fall passionately in love and vow to live happily ever after. However, with the passage of more time, each individual realizes that the other is not the eighth wonder of the world after all. Behaviors that one tolerated early on, such as leaving the toilet seat up or squeezing the toothpaste from the middle, become increasingly annoying. Favors that one once did quite happily and willingly for the other person now become demands on one's time. Having never dreamed that you would intentionally do anything to hurt your partner, suddenly you find yourself making that person feel guilty for not having dinner ready. In an effort to appear in control of the relationship, you tease your partner mercilessly in front of your friends. Of course, you don't mean anything negative by this; you are really "just kidding."

An examination of research on interpersonal relationships reveals that this time table of events in personal relationships parallels the development of research in this area. Researchers, like people in the early stages of relationships, blissfully and energetically began exploring why we choose to affiliate with other people and the variables that influence with whom we choose to affiliate (Sarnoff & Zimbardo, 1961; Schachter, 1959). Then, they initiated programs of research into the variables that determine attraction (Berschied & Walster, 1978; Byrne, 1971; Newcomb, 1961). Soon afterwards, they began investigations into love (Rubin, 1970; 1973). Much as people who are falling in love have difficulty determining what love is and if, in fact, they are in love, so, too, researchers had difficulty articulating precisely what they meant by the term. Nevertheless, research progressed. Just as conflicts and disagreements arise in relationships when people do not always act as we would like or expect them to or when they engage in behaviors that we find truly annoying, so, too, researchers have now reached a point where a focus on the aversive side of interpersonal behaviors is at hand (Cupach & Spitzberg, 1994).

In light of this, the primary purpose of the present volume is to round out the theoretical picture of personal relationships and social interactions by examining the aversive interpersonal behaviors in which people all too often engage. By doing so, however, I do not mean to suggest that positive and negative interpersonal behaviors are the antithesis of one another. The positive and negative sides of relationships are not mutually exclusive any more than a person is either altogether nice or altogether mean. Just as the same individual can be "sweet as pie" one minute and "mean as a snake" the next, so any particular interpersonal relationship will show variations in the degree of positivity or negativity characterizing that relationship.

INEVITABILITY OF AVERSIVE INTERPERSONAL BEHAVIORS

Aversive interpersonal behaviors should not be viewed as an anomoly. Rather, they are an integral and inevitable part of all relationships, whether they be with romantic partners, close friends, acquaintances, co-workers, or family members. Any time two or more people relate to one another, they bring to that interaction their own relationship history, personality, attitudes, and values, as well as their own experiences with aversive interpersonal behaviors. Based upon these factors, each individual will have different perceptions of the use of aversive interpersonal behaviors, such as intentional embarrassment, teasing, or guilt-induction. For example, a person who has previously been involved with chronic teasers will display one of two reactions toward a current partner or friend who teases. On one hand, he or she may be immune to the behavior and simply ignore it. On the other hand, he or she may be hypersensitive to teasing and overreact to the other's taunts.

Aversive interpersonal behaviors are also inevitable because of the larger social and cultural dynamic in which relationships exist. Dyadic interactions do not exist in a vacuum. If they did, couples would probably get along much better than they do. Rather, a developmental-contextual perspective on relationships suggests that dyadic interpersonal interactions take place within a larger social and cultural context that limits the nature and type of particular interactions (Lerner, 1991). For example, dyadic interactions at school or work are at least partly regulated by the normative constraints of those particular settings. The school and work settings, in turn, are set within a larger community and cultural environment.

Relatedly, at the dyadic level of interaction, time spent in one relational interaction draws time away from others. In this way, interactional networks with friends and family (i.e., in-laws) can create situations that set up aversive interpersonal interactions. For example, one partner to a relationship may make the other feel guilty for spending too much time with his friends and not enough with her.

Third, no matter how perfect a match you feel a partner, friend, or roommate is, he or she will not do everything exactly as you do or perhaps as you would like it done. Although compatible in most dimensions, he may repeatedly leave the toilet seat up, she may continue to hang her panty hose in the shower, or he may squeeze the toothpaste from the middle as opposed to the bottom. Friends may fail to follow through, show up late for appointments, or betray our confidences. Although reflecting our own idiosyncratic ways of behaving, any one of these behaviors may become a pet peeve, thereby setting the stage for aversive interpersonal interactions.

THE POSITIVE SIDE OF AVERSIVE INTERPERSONAL BEHAVIORS

Although negative in their connotations, aversive interpersonal behaviors are not necessarily perceived the same way by all individuals (Spitzberg & Cupach, 1994). Positivity and negativity in relationships are relative terms. Due in part to their past relationship history, many people are seemingly more comfortable with negative than positive interpersonal behaviors. For example, people with negative self-conceptions may seek out relationships with individuals who will confirm those self-conceptions (Swann, 1983). Someone with a history of abusive relationships may be distrustful of "healthy" relationships. Many people fear intimacy and close attachments with others (Duck, 1994) and, thus, are more content in relationships in which interpersonal behaviors allow for some distance between the partners. Thus, at least for some individuals, what some people perceive as aversive interpersonal behaviors actually establish a comfort zone in relationships.

In addition, negative interpersonal behaviors are not necessarily detrimental to a relationship. Rather, the aversive behavior may ultimately benefit the relationship. In a statement that applies to both positive and negative interpersonal behaviors, Kiesler (1983) noted that, "our interpersonal actions are designed to invite, pull, elicit, draw, entice, or evoke 'restricted classes' of reactions from persons with whom we interact, especially from significant others" (p. 198). For example, people may tease or intentionally embarrass their relationship partner or friends to demonstrate camaraderie to others. Similarly, people may complain about another's behavior or induce guilt in others to get the individual to change behaviors that are, themselves, undermining the quality of the relationship. Nicely asking people to change particular behaviors is not always effective. Thus, to produce the desired effect, aversive interpersonal behaviors are invoked. On a recent episode of the television show "Real Life," cadets at the Citadel were interviewed regarding the manner in which they degrade and humiliate the first-year students. The cadets stated that their purpose for using these techniques was to induce discipline. Without the fear and humiliation, they said, the plebes would be less likely to acquire respect and discipline.

Finally, aversive interpersonal behaviors add a little excitement to most relationships. How would people ever get to make up if they never fought? Imagine how boring relationships would be if there were never any conflicts. Some of the best laughs in a relationship stem from good-natured teasing. As Duck (1994) observed, "part of the delights of intimacy comes from knowledge of the horrors of rejection; a certain measure of the satisfaction from being in good relationships comes from reflection on the opposite situation" (p. 15).

CARRYING AVERSIVE BEHAVIORS TOO FAR

Although potentially adaptive to relationship functioning, aversive interpersonal behaviors may be taken too far. Some people overstep the bounds of appropriate interpersonal interactions. For example, nearly everyone has had an experience with an individual who did not know when to stop teasing. People who go too far in their use of aversive interpersonal behaviors are perceived as maladjusted (Kiesler, 1991). Most of the aversive interpersonal behaviors that one could enumerate represent interpersonal transactions with an individual with whom one has at least passing familiarity. For example, rarely, if ever, would a person tease someone whom they did not know or intentionally embarrass a total stranger. Maladjusted people, however, appear to be unable to regulate the appropriateness of their interpersonal behaviors.

In addition, the aversive interpersonal behaviors that are invoked by "maladjusted" individuals are typically more extreme than those enacted by "normal" individuals. Thus, episodes of intentional embarrassment initiated by maladjusted people will be carried much farther than similar episodes commenced by more adjusted individuals.

Finally, maladjusted individuals adopt a rigid interpersonal style, reflecting their limited repertoire of interpersonal behaviors (Kiesler, 1991). Thus, not only are their behaviors more likely to be aversive than those of more interpersonally adjusted people in terms of their interpersonal impact, but they are also more likely to be aversive simply in terms of their repetitiveness. Thus, although aversive interpersonal behaviors may themselves not be detrimental to relationships when enacted in moderation, the extreme, continuous, and inappropriate use of such behaviors may hurt relationships deeply.

HOW AVERSIVE INTERPERSONAL BEHAVIORS WORK

Although each of the behaviors examined in this volume differs from the others in its specifics, the aversiveness of aversive interpersonal behaviors is triggered, in part, by the unexpected, unexplainable nature of the behaviors. That people would ostracize others, induce guilt, or intentionally embarrass someone flies in the face of the notion that interpersonal relationships are mutually satisfying and fulfilling. We expect people to be nice to one another and to treat each other kindly. Of course, when they do, their good behavior is seldom acknowledged. It is taken simply as common courtesy. Let that same individual, however, have a bad day, display a negative emotion, or say something untoward to us and the whole nature of an interpersonal interaction changes. We may well remember any misdeed for some time to come and not hesitate to raise reminders of a particular incident.

Unlike positive events and behaviors, negative actions trigger attributional searches (Holtzworth-Munroe & Jacobson, 1985). We immediately seek to understand why we were made to feel the way we were or why another person would have chosen to behave negatively toward us. In essence, we are far less likely to seek meaning for positive than negative behaviors. "People are quite willing to endure pain, deprivation, and other aversive events if there is some meaning such as a purpose or justification or an increase in self-worth" (Baumeister, 1991, p. 233). When interactions proceed blissfully, we seldom question why things are going so well. However, when the interaction gets derailed, we attempt to find explanations for the events that transpired.

OVERVIEW OF THE PRESENT VOLUME

The topics covered in this book represent only a fraction of the aversive interpersonal behaviors in which people engage. To have included all such behaviors within a single volume would have presented an aversive situation all of its own. The topics that are included represent aversive interpersonal behaviors that have only recently begun to be investigated but that reveal remarkable similarities as will be discussed in the final chapter. In Chapter 2, Rowland Miller discusses the fact that the majority of our aversive behaviors are directed toward those to whom we are closest. In the context of this discussion, he describes eight specific sources of aversiveness in close relationships. Kristin Sommer and Roy Baumeister discuss guilt-induction in Chapter 3, including an examination of both the positive and negative implications of inducing guilt in others. They point, specifically, to the relationship-enhancing functions of guilt-induction through the spreading of emotional distress among the relationship partners and through the enacting of reparative behaviors on the part of the target of the guilt-induction. Following this, William Sharkey examines the "aversiveness" of intentional embarrassment in Chapter 4, raising the question of why people would desire intentionally to lead others to lose face. As with guilt-induction, however, Sharkey points out some of the positive relationship functions and implications of intentional embarrassment. In Chapter 5, Kowalski and Erickson discuss the motivations for and consequences of complaining, an interpersonal behavior in which everyone engages at least occasionally. After discussing the elements that make complaining aversive, they focus on perhaps the most aversive of complainers, the help-rejecting complainer. Mark Leary and his colleagues discuss egotism, narcissism, and conceit in Chapter 6. Following a discussion of why egotism is aversive, they examine why people would elect to convey their egotism to others. In Chapter 7, Kipling Williams discusses the aversiveness of ostracism within the context of a need-threat model of ostracism. Specifically, he proposes that ostracism prevents people from satisfying their needs for belonging, self-esteem, control, and meaningful existence. Deborah Richardson and Laura Green focus on nondirect aggression in Chapter 8. Unlike direct aggressive strategies, indirect aggression frequently allows the aggressor to remain unidentified—or at least his or her intention unknown. According to Michael Cunningham and his colleagues (Chapter 9), any of the aversive behaviors may initially be perceived by the targets of the behaviors as minor irritations. However, much like the physical allergy process, repeated exposure to these behaviors may lead individuals to develop social allergies. The book concludes in Chapter 10 with an integrative look at features common to aversive interpersonal behaviors, including an examination of the positive, relationship-enhancing side of these behaviors.

REFERENCES

Baumeister, R. (1991). *Meanings of life*. New York: Guilford.

Berscheid, E., & Walster, E. (1978). *Interpersonal attraction* (2nd ed.). Reading, MA: Addison-Wesley.

Bolger, N., Foster, M., Vinokur, A.D., & Ng, R. (1996). Close relationships and adjustment to a life crisis: The case of breast cancer. *Journal of Personality and Social Psychology, 70,* 283–294.

Byrne, D. (1971). *The attraction paradigm*. New York: Academic Press.

Cupach, W.R., & Spitzberg, B.H. (Eds.) (1994). *The dark side of interpersonal communication*. Hillsdale, NJ: Lawrence Erlbaum.

Duck, S. (1994). Strategems, spoils, and a serpent's tooth: On the delights and dilemmas of personal relationships. In W.R. Cupach & B.H. Spitzberg (Eds.), *The dark side of interpersonal communication* (pp. 3–24). Hillsdale, NJ: Lawrence Erlbaum.

Holtzworth-Munroe, A., & Jacobson, J.S. (1985). Causal attributions of marital couples: When do they search for causes? What do they conclude when they do? *Journal of Personality and Social Psychology, 48,* 1398–1412.

Kiesler, D.J. (1983). The 1982 interpersonal circle: A taxonomy for complementarity in human transactions. *Psychological Review, 90,* 185–214.

Kiesler, D.J. (1991). Interpersonal methods of assessment and diagnosis. In C.R. Snyder & D.R. Forsyth (Eds.), *Handbook of social and clinical psychology* (pp. 438–468). New York: Pergamon.

Leary, M.R., & Kowalski, R.M. (1995). *Social anxiety*. New York: Guilford.

Lerner, R.M. (1991). Changing organism-context relations as the basic process of development: A developmental contextual perspective. *Developmental Psychology, 27,* 27–32.

Newcomb, T.M. (1961). *The acquaintance process*. New York: Holt.

Peplau, L.A., & Perlman, D. (1982). Perspectives on loneliness. In L.A. Peplau & D. Perlman (Eds.), *Loneliness: A sourcebook of current theory, research, and therapy*. New York: Wiley.

Rubin, Z. (1970). Measurement of romantic love. *Journal of Personality and Social Psychology, 16,* 265–273.

Rubin, Z. (1973). *Liking and loving: An invitation to social psychology*. New York: Holt, Rinehart, & Winston.

Sarnoff, I., & Zimbardo, P.G. (1961). Anxiety, fear, and social affiliation. *Journal of Abnormal and Social Psychology, 62,* 356–363.

Schachter, S. (1959). *The psychology of affiliation*. Stanford, CA: Stanford University Press.

Spitzberg, B.H., & Cupach, W.R. (1994). Dark side dénouement. In W.R. Cupach & B.H. Spitzberg (Eds.), *The dark side of interpersonal communication* (pp. 315–320). Hillsdale, NJ: Lawrence Erlbaum.

Swann, W.B., Jr. (1983). Self-verification: Bringing social reality into harmony with the self. In J. Suls & A.G. Greenwald (Eds.), *Social psychology perspectives* (Vol. 2, pp. 33–66). Hillsdale, NJ: Erlbaum.

Tangney, J.P., & Fischer, K.W. (1995). *Self-conscious emotions: The psychology of shame, guilt, embarrassment, and pride*. New York: Guilford.

CHAPTER 2

WE ALWAYS HURT THE ONES WE LOVE

AVERSIVE INTERACTIONS IN CLOSE RELATIONSHIPS

ROWLAND S. MILLER

Some marriages work. Now and then, two people somehow manage to fulfill the many psychological and practical duties of marital partners with contentment and delight, remaining intimate, interdependent, and happy with each other for several straight decades. *Most* marriages do *not* work, however, especially by a criterion of unbroken bliss. The chance that a new marriage will ultimately end in divorce continues to exceed 50% in the United States (U.S. Bureau of the Census, 1995), but that datum unquestionably underestimates the actual base rate of distress: If one also accepts as broken those marriages in which the spouses (a) are separated but not divorced or (b) are simply miserable, the real rate of failure probably exceeds 70% (Martin & Bumpass, 1989; U.S. Bureau of the Census, 1995).

This really isn't news to most people. For instance, students who take my college course in Close Relationships know exactly what the current American divorce rate is (Miller, 1991a). On the other hand, my students are also quite certain that a high risk of divorce doesn't apply to *them*. When

---

ROWLAND S. MILLER • Department of Psychology and Philosophy, Sam Houston State University, Huntsville, Texas 77341-2447. psy_rsm@shsu.edu

Aversive Interpersonal Behaviors, edited by Kowalski
Plenum Press, New York, 1997

I asked, the same people who cited a population divorce rate of 53% calculated that their personal chances of ever getting a divorce were only 18%. (Many of them undoubtedly had some unwelcome surprises ahead.) Unrealistic optimism like this is rather routine; people ordinarily underestimate their personal risks of encountering a wide variety of unwanted events (Taylor & Brown, 1988). However, cockeyed confidence may leave people unprepared for the inevitable difficulties they will face, especially if misplaced surety leads them to fail to prevent problems that would have otherwise been avoidable.

It is in this light that one can argue that our modern science of relationships, as rich as it is, does us a disservice. People may underestimate the difficulties involved in maintaining a satisfying close relationship in part because studies of intimacy routinely emphasize its benefits rather than its drawbacks. Science has been preoccupied with the rewards and attractions that draw us to close relationships (e.g., Baumeister & Leary, 1995). It has had relatively little to say about the pains and perils we face when we get there. As Steve Duck (1994, p. 5) observed, "in the bulk of personal relationships research, the underlying assumption is not only that relationships should be nice but also that people are nice." According to the typical textbook, people thoughtfully strive to make themselves attractive to one another, they share important disclosures to build trust and intimacy, and they considerately pleasure one another in order to maintain interdependent satisfaction. Only rarely, if ever, are they obstinate, tactless, sullen, selfish, impolite, careless, and neglectful.

In real life, however, people seem to be less adorable. They come to dinner unwashed and unkempt, they misrepresent their heartfelt feelings, and they fail to call when they are running late. They disclose secrets, ignore others' wishes, and argue about who did the dishes last. Too often, the actual transactions shared by family members fail to approximate the rosy, supportive, intimate ideal that implicitly underlies a "happy" marriage (Stafford & Dainton, 1994). Most models of close relationships take too little heed of this fact and, to an important degree, relationship researchers have overlooked a vital truth (Miller, 1991b): *Married people are meaner to each other than they are to total strangers.*

In fact, Birchler, Weiss, and Vincent (1975) compared the manners in which people interacted with their spouses and with total strangers. In both casual conversation and during a problem-solving task, people were decorous and polite when dealing with a person they did not know well. They refrained from criticism, suppressed any frustration, and swallowed signs of disapproval. With their spouses, however, people were much more obnoxious. They were often inattentive. They interrupted their spouses, criticized and disparaged them, and openly disagreed. Compared to their congenial behavior toward the strangers, they were quite impolite, and it was clear that "loving" others had little to do with treating them cordially.

Indeed, many of us are routinely less courteous and tactful with our spouses than we are with most others (see Miller, 1991b). If a friend serves us a meal and the peas are cold, the mashed potatoes are lumpy, the steak is gristly, and the beer is lukewarm, we may keep on smiling, say the meal is "fine," and be grateful for the favor. In contrast, if our spouses serve us a similar meal, few of us may be able to refrain from mentioning its deficiencies. Worse, our feedback may not be delivered mildly; whether intended or not, abrasive sarcasm or caustic rebuke may creep into our voices. In a similar manner, a coworker's halitosis is rarely mentioned, but a spouse's bad breath is routinely announced and often ridiculed.

This abiding tendency to treat close intimates more harshly than most others is the topic of this chapter. Obviously, intimacy does not make us immune from unpleasantness. To the contrary, I think that we should *expect* close relationships to develop a seamy underbelly over time. Please allow me to explain in the pages that follow.

OUR FOCUS OF ATTENTION

Along with the many riches we obtain from close partnerships there usually come more frequent frustrations, aggravations, and annoyances than we encounter anywhere else. In addition, the most hurtful interactions we are ever likely to have will probably be with those who say (or once said) they love us. Close relationships are the source of our most meaningful interpersonal rewards, but they are also the source of our most hurtful and most frequent punishments.

In focusing on this "dark side" of close relationships, I do not mean to diminish the value of interdependent intimacy with others. Few people wish to live without meaningful interpersonal attachments. Indeed, a "need to belong," a fundamental drive to establish a minimal level of inclusion, acceptance, and closeness with other people, may be a basic motive that characterizes our species (Baumeister & Leary, 1995). A happy marriage is of enormous benefit to one's health, inoculating one against a variety of stressors that would otherwise take a toll (Burman & Margolin, 1992; Coombs, 1991), and most marriages are apparently healthier, on average, than being single, widowed, or divorced (Lynch, 1979). Close relationships are vital, irreplaceable, essential parts of our lives. That doesn't mean that they are always (or even *routinely*) wonderful, however, and I think that evenhanded explication of the aversive aspects of close relationships is long overdue.

I should also note that the drawbacks of close relationships have not been overlooked entirely; some relationship researchers *have* taken note of the downside of intimacy. In a cautionary chapter, Elaine Hatfield (1984) argued that there are several sensible reasons why people might be reluctant to make the cognitive, emotional, and behavioral commitments that intimacy entails. Because openness and self-disclosure are defining elements of intimacy, people may fear that their sensitive secrets will be revealed or turned against them. They may dread the loss of autonomy and control that comes from sharing one's life with others. They may also shudder at the prospect that they may someday be abandoned by those on whom they rely. Hatfield insightfully noted that intimacy could be frightening as well as alluring.

This point was also evident in several contributions to a marvelous volume edited by Bill Cupach and Brian Spitzberg (1994) that focused exclusively on botched interactions and relational dysfunction. Spitzberg and Cupach reported that "closeness often breeds undue influence, loss of identity, loss of privacy, frustrations of individual goals and personal projects, and the possibilities of great psychological and even physical harm" (1994, p. 317). Thus, the disadvantages of close relationships have attracted some attention, and some particular problems, such as the difficulties faced by people who are married to alcoholic (e.g., Schafer, Birchler, & Fals-Stewart, 1994) or abusive (e.g., Marshall, 1994) spouses, have been studied extensively.

On the other hand, a striking asymmetry in relationship research still exists. Studies examine "attraction" and "relationship maintenance"; they rarely inspect "rejection" and "ennui and decay." Investigators rarely set out to scrutinize the *negative* interchanges that characterize close relationships just as thoroughly as rewarding ones do (but see Gottman, 1994). This is regrettable because, as Duck (1994) asserted, "an understanding of the full range of relationship processes can only be increased if one extends our timely detailed lists of overlooked behaviors that doom, disturb, or challenge relationships; or of the distressing side effects of relationships themselves; or of the incompetent performance of the behaviors that normally promote relationships" (p. 14). With that exhortation in mind, this chapter focuses on the ordinary but insensitive, untidy, thoughtless, and indecorous things people do around intimates that they are careful not to do around strangers.

My primary concern will be with the many small *unanticipated* hassles, frustrations, nuisances, and disappointments that relational partners impose on one another *when they do not intend to injure* each other, and want the relationship to continue. There are occasions, of course, when angry partners are momentarily aggressive or vengeful, and want to inflict harm. However, as important as those episodes may be (see Marshall, 1994), I will focus instead on the nature of *ordinary* interaction in close relationships, which is often less supportive, affirming, and pleasant than loving partners want it to be. In general, over time, the net outcomes close partners extract from their relationships will be lower than they anticipated because they encounter more lazy neglect and impoliteness from their partners than they thought they would. I think this is typically true of close relationships but too often has been overlooked.

Of course, no one has missed the universal fact that unhappy partners are meaner to each other than happy partners are. A robust literature demonstrates that dissatisfaction both results from and causes reduced rewards in close relationships (e.g., Birchler et al., 1975; Gottman, 1994; Gottman & Levenson, 1992). Dissatisfaction unquestionably intensifies several of the unwanted phenomena I will describe.

However, I will assert the broader point that *normal* processes that pervade *most* partnerships ordinarily make close relationships more aversive than the participants expected them to be. This is not to say that, on balance, close relationships are usually more punishing than they are rewarding (although, if one judges by the American marital record, most of them may be!). Certainly, the rewards of closeness are unique and irreplaceable and often outweigh the costs. On the other hand, the simple truth is that the usual base rate of thoughtless, churlish impoliteness is higher in close relationships than in most of the other meaningful interpersonal exchanges we transact (Birchler et al., 1975; Vincent, Weiss, & Birchler, 1975). On any given day, 44% of us are likely to be annoyed by a close relational partner (Averill, 1982). On average, young adults encounter 8.7 aggravating hassles in their romantic relationships *each week* (Perlman, 1989). Most people (66%) get angry at somebody in any given week (Averill, 1982), and every seven days *most* young adults will be distressed by different encounters with a lover's (a) criticism, (b) stubbornness, (c) selfishness, *and* (d) lack of conscientiousness, at least once (Perlman, 1989). Over time, people are meaner to their intimate partners than to anyone else they know. Why is that?

SOURCES OF AVERSIVENESS IN CLOSE RELATIONSHIPS

A variety of discrete (although occasionally overlapping) influences contribute to unanticipated indecorous behavior and unwanted outcomes among relational partners. Most of them are *passive* events that occur naturally as relationships develop, making them very hard—if not impossible—to avoid. At least one of them is a more active phenomenon, however, emerging from partners' intentional (if inept) behavior toward each other. I will save that one for last.

ACCESS TO WEAPONRY

As intimacy develops, partners become privy to increasingly detailed and sensitive information about each other. In the terms of social penetration theory (Altman & Taylor, 1973), both the "breadth" and "depth" of the knowledge partners have of one another gradually increase over time. Slowly but surely, our close partners learn things about us that are known to few others.

Most partners self-disclose willingly, and the exchange of personal secrets is one of the defining characteristics of intimacy (Walster, Walster, & Berscheid, 1978). Nevertheless, access to sensitive information gives intimate partners unique weapons with which injury, accidental or otherwise, may be done. "Since intimates know each other's essential weaknesses, they are in a position to wound each other in the worst possible way" (Davis, 1973, p. 265). They need not intend such harm for it to occur. Without wishing to, people may inadvertently reveal partners' secrets (Petronio, Olson, & Dollar, 1989), hurt their feelings (Shapiro, Baumeister, & Kessler, 1991), or cause them chagrin (Miller, 1996), because of their special knowledge. Intimacy gives partners the power to do more harm, even involuntarily, than anyone else can.

MISPLACED EXPECTATIONS AND UNWELCOME SURPRISES

Some of the things we learn about our partners are likely to be both unanticipated and undesired. Intimate partners are much more likely than other people to become aware of a person's current addictions and eccentricities, and past convictions and breakdowns. This may take some time, however, and partners may have made substantial investments in a partnership before the bad news surfaces. People may find themselves intimately connected to someone who now seems less desirable than he or she first appeared.

This may not be an uncommon occurrence. Bernard Murstein (1987) noted that information about a prospective partner may vary in its salience and utility as a relationship develops. A premarital couple may be fully informed about their joint tastes in food and music, for instance, but be completely unaware of their divergent interests in parenting. Too often, couples may not stumble upon their consequential incompatibilities until they have already become quite inconvenient.

Further, there may be two ways in which such unwelcome surprises can occur. First, people may learn undesired things they didn't know; these may be either idiosyncratic data that are unique to a particular relationship (as described above), or generic dilemmas that confront most partnerships. As an example of the latter, consider the effects of parenting on most marriages. The common expectations are that rearing children is fun, the kids themselves are sweet and precious, and that having children will bring the parents "closer together" (LeMasters & DeFrain, 1989). The reality, of course, is that "after the birth of a child the prognosis for the course of the marital relationship is unequivocally grim" (Stafford & Dainton, 1994, p. 270). There are things one learns for the first time about a partner's generosity, compassion, and responsibility when one is faced with a squalling, colicky infant at 3:19 a.m. The same events that are often expected to cement and reinforce a couple's love for one another instead provide unparalled potential for "disappointment with the spouse, anger at the spouse, resentment toward the spouse, and marital dissatisfaction" (Reichle & Montada, 1994, p. 222).

Unfortunate surprises can also occur when data that are already known prove to have been misread or misunderstood. In almost a third of romantic relationships, for instance, a quality that initially attracts one partner to another later becomes a source of dissatisfaction (Felmlee, 1995). Remarkably often, desirable "virtues" in a fiancé(e) become unattractive "vices" in a spouse as the partners' perceptions and roles change; initial caring and attentiveness can turn out to be jealous possessiveness, and carefree playfulness may later be judged to be irresponsible immaturity (Whitehouse, 1981). In this fashion, through both lack of information and the misuse of what they know, too many people probably find themselves cruelly disillusioned when their romantic expectations about the joys of their close relationships are replaced with a disappointing reality.

THE LOSS OF ILLUSION

Not only may people have insufficient information about their partners, some of what they think they know simply isn't true. People ordinarily construct idealized images of their romantic partners that portray their lovers as (a) more desirable people than they really are (Murray, Holmes, & Griffin, 1996) who have (b) more in common with them than they really do (Levinger & Breedlove, 1966). In this sense, love really *is* "blind"; people routinely ignore or underestimate the faults of those they otherwise find attractive (Murray & Holmes, 1996). They also tend to think their partners love them just as much as they love their partners, even when that isn't true (Miller, 1993). As a result, people glorify their close relationships, unrealistically believing them to be better than those of other people (Van Lange & Rusbult, 1995).

These positive illusions are pleasant fictions that help people shrug off their partners' improprieties as unintended, unimportant accidents (Bradbury & Fincham, 1990). However, because they *are* illusions, they are likely to be adversely affected by time and experience. In particular, a partner's transgressions are likely to have a disproportionate impact on one's attributions and judgments as they inevitably accumulate over time. Negative, unexpected behavior is especially salient and memorable, leading observers to form more extreme judgments of an actor than analogous positive behavior does (Fiske, 1980). This asymmetry in interpersonal perception, coupled with the initial glorification of the partner that typifies closeness, leads to only one path that evaluations of our intimates can follow: *down*. Over time, small irritations that are initially minimized or ignored may gain considerable weight as truth gradually replaces illusion. Before they are married, for example, a couple's conflicts may be completely unrelated to their love for each other, whereas, two years later, the same conflicts may predict a couple's (lack of) love quite well (Kelly, Huston, & Cate, 1985).

The Erosion of Novelty

The passage of time and experience also adversely affects the exciting freshness and sense of discovery that can underlie new relationships. To the extent new partners are alluring because of their sheer *novelty*, they will become less attractive as they become well known.

Falling in love is invigorating. In other species, for example, novelty has a rather dramatic influence on sexual arousal. When a male rat is paired with a receptive female, he will copulate repeatedly until he seems to be sexually exhausted and is uninterested in further mating; however, if the original partner is then replaced with a new female in estrus, his interest and energy are renewed. By continuing to replace an old partner with a new one, researchers can elicit two to three times as many ejaculations from a male as would have been possible with only the single partner (Dewsbury, 1981).

The generalizability of this effect to humans is uncertain, but it's not unlikely. Certainly, both romantic love for our partners (Tucker & Aron, 1993) and the frequency of our sexual intercourse with them (Blumstein & Schwartz, 1983) decline markedly over time. When people are infatuated with a new attraction, they may be unable to appreciate how thoroughly familiar, predictable, and potentially unexciting that same lover will be 30 years later.

Reduced Effort

The amount of effort people put in to pleasing a partner is likely to wane as well. Once a courtship is over and a partner has been won, people ordinarily relax their careful crafting of their self-presentations and try less hard to make consistently favorable impressions on those from whom acceptance is assured. In fact, it is a curious irony of intimacy that we are typically more concerned with impressing those who do not know us well than we are with impressing those who already like us. Mark Leary and John Nezlek tracked all the interactions of 179 college students for a week and found that the students reported steadily lower motivation to impress their same-sex friends than to make good impressions on (a) same-sex acquaintances and strangers and on (b) anyone of the opposite sex (Leary et al., 1994). When we can rely on others' approbation and approval, we stop trying so hard to get them to like us. Thus it is that a suitor who never appears for breakfast without his beard well trimmed and his cologne apparent becomes a spouse who shows up in his underwear, unwashed and unshaven, and then steals the last doughnut.

In fact, people are generally lazy social animals. Much of their social behavior is rather mindless (Langer, 1989), they constantly take shortcuts in reasoning and fail to think things through (Krull & Erickson, 1995), and they reduce effort on group tasks when they can get away with it (Karau & Williams, 1993). Our default strategy is to coast when we can. This means that, everything else being equal, the active, effortful things that people do to pleasure their partners and maintain their relationships are likely to diminish over time.

Indeed, several relationship maintenance strategies take work (Baxter & Dindia, 1990). Active attention, consideration, and restraint are all routinely involved in keeping a partner happy, and each may decline as habituation to a partner—and simple fatigue—set in. Consider the desirable technique of accommodation. Committed individuals often actively suppress their authentic, angry responses to rudeness or thoughtlessness from their partners, biting their tongues and allowing the partner's malfeasance to go unanswered (Rusbult, Yovetich, & Verette, 1996). Such restraint takes *effort*, however, and, over time, partners may be more likely to "let him (or her) have it" not because they love each other any less but because they are not trying as hard to be adorable.

Interdependency Ups the Ante

Even as disillusionment sets in and excitement begins to wane, partners may find themselves interacting more closely and more frequently with each other than ever before. Our intimate partners control particularly valuable, sometimes exclusive rewards, and our interactions with them are especially broad and frequent. This gives them unmatched *opportunity* to cause us grief. Even if they are ordinarily nicer to us than most people are, and even if they are nice to us most of the time, we are still likely to encounter more thoughtless or accidental mistreatment at the hands of our intimates than from anyone else.

This is true in part because people tend to reduce their other social contacts as they invest more of their time and energy in a close relationship. As a primary partnership develops, people see less of their friends (Johnson & Leslie, 1982), and generally interact with fewer other people, less often, and for shorter periods of time (Milardo, Johnson, & Huston, 1983). Close relationships usurp disproportionate amounts of the time we spend in meaningful contact with others.

This close, prevalent contact means that we will be more affected by, for instance, the emotional distress (Hokanson, Hummer, & Butler, 1991) and work stress (MacEwen & Barling, 1994) of intimate partners than by the similar difficulties of others. Our partners' problems *are* our problems, too (Turner, 1994), and interdependency magnifies the burdens of social support well beyond those we face in our casual relations with coworkers and acquaintances.

Moreover, because we depend on our close partners for specialized, highly prized rewards that are not available elsewhere (Turner, Foa, & Foa, 1971), they have an unique ability to hurt us by failing to provide the goods we expect. When close relationships falter, there is farther for us to fall.

Contrast Effects

There is a special pain associated with the *loss* of approval and regard from others that may exceed the distress of never having had that acceptance in the first place. Aronson and Linder (1965) demonstrated that people were especially sensitive to gains and losses in esteem from others, so that, for instance, losing a friend was more hurtful than having a constant enemy.

In fact, the influence of such gains and losses in interpersonal benefits led Aronson (1992) to formulate a wry "law of marital infidelity": Once a relationship's heady and exciting developmental period is finished, the best new gains can only come from newcomers outside the established partnership, whereas the worst losses one can possibly incur can only come from those on whom one already depends. Partners are enticed by new attractions outside the relationship and punished by losses they encounter within, putting an existing partnership at a disadvantage over time.

Whether or not this occurs, there's little doubt that inattention, thoughtlessness, or outright betrayal by a close, trusted partner is much more painful than similar treatment from a stranger or foe (e.g., Jones & Burdette, 1994). Basic perceptual processes may help make this so. When trust is violated and close partners treat us badly, the stark contrast between their past kindnesses and their current neglect can make their inconsiderateness seem worse than it is; past experiences routinely influence our perception of current events (Gleitman, 1991). In addition, people's subjective utility curves are ordinarily steeper for losses than for gains (Kahneman & Tversky, 1982). That is, people are *loss-averse;* they react more strongly to the threat of losing what they already have than they do to the promise of gaining comparable outcomes that they do not yet have, even when the two results are logically equivalent. In this sense, relational partners really are able to hurt us more powerfully than they can reward us, both because the harm seems greater and because it touches us more deeply.

The Threat of Exclusion

Loss-aversion may motivate a final source of difficulty that is somewhat less passive than the preceding problems in resulting from a specific shift in behavioral strategy that occurs after a relationship is formed. The process of *seeking* acceptance and approval one does not yet have may engender more appropriate, more desirable behavior in people than does the desire to *avoid losing* esteem one already possesses. This asymmetry may mean that people who are perfectly adept at pleasing a partner during a courtship may have difficulty later on when they try to avoid antagonizing the same partner. When they try to keep others from falling out of love with them, people may behave less effectively than they do when they get those others to fall in love with them in the first place.

For example, Schreindorfer, Leary, and Keith (1996) placed young adults in interviews with a stranger who, they believed, could decide to (a) put them in a desirable group which was just being formed or (b) exclude them from the new group. In the context of the experiment, these were simply two different ways of saying the same thing: The stranger would decide whether they were in or out. However, the first situation emphasized social inclusion whereas the other underscored exclusion, and people behaved differently in the two conditions. When they were threatened with exclusion and were trying to avoid rejection, people made poorer impressions on observers than they did when they sought inclusion and acceptance; they said more negative things about themselves, portrayed themselves less positively, and were less liked.

Thus, as unwelcome surprises, reduced effort, and the erosion of novelty gradually make a close relationship less and less delightful, people may respond to the specter of disappointment and decay with behavior that is noticeably less appealing than the actions that originally attracted their partners. In this fashion, instead of continuing to woo their partners, they may actually begin to worry them.

ADDITIONAL COMPLICATIONS

All eight of the phenomena described above *routinely* occur in close relationships and, collectively, they produce unanticipated outcomes that make those partnerships more aversive than they were expected to be. Through unavoidable opportunity and lazy lack of restraint, intimate partners are likely to say and do more hurtful things to those they love than to anyone else. These are pervasive processes that will probably confront all close relationships at one time or another, but there are further factors that may influence how unmanageable they are and how much damage they do. I'll consider three additional complications.

INDIVIDUAL DIFFERENCES

When a partner disappoints, various personality traits may influence a person's response. Some people manage their anger better than others (Tangney et al., 1996), for instance, and destructive responses to anger are linked to fundamental individual differences such as insecure attachment styles (Dutton, Saunders, Starzomski, & Bartholomew, 1994) and the Big Five personality traits of (high) neuroticism and (low) agreeableness and conscientiousness (Buss, 1991). Clearly, different people may react to a particular provocation in quite different ways.

Anger management is just one example, however, and individual differences in attachment style, negative affectivity, gender role, hostility, defensiveness, and a variety of other traits unquestionably have broad effects on incipient dissatisfaction in close relationships (e.g., Karney, Bradbury, Fincham, & Sullivan, 1994; Newton, Kiecolt-Glaser, Glaser, & Malarkey, 1995; Shaver & Hazan, 1994). Moreover, to the extent that influential traits are distributed differently among men and women, heterosexual relationships may be especially complex.

In fact, women tend to experience more intense emotions than men do (Brody & Hall, 1993) and are more likely to express their feelings to their partners (Ickes, 1993). They also think about their relationships more often and more thoroughly than men do (Acitelli & Young, 1996). As a result, when women initiate complaints and criticisms, they are likely to be met, more often than they would like, by passive retreat and withdrawal by men who are reluctant to engage in an emotional exchange (Christensen & Heavy, 1990). This can be very frustrating (Markman, Stanley, & Blumberg, 1994), and may easily exacerbate the discontent that prompted the complaint.

THE ROLE OF CULTURE

Even as our personalities leave some of us impulsively unable to delay gratification (Shoda, Mischel & Peake, 1990), our culture encourages us to insist on personal fulfillment and immediate gratification in our close relationships. A sense of entitlement pervades modern marriages, so that nothing less than full-fledged delight is to be tolerated (Attridge & Berscheid, 1994).

This has not always been so. Historically, marriage has more often been considered a practical convenience than a matter of love (Brehm, 1992). Only in this century, for instance, has romantic love been considered to be a necessary prerequisite for marrying someone. It is now, however; almost no one says they would marry a person perfect in every other way, if they did not love him or her (Simpson, Campbell, & Berscheid, 1986). Nevertheless, such love is not supposed to infringe overmuch on one's autonomy; where the culture once praised selflessness and self-restraint, it now promotes personal freedom and speaking one's mind (Kidd, 1975).

Worse, if disappointment occurs, we are implicitly urged to move on and pursue contentment elsewhere. In the last few generations, many economic, legal, religious, filial, and social barriers to divorce have been dismantled, while access to potential alternative partners has skyrocketed (Attridge & Berscheid, 1994). Combine (a) our greedy orientations to marriage with (b) the culture's support for relational impermanence and (c) the unexpected aversiveness that characterizes closeness, and you get a mixture that is lethal to most marriages.

SEVERE CONSEQUENCES

Of course, not everyone has the resources to flit from partner to partner. Whether or not one is happy, one's ability to leave a relationship depends on one's investments, the resources one would lose by departing (Rusbult, Drigotas, & Verette, 1994). Unfortunately, when aversiveness rises beyond tolerable limits, people may find themselves *entrapped*, stuck in miserable relationships that they cannot leave (because of what they would lose by leaving).

These are very difficult situations that, over time, may adversely affect the participants' *health*. Marital conflict depresses spouses' immune systems, leaving them at increased risk for a variety of infections (Kiecolt-Glaser et al., 1993). There may also be *innocent bystanders* who are gradually injured. Children who are exposed to chronic marital conflict suffer undue stress (Cummings, 1994), and may learn maladaptive ways of managing their own frustrations (Doumas, Margolin, & John, 1994; Grych & Fincham, 1990). Unexpected aversiveness in close relationships may not only do real harm to the partners themselves, but to others as well.

THE BRIGHTER SIDE

There appear to be many good reasons to expect our close relationships to be more aversive than we would wish them to be. They involve normal processes that are hard to avoid, and most relationships will be at risk. This is solemn news, and in raising these points and asserting caution, I may seem a curmudgeon. Nevertheless, at bottom, I do not mean this to be a pessimistic perspective. To the contrary, I think it is merely *realistic*, and I think it can be a profitable outlook.

Most relationships have surprising costs, at least in comparison to the way they start and what the partners expect (Eidelson, 1980). I think it's likely that, if partners objectively understand the likely dynamics of their relationship over time, they may be able to avoid needless disappointment and may even be better equipped to forestall the creeping invasion of increasing aversiveness. If people *expected* their lovers to be increasingly impolite over time, they might be more likely to appreciate the many thoughtful things their partners do and less likely to attach momentous portent to an occasional lack of decorum.

Certainly, useful insights have emerged from the studies that have focused on the negative interactions that accompany closeness (e.g., Gottman, 1994). Studies of argument and conflict between spouses clearly show that spouses are routinely mean to each other but that happy spouses provide a consistently high ratio of positive to negative actions that compensates for their meanness (Gottman & Levenson, 1992); in addition, they are able to resist responding in kind to all the mean things their partners do (Gottman, 1994). The ability to manage an aversive interaction without high emotion and evil counterattack is a key talent in maintaining a happy marriage.

Altogether, then, expecting the worst and being ready to deal with it seem much more efficacious than romantically (and naively) believing one's love is special and will be immune. If we eschew romanticism and dispel illusion, we might be better off for expecting inattention and impoliteness from those who love us. For one thing, we may be less likely to blame our partners unduly for their occasional lapses of decorum. For another, expecting the worst allows contrast effects to work for us—magnifying our partners' kindnesses instead of their slights—rather than against us. Moreover, when our relationships turn out to be merely contented rather than ecstatic and superb, we can avoid the nagging and dangerous suspicion that we are somehow being cheated.

I suggest that we strive for "relational realism" in our expectations for and perceptions of our close relationships. Along with their many riches and rewards, our partnerships will produce some aches and pains. Acknowledging this, and understanding that aversiveness is normal even in *good* relationships, is a freeing, and effective, perspective. On the other hand, please do not interpret my remarks as providing implicit permission to be lazily mean to your partners. Aversiveness is unavoidable but nobody likes it, and partners are always responsible for being as pleasant as possible to those whose company they value.

Indeed, the good news is that, of course, partners often do manage to be much nicer to each other than they are mean (Gottman, 1994). Moreover, over time (if they can stay married that long), couples are often able to resolve conflicts less negatively and more affectionately (Carstensen, Gottman, & Levenson, 1995). Teaching and training can help people manage conflict more constructively as well (Markman et al., 1994). We should not stop striving for the kindest treatment of our close partners that we can manage. Still, it may help to be realistic and acknowledge that, despite our hopes and romantic ideals, most of our close relationships will be more aversive than we thought they would be.

REFERENCES

Acitelli, L.K., & Young, A.M. (1996). Gender and thought in relationships. In G.J.O. Fletcher & J. Fitness (Eds.), *Knowledge structures in close relationships: A social psychological approach* (pp. 147–168). Mahwah, NJ: Erlbaum.

Altman, I., & Taylor, D.A. (1973). *Social penetration: The development of interpersonal relationships.* New York: Holt, Rinehart and Winston.

Aronson, E. (1992). *The social animal* (6th ed.). New York: Freeman.

Aronson, E., & Linder, D. (1965). Gain and loss of esteem as determinants of interpersonal attractiveness. *Journal of Experimental Social Psychology, 1,* 156–171.

Attridge, M., & Berscheid, E. (1994). Entitlement in romantic relationships in the United States: A social-exchange perspective. In M.J. Lerner & G. Mikula (Eds.), *Entitlement and the affectional bond: Justice in close relationships* (pp. 117–147). New York: Plenum Press.

Averill, J.R. (1982). *Anger and aggression: An essay on emotion.* New York: Springer.

Baumeister, R.F., & Leary, M.R. (1995). The need to belong: Desire for interpersonal attachments as a fundamental human motivation. *Psychological Bulletin, 117,* 497–529.

Baxter, L.A., & Dindia, K. (1990). Marital partners' perceptions of marital maintenance strategies. *Journal of Social and Personal Relationships, 7,* 187–208.

Birchler, G.R., Weiss, R.L., & Vincent, J.P. (1975). Multimethod analysis of social reinforcement exchange between maritally distressed and nondistressed spouse and stranger dyads. *Journal of Personality and Social Psychology, 31,* 349–360.

Blumstein, P., & Schwartz, P. (1983). *American couples: Money, work, sex.* New York: Morrow.

Bradbury, T.N., & Fincham, F.D. (1990). Attributions in marriage: Review and critique. *Psychological Bulletin, 107*, 3–33.

Brehm, S.S. (1992). *Intimate relationships* (2nd ed.). New York: McGraw-Hill.

Brody, L.R., & Hall, J.A. (1993). Gender and emotion. In M. Lewis & J.M. Haviland (Eds.), *Handbook of emotions* (pp. 435–446). New York: Guilford Press.

Burman, B., & Margolin, G. (1992). Analysis of the association between marital relationships and health problems: An interactional perspective. *Psychological Bulletin, 112*, 39–63.

Buss, D.M. (1991). Conflict in married couples: Personality predictors of anger and upset. *Journal of Personality, 59*, 663–688.

Carstensen, L.L., Gottman, J.M., & Levenson, R.W. (1995). Emotional behavior in long-term marriage. *Psychology and Aging, 10*, 140–149.

Christensen, A., & Heavy, C.L. (1990). Gender and social structure in the demand/withdraw pattern of marital conflict. *Journal of Personality and Social Psychology, 59*, 73–81.

Coombs, R.H. (1991). Marital status and personal well-being: A literature review. *Family Relations, 40*, 97–102.

Cummings, E.M. (1994). Marital conflict and children's functioning. *Social Development, 3*, 16–36.

Cupach, W.R., & Spitzberg, B.H. (Eds.). (1994). *The dark side of interpersonal communication*. Hillsdale, NJ: Erlbaum.

Davis, M.S. (1973). *Intimate relations*. New York: Free Press.

Dewsbury, D.A. (1981). Effects of novelty on copulatory behavior: The Coolidge effect and related phenomena. *Psychological Bulletin, 89*, 464–482.

Doumas, D., Margolin, G., & John, R.S. (1994). The intergenerational transmission of aggression across three generations. *Journal of Family Violence, 9*, 157–175.

Duck, S. (1994). Strategems, spoils, and a serpent's tooth: On the delights and dilemmas of personal relationships. In W.R. Cupach & B.H. Spitzberg (Eds.), *The dark side of interpersonal communication* (pp. 3–24). Hillsdale, NJ: Erlbaum.

Dutton, D.G., Saunders, K., Starzomski, A., & Bartholomew, K. (1994). Intimacy-anger and insecure attachment as precursors of abuse in intimate relationships. *Journal of Applied Social Psychology, 24*, 1367–1386.

Eidelson, R.J. (1980). Interpersonal satisfaction and level of involvement: A curvilinear relationship. *Journal of Personality and Social Psychology, 39*, 460–470.

Felmlee, D.H. (1995). Fatal attractions: Affection and disaffection in intimate relationships. *Journal of Social and Personal Relationships, 12*, 295–311.

Fiske, S. (1980). Attention and weight in person perception: The impact of negative and extreme behavior. *Journal of Personality and Social Psychology, 38*, 889–906.

Gleitman, H. (1991). *Psychology* (3rd ed.). New York: Norton.

Gottman, J.M. (1994). *What predicts divorce? The relationship between marital processes and marital outcomes*. Hillsdale, NJ: Erlbaum.

Gottman, J.M., & Levenson, R.W. (1992). Marital processes predictive of later dissolution: Behavior, physiology, and health. *Journal of Personality and Social Psychology, 63*, 121–133.

Grych, J.H., & Fincham, F.D. (1990). Marital conflict and children's adjustment: A cognitive-contextual framework. *Psychological Bulletin, 108*, 267–290.

Hatfield, E. (1984). The dangers of intimacy. In V.J. Derlega (Ed.), *Communication, intimacy, and close relationships* (pp. 207–220). Orlando: Academic Press.

Hokanson, J.E., Hummer, J.T., & Butler, A.C. (1991). Interpersonal perceptions by depressed college students. *Cognitive Therapy and Research, 15*, 443–457.

Ickes, W. (1993). Traditional gender roles: Do they make, and then break, our relationships? *Journal of Social Issues, 49*, 71–85.

Johnson, M.P., & Leslie, L. (1982). Couple involvement and network structure: A test of the dyadic withdrawal hypothesis. *Social Psychology Quarterly*, 45, 34–43.

Jones, W.H., & Burdette, M.P. (1994). Betrayal in relationships. In A.L. Weber & J.H. Harvey (Eds.), *Perspectives on close relationships* (pp. 243–262). Boston: Allyn and Bacon.

Kahneman, D., & Tversky, A. (1982). The psychology of preferences. *Scientific American, 246,* 160–173.

Karau, S.J., & Williams, K.D. (1993). Social loafing: A meta-analytic review and theoretical integration. *Journal of Personality and Social Psychology, 65,* 681–706.

Karney, B.R., Bradbury, T.N., Fincham, F.D., & Sullivan, K.T. (1994). The role of negative affectivity in the association between attributions and marital satisfaction. *Journal of Personality and Social Psychology, 66,* 413–424.

Kelly, C., Huston, T.L., & Cate, R.M. (1985). Premarital relationship correlates of the erosion of satisfaction in marriage. *Journal of Social and Personal Relationships, 2,* 167–178.

Kidd, V. (1975). Happily ever after and other relationship styles: Advice on interpersonal relations in popular magazines, 1951–1973. *Quarterly Journal of Speech, 61,* 31–39.

Kiecolt-Glaser, J.K., Malarkey, W.B., Chee, M., Newton, T., Cacioppo, J.T., Hsiao-Yin, M., & Glaser, R. (1993). Negative behavior during marital conflict is associated with immunological down-regulation. *Psychosomatic Medicine, 55,* 395–409.

Krull, D.S., & Erickson, D.J. (1995). Inferential hopscotch: How people draw social inferences from behavior. *Current Directions in Psychological Science, 4,* 35–38.

Langer, E.J. (1989). *Mindfulness.* Reading, MA: Addison-Wesley.

Leary, M.R., Nezlek, J.B., Downs, D., Radford-Davenport, J., Martin, J., & McMullen, A. (1994). Self-presentation in everyday interactions: Effects of target familiarity and gender composition. *Journal of Personality and Social Psychology, 67,* 664–673.

LeMasters, E.E., & DeFrain, J. (1989). *Parents in contemporary America: A sympathetic view.* Belmont, CA: Wadsworth.

Levinger, G., & Breedlove, J. (1966). Interpersonal attraction and agreement: A study of marriage partners. *Journal of Personality and Social Psychology, 3,* 367–372.

Lynch, J.J. (1979). *The broken heart: The medical consequences of loneliness.* New York: Basic Books.

MacEwen, K.E., & Barling, J. (1994). Daily consequences of work interference with family and family interference with work. *Work and Stress, 8,* 244–254.

Markman, H., Stanley, S., & Blumberg, S.L. (1994). *Fighting for your marriage: Positive steps for preventing divorce and preserving a lasting love.* San Francisco: Jossey-Bass.

Marshall, L.L. (1994). Physical and psychological abuse. In W.R. Cupach & B.H. Spitzberg (Eds.), *The dark side of interpersonal communication* (pp. 281–311). Hillsdale, NJ: Erlbaum.

Martin, T.C., & Bumpass, L. (1989). Recent trends in marital disruption. *Demography, 26,* 37–51.

Milardo, R.M., Johnson, M.P., & Huston, T.L. (1983). Developing close relationships: Changing patterns of interaction between pair members and social networks. *Journal of Personality and Social Psychology, 44,* 964–976.

Miller, R.S. (1991a, April). *"It won't happen here": Demonstrating overconfidence in expectations of divorce.* Paper presented at the meeting of the Southwestern Psychological Association, New Orleans.

Miller, R.S. (1991b). On decorum in close relationships: Why aren't we polite to those we love? *Contemporary Social Psychology, 13,* 74–76.

Miller, R.S. (1993, June). *Is love blind? Perceptions of partners in developing relationships.* Paper presented at the meeting of the International Network on Personal Relationships, Milwaukee.

Miller, R.S. (1996). *Embarrassment: Poise and peril in everyday life.* New York: Guilford Press.

Murray, S.L., & Holmes, J.G. (1996). The construction of relationship realities. In G.J.O. Fletcher & J. Fitness (Eds.), *Knowledge structures in close relationships: A social psychological approach* (pp. 91–120). Mahwah, NJ: Erlbaum.

Murray, S.L., Holmes, J.G., & Griffin, D.W. (1996). The benefits of positive illusions: Idealization and the construction of satisfaction in close relationships. *Journal of Personality and Social Psychology, 70,* 79–98.

Murstein, B.I. (1987). A classification and extension of the SVR theory of dyadic pairing. *Journal of Marriage and the Family, 42,* 777–792.

Newton, T.L., Kiecolt-Glaser, J.K., Glaser, R., & Malarkey, W.B. (1995). Conflict and withdrawal during marital interaction: The roles of hostility and defensiveness. *Personality and Social Psychology Bulletin, 21,* 512–524.

Perlman, D. (1989, August). *You bug me: A preliminary report on hassles in relationships.* Paper presented at the meeting of the American Psychological Association, New Orleans.

Petronio, S., Olson, C., & Dollar, N. (1989). Privacy issues in relational embarrassment: Impact on relational quality and communication satisfaction. *Communication Research Reports, 6,* 21–27.

Reichle, B., & Montada, L. (1994). Problems with the transition to parenthood: Perceived responsibility for restrictions and losses and the experience of injustice. In M.J. Lerner & G. Mikula (Eds.), *Entitlement and the affectional bond: Justice in close relationships* (pp. 205–228). New York: Plenum Press.

Rusbult, C.E., Drigotas, S.M., & Verette, J. (1994). The investment model: An interdependence analysis of commitment processes and relationship maintenance phenomena. In D.J. Canary & L. Stafford (Eds.), *Communication and relational maintenance* (pp. 115–139). San Diego: Academic Press.

Rusbult, C.E., Yovetich, N.A., & Verette, J. (1996). An interdependence analysis of accommodation processes. In G.J.O. Fletcher & J. Fitness (Eds.), *Knowledge structures in close relationships: A social psychological approach* (pp. 91–120). Mahwah, NJ: Erlbaum.

Schafer, J., Birchler, G.R., & Fals-Stewart, W. (1994). Cognitive, affective, and marital functioning of recovering male polysubstance abusers. *Neuropsychology, 8,* 100–109.

Schreindorfer, L.S., Leary, M.R., & Keith, J.M. (1996). *In pursuit of acceptance: Interpersonal strategies and consequences of seeking inclusion vs. avoiding exclusion.* Manuscript submitted for publication.

Shapiro, J.P., Baumeister, R.F., & Kessler, J.W. (1991). A three-component model of children's teasing: Aggression, humor, and ambiguity. *Journal of Social and Clinical Psychology, 10,* 459–472.

Shaver, P.R., & Hazan, C. (1994). Attachment. In A.L. Weber & J.H. Harvey (Eds.), *Perspectives on close relationships* (pp. 110–130). Boston: Allyn and Bacon.

Shoda, Y., Mischel, W., & Peake, P.K. (1990). Predicting adolescent cognitive and self-regulatory competencies from preschool delay of gratification: Identifying diagnostic conditions. *Developmental Psychology, 26,* 978–986.

Simpson, J.A., Campbell, B., & Berscheid, E. (1986). The association between romantic love and marriage: Kephart (1967) twice revisited. *Personality and Social Psychology Bulletin, 12,* 363–372.

Spitzberg, B.H., & Cupach, W.R. (1994). Dark side dénouement. In W.R. Cupach & B.H. Spitzberg (Eds.), *The dark side of interpersonal communication* (pp. 315–320). Hillsdale, NJ: Erlbaum.

Stafford, L., & Dainton, M. (1994). The dark side of "normal" family interaction. In W.R. Cupach & B.H. Spitzberg (Eds.), *The dark side of interpersonal communication* (pp. 259–280). Hillsdale, NJ: Erlbaum.

Tangney, J.P., Hill-Barlow, D., Wagner, P.E., Marschall, D.E., Borenstein, J.K., Sanftner, J., Mohr, T., & Gramzow, R. (1996). Assessing individual differences in constructive versus destructive responses to anger across the lifespan. *Journal of Personality and Social Psychology, 70,* 780–796.

Taylor, S.E., & Brown, J.D. (1988). Illusion and well-being: A social psychological perspective on mental health. *Psychological Bulletin, 103,* 193–210.

Tucker, P., & Aron, A. (1993). Passionate love and marital satisfaction at key transition points in the family life cycle. *Journal of Social and Clinical Psychology, 12,* 135–147.

Turner, H.A. (1994). Gender and social support: Taking the bad with the good? *Sex Roles, 30,* 521–541.

Turner, J.L., Foa, E.B., & Foa, U.G. (1971). Interpersonal reinforcers: Classification, interrelationship, and some differential properties. *Journal of Personality and Social Psychology, 19,* 168–180.

U.S. Bureau of the Census. (1995). *Statistical abstract of the United States* (115th ed.). Washington, DC: U.S. Government Printing Office.

Van Lange, P.A.M., & Rusbult, C.E. (1995). My relationship is better than—and not as bad as—yours is: The perception of superiority in close relationships. *Personality and Social Psychology Bulletin, 21,* 32–44.

Vincent, J.P., Weiss, R.L., & Birchler, G.R. (1975). A behavioral analysis of problem solving in distressed and nondistressed married and stranger dyads. *Behavior Therapy, 6,* 475–487.

Walster, E., Walster, G.W., & Berscheid, E. (1978). *Equity: Theory and research.* Boston: Allyn and Bacon.

Whitehouse, J. (1981). The role of the initial attracting quality in marriage: Virtues and vices. *Journal of Marital and Family Therapy, 7,* 61–67.

CHAPTER 3

MAKING SOMEONE FEEL GUILTY

CAUSES, STRATEGIES, AND CONSEQUENCES

KRISTIN L. SOMMER AND ROY F. BAUMEISTER

INTRODUCTION

Guilt is an aversive emotion. It involves a sense of remorse, regret, tension, and arousal (Baumeister, Reis, & Delespaul, 1995; Tangney, 1995) and often co-occurs with shame (Ferguson & Stegge, 1995; Tangney, 1995). Because guilt is experientially bad, the act of making another person feel guilty clearly qualifies as an aversive interpersonal behavior. To make someone feel guilty is to inflict a negative, undesired emotional state that most people normally try to avoid.

Despite the aversiveness of guilt, people who induce guilt do not appear to be motivated by malicious or aggressive desires to inflict anxiety or suffering. There may be some circumstances which lead individuals to induce guilt for the sole purpose of exploiting or punishing their relationship partners, yet these are probably more the exception than the rule. Instead, we believe that guilt is most often used by one

KRISTIN L. SOMMER AND ROY F. BAUMEISTER • Department of Psychology, Case Western Reserve University, Cleveland, Ohio 44106-7123. kxs16@po.cwru.edu

Aversive Interpersonal Behaviors, edited by Kowalski
Plenum Press, New York, 1997

partner with the intention of securing long-term, positive outcomes. Individuals who are made to feel guilty will reaffirm both their concern for their partners and their commitment to the relationship. Guilt serves important relationship-enhancing functions (Baumeister, Stillwell, & Heatherton, 1994), and thus guilt induction provides a powerful and effective method for strengthening the interpersonal bond. Put simply, inducing guilt is an aversive interpersonal behavior precisely because it makes its targets feel so bad, but it is usually done in the service of something that is desirable and good.

The purpose of this chapter is first to give some understanding to the nature of guilt, particularly its interpersonal functions. Following this is a brief presentation of the various strategies for inducing guilt and a discussion of when guilt will be used as an influence tactic within close relationships. In our analysis, we emphasize the benefits of guilt induction to the inducer and to the relationship as a whole. Later, we illustrate how misuse of guilt induction as a tool for getting what one wants out of a relationship can alter the interpersonal outcomes of guilt. Normally, guilt promotes and sustains the interpersonal bond, yet there are some paths by which guilt can have destructive rather than constructive effects on a relationship. These are reviewed briefly. We conclude with a summary of the chapter and some suggestions for future work on the topic.

THE INTERPERSONAL NATURE OF GUILT

Traditional concepts of guilt have treated it as an intrapsychic phenomenon. The prototype of these views would perhaps involve a person sitting alone, reflecting on some past action and comparing it to internal, personal standards. When the action violates the standards, the person feels guilty as a result. No one else need be involved (e.g., Buss, 1980).

In contrast, recent work has pointed toward a radically different notion of guilt (Baumeister et al., 1994; Tangney, 1992). In this new view, guilt is rooted in the interpersonal bonds and connections between people and serves the function of strengthening and maintaining those bonds. From this interpersonal perspective, the prototype cause of guilt would be inflicting harm or distress on a relationship partner. Guilt feelings might indeed arise when the person sits alone and reflects on his or her actions, but the roots of the feeling lie in the interpersonal bond that could be damaged or jeopardized by one's acts.

The interpersonal nature of guilt is evidenced in several recent theoretical and empirical papers. For example, an edited book devoted to the study of "self-conscious" emotions (Tangney & Fischer, 1995) included several chapters on guilt, and the conclusion drawn by experts on the topic (based on research using different methods and populations) was that guilt occurs primarily within social, interpersonal contexts. For example, Jones, Kugler, and Adams (1995) revealed that both trait and state guilt were positively associated with relationship transgressions (e.g., coercion, deceit) but not nonrelational transgressions (e.g., substance use, deviant sexual behaviors). Guilt resulted mainly from the perception of having inflicted harm on others. Baumeister, Stillwell, and Heatherton (1995a) found that guilt was positively associated with high regard for the victim. They further asserted that the capacity to experience guilt should approach zero as the emotional distance between individuals increases (Baumeister et al., 1994).

A developmental analysis of guilt also sheds light on the role of others in the experience of guilt. Zahn-Waxler and Robinson (1995) demonstrated that guilt emerges around the second year of life, when children develop the capacity for empathy and begin to learn moral codes that differentiate right from wrong—including how one should treat others (see also Hoffman, 1982). The capacity to empathize and the internalization of norms appear to be antecedent conditions of guilt (Zahn-Waxler, Radke-Yarrow, Wagner, & Chapman, 1992). Mascolo and Fischer (1995) illustrated the transformation of guilt over time. They stated that guilt begins with simple awareness of a contingency between one's behavior and another's distress, but guilt then develops into an emotional response that may result from more complex conditions—such as failing to fulfill interpersonal obligations or exhibiting "less moral" behavior than a similar other. Barrett and Campos's (1987) functionalist analysis of emotions distinguishes "primordial," "concurrent-goal," and "social" emotions. Guilt, they argue, falls in the category of social emotions because socialization processes are seen as precursors to the capacity to experience guilt, and because guilt serves important interpersonal functions (Barrett, 1995; Barrett & Campos, 1987).

A pair of studies by Baumeister et al. (1995) investigated the patterns of guilt in daily life and the interpersonal contexts that give rise to guilt. In the first study, they used an experience sampling method in which subjects were signaled (via a beeper) to record the intensity with which they were currently experiencing each of several emotions. Participants recorded both their emotions and qualitative aspects of their current social interactions (e.g., degree of intimacy, social support, desire to be alone). Some guilt was experienced nearly 13% of the time and was associated significantly with the presence of other negative emotions such as loneliness, anxiety, discontent, and rejection. Guilt was distributed about equally across all categories of thoughts and actions used in the study, with one major exception: Rates of guilt were significantly higher when subjects were thinking about self in relation to others, as compared with all other topics of thought. Baumeister et al. did find that guilt occurred almost as often when alone as when in the company of others. Thus, guilt is interpersonal in its focus (on self in relation to others) but it does not require the immediate physical presence of others. The results from this first study paralleled those from a previous study by Vangelisti, Daly, and Rudnick (1991, Study 1) which revealed that 80% of autobiographical narratives about guilt involved interactions with very close others.

A second study by Baumeister et al. (1995) was designed to compare several aversive emotions (including guilt) as to how interpersonal and relationship-oriented they are. Baumeister et al. had participants write stories about the last time they experienced each of six emotions, and these narratives were coded for the strength of interpersonal attachments between the narrator and other characters in the stories. (If there were multiple others in the story, the main other character was the basis for coding, and, if there were several important ones, the strongest relationship was coded.) Close relationship partners received the maximum coding of 5, and the codings ranged downward through other friends (4), casual acquaintances or role relationships (3), strangers with whom future interaction was expected (2), strangers with no future interaction (1), and solitary stories (0). Each subject wrote one story each about the most recent experience of guilt, anger/irritation, anxiety, fear, sadness, and frustration. The guilt stories received the highest scores on interpersonalness of the six emotions, and guilt was significantly higher in interpersonalness than a pool of the other five emotions as well as significantly higher than each of the others individually (except sadness, for which guilt was nonsignificantly higher). The guilt stories were also the most likely to receive the maximal coding of 5, confirming the view that guilt is linked to close relationships.

In all, several recent empirical investigations of guilt have highlighted the role of (perceived or actual) others in individuals' subjective experiences of guilt (see Baumeister et al., 1994, for a review). Guilt may be experienced when alone, but the cause is usually reflecting on some interpersonal misdeed or transgression. Guilt coincides developmentally with the onset of cognitive capacities for empathy (perspective taking), and even in adulthood guilt is linked to greater abilities to understand another person's perspective as well as a greater likelihood of spontaneously doing so (Leith & Baumeister, in press). Although guilt is often associated with violating societal standards about how to treat other people, the violation of standards is probably not sufficient to cause guilt. Instead, guilt seems to be based on vicarious involvement in another's suffering, combined with the belief that one is responsible for that suffering. Moreover, the intensity of guilt feelings appears to vary decisively with the closeness of the relationship. People are most likely to experience guilt as a result of transgressing against others with whom they have formed long-term, emotional attachments. The less one cares about the victim of one's transgression, the less guilt one feels, even if the transgressions are identical and the standards are the same.

ORIGINS OF GUILT

Why is guilt so fundamental to interpersonal attachments? Inflicting harm on an emotionally distant other will have far fewer implications for guilt than will bringing harm to a close other. But why? We address this question by examining the root or core (as opposed to proximate or immediate) causes of guilt. The origins of guilt should also shed light on why guilt is experientially so negative and yet simultaneously credited with creating positive outcomes.

According to Baumeister et al. (1994), guilt derives from two main affective roots. The first of these is empathy. We have already mentioned the research linking guilt with the development of empathy in children. According to Hoffman (1982), empathic distress is particularly important in the development of guilt. Nearly all human beings are capable of feeling upset merely upon being exposed to another person who is suffering visibly. This empathic distress becomes guilt when the self is associated with (or especially responsible for) that person's suffering. Well-documented links between guilt and empathy (Leith & Baumeister, in press; Tangney, Burggraf, & Wagner, 1995) indicate that the stronger a person's ability to feel distress in response to another's suffering, the greater the proneness to guilt. Given that empathy is strongest among partners in close relationships, including people who know and care about each other and feel similar to each other, it is not surprising that guilt flourishes mainly in such close relationships.

The other affective root of guilt, according to Baumeister et al. (1994), is anxiety over social exclusion—in other words, the fear that important social attachments may be broken off or lost, or that one will be rejected, ostracized, or otherwise cut off from other people. Such fears are probably the single most important and prevalent cause of anxiety in general (Baumeister & Tice, 1990; see also Bowlby, 1969, 1973). If managing guilt were simply a matter of regulating affect, that is, of getting rid of anxiety or remorse, there should be ways to do this that do not directly involve the victimized partner. That is, getting rid of bad feelings might be accomplished in simpler ways than by apologizing, reiterating concern for the victim, and engaging in reparative behaviors. Yet people do attempt to compensate for past transgressions, which suggests that guilt reflects not only consideration of another's feelings but also concerns for maintaining the relationship. Any event that disrupts the relationship thus should have the potential to evoke guilt, especially when one partner assumes responsibility for the disruptive event.

The concern over relationship termination and its implications for guilt are apparent given the vital importance of interpersonal attachments to human functioning. There is considerable evidence that people are fundamentally and pervasively motivated to form and maintain strong interpersonal attachments (see Baumeister & Leary, 1995, for a review). Threats to a sense of belongingness lead to feelings of loneliness and worthlessness as well as more extreme cases of mental and physical illness. Guilt may be among the ways that the human psyche has adapted to this basic need for attachments. Put simply, guilt alerts individuals to the potential exclusion by others with whom they have formed strong, emotional bonds. It is true that partners in close, communal relationships (or those characterized by mutual concern for the other's welfare) do show fewer concerns over day-to-day issues of fairness or justice (Clark, 1984; Clark & Chrisman, 1994). Yet in the long run, people want their relationship investments to be reciprocated. They want to feel that their partners value and respect them and that they are not being taken for granted (Attridge & Berscheid, 1994). Thus, the capacity or potential for guilt increases as relationships progress toward a communal state (Baumeister et al., 1994). Guilt feelings serve as "centripetal forces," binding relationship partners and making them resistant to separation (Miceli, 1992).

These origins of guilt shed light on why guilt is so aversive. First, empathy allows individuals to relate subjectively to the pain or suffering they have caused their partners. Significant others, such as spouses, family members, and close friends, can be viewed as extensions of the self (Aron, Aron, Tudor, & Nelson, 1991; Josephs, Markus, & Tafarrodi, 1992). Thus, the emotional outcomes of others become incorporated into one's own affective state. Second, because guilt alerts individuals to potential threats to their relationships, it should activate the potential for anxiety, depression, and lowered self-esteem (Baumeister & Leary, 1995; Baumeister & Tice, 1990; Leary, Tambor, Terdal, & Downs, 1995). Even if guilt does not directly cause these other affective states, it should activate the *possibility* of these emotions in the event that the relationship is not restored to its previous status.

These origins of guilt underscore the interpersonal benefits of guilt. Guilty people want to escape the psychological distress they experience from seeing a close other suffer, and they want to preserve their interpersonal attachments. Both empathy and fear of exclusion will cause guilty individuals to engage in compensatory or reparative behaviors that function to strengthen the bond with their partners.

WHY INDUCE GUILT?

Why would someone want to induce guilt in his or her relationship partner? The first general reason is that sometimes people need to be reminded of the existence and severity of their transgressions. Baumeister, Stillwell, and Wotman (1990) found that perpetrators and victims show memory differences for transgressions, with perpetrators forgetting more quickly. This suggests that victims would benefit from reminding their perpetrators of the transgressions. Baumeister et al. (1990) also found that victims and perpetrators disagreed systematically about the severity of transgressions, which suggests that victims and perpetrators are likely to disagree about the "appropriate" level of guilt the perpetrator should experience. Not surprisingly, perpetrators tended to downplay or minimize the severity of the transgressions, as compared with victims. If the victim wants to ensure that the transgression will not be minimized or forgotten, he or she may find it necessary to remind the perpetrator of the magnitude of harm or suffering that the transgression wrought.

Aside from the desire to focus the perpetrator on the transgression and its negative effects, we believe that the primary, compelling motive for inducing guilt is to gain control in the relationship. Consider the three main interpersonal functions of guilt proposed by Baumeister et al. (1994). First, guilt reduces damage to relationships, because it makes people avoid doing things that may harm, disappoint, or upset relationship partners, and after the fact of such a transgression guilt motivates people to take steps to make amends and reaffirm the relationship. Second, guilt redistributes emotional distress within the relationship, by making the transgressor feel bad and often helping the victim to feel better. Third, guilt serves as a means of interpersonal influence, because it helps people—especially people who may lack formal power and means of influence within the relationship—to get their way.

The third of these functions (guilt as influence) is most relevant to the theme of this chapter, namely the induction of guilt feelings. People induce guilt because they want to alter something that is undesirable or unsatisfactory about their relationships. The remaining two functions (reducing damage through reparation and redistributing emotional distress) may be viewed broadly as the two main paths by which individuals achieve influence or power through use of guilt. The former involves controlling the partner's behaviors; the latter involves controlling the partner's emotions. We consider each of these briefly.

Guilt leads transgressors to apologize, express affection, or engage in other reparative behaviors. Baumeister, Stillwell, and Heatherton (1995b, Study 1) asked participants to write two stories about instances in which they made another person angry. One story involved an event that made them feel guilty, whereas the other described an event that did not lead to guilt. Compared to no-guilt stories, narrators of the guilt stories were significantly more likely to report making apologies, learning a lesson, and changing their behaviors. There is also some evidence that transgressors are more likely than nontransgressors subsequently to engage in helping behavior in an unrelated sphere, especially if they are made to feel obligated (Cunningham, Steinberg, & Grev, 1980). Thus, guilt invokes action tendencies toward engaging in reparation and prosocial behavior (see also Vangelisti et al., 1991).

Also, victims of transgressions initially suffer a disproportionate amount of negative affect, such as anger, sadness, or hostility. Making the perpetrator feel guilty prevents the perpetrator from possessing an emotional advantage and redistributes emotional distress in the relationship. Evidence for this comes from additional findings from the same study mentioned earlier (Baumeister et al., 1995b, Study 1). In addition to trying to remedy their partners' emotional states through apologies and reparation, narrators of guilt (relative to no-guilt) stories reported feeling worse, more selfish, and ultimately less happy with the outcomes of the events they were describing.

Thus people will induce guilt for the general purpose of regaining a sense of control or power in a relationship. The reason that guilt induction is successful in this regard is related to the other two interpersonal functions of guilt, namely increased emotional distress in the guilty party and subsequent attempts at reparation. The inducer benefits both emotionally and behaviorally from the partner's guilt.

Guilt induction is an influence tactic that should be exercised more frequently among low as opposed to high status individuals. To induce fear or anger or sadness may require some degree of status or dominance, but guilt induction does not require power or status. Instead, guilt is power-equalizing; it allows the less powerful person to get his or her way. Whereas high status (compared to low status) individuals will have greater success in changing their partners' behavior by issuing demands or ultimatums, low status partners must adopt more indirect methods of social influence. Guilt induction is a relatively effortless yet highly effective way to elicit desired changes in a partner's behavior. The inducer gains an "edge" from the partner's guilt. Because the guilty partner is willing (and even eager) to make amends, the inducer is placed in the new and advantageous position of exerting control over both the partner's emotions and behaviors.

One context where one should see guilt induction as a means of gaining power is in filial relationships, specifically, in mother–child attachments. Fathers traditionally get their way with overt power, from physical dominance to control over material resources, but mothers often lack this power. A young college student who returns from school and spends every day with her friends may be responsive to a father's insistence that she spend more time with her parents. The mother, lacking this direct power over the child, may opt for a different approach, such as expressing to the child her disappointment and hurt for not receiving the attention to which she feels entitled. To the degree that fathers do have relatively more direct control over their children's actions, mothers may be more likely than fathers to use guilt as a tool for getting what they want from their children. As parents forsake corporal punishment and direct control over the material resources is diminished by societal changes, however, fathers will probably become increasingly similar to mothers in the reliance on guilt to influence the child.

Using guilt to equalize power should also emerge in close relationships in which one partner feels that his or her relative lack of power and influence has created a chronic state of inequity. High status partners can derive maximum benefits from their relationships, whereas low status partners experience fewer positive outcomes and are relatively more dependent and distressed. One way to balance this distress and gain control in the relationship is to make the overbenefitted partner feel guilty (VanYperen & Buunk, 1994). Sprecher (1992) found that people who imagined themselves as an underbenefitted partner in a relationship reported greater overall distress than when imagining themselves as the overbenefitted partner. The only emotion experienced significantly more frequently among overbenefittors was guilt. In this study, participants were also asked a series of questions pertaining to equity in their own, real-life relationships. Women were more likely than men to report *raising* issues of fairness, even though both genders rated their relationships equally in overall fairness. Because women on average tend to be more economically vulnerable outside of marriage, and thus relatively powerless, guilt may provide them with a valuable tactic for strengthening the relationship and keeping the husband committed (Baumeister, Sommer, & Cicora, in press).

This analysis sheds light on the continuing gender inequities in romantic or spousal relationships. Several studies investigating equity or equality in these relationships consistently reveal gender differences in the amount of childcare and housework responsibilities assumed by each partner. Even after controlling for biased reporting, type of housework, and work responsibilities outside the home, women still do more (Steil, 1995; VanYperen & Buunk, 1995). Surprisingly, these findings emerge despite an apparent lack of any systematic complaints among underbenefitting women. Such results make more sense, however, if one considers the possibility of elevated guilt levels among overbenefitting men.

Hochschild (1989) maintains that, as women do more housework, they achieve a sense of moral superiority. Contributing more to daily tasks around the home may thus provide a useful tactic for some women for sustaining a moderate degree of guilt in their partners. This guilt, in turn, leads male partners to maintain high appreciation for their spouses and exhibit a greater willingness to make future compromises.

Thus individuals can use guilt to exert control over others and bind others to them. Considering the importance of the basic gift of life, children can never pay off their debt to their mother, and the mother can use this fact (with judicious reminders) to make sure the kids keeps calling and visiting long after the delight of her companionship has worn off. A spouse who lacks traditional forms of power or influence in the relationship may create an underbenefitting status by putting extra effort into household chores and calling the partner's attention to her (or his) sacrifices. This provides an effective way to rack up "guilt points" and thereby increase the partner's sense of indebtedness and committment to the relationship.

Although inducing guilt does not require power or status, it will be ineffective when the transgressing partner shows little concern for maintaining the relationship. Recall that guilt originates in empathy and fear of exclusion. Close relationships are characterized by mutual concern and sensitivity to the other's emotional outcomes as well as an investment in maintaining the attachment. The magnitude of guilt experienced by the partner will depend on these factors. To the degree that a partner has lost concern for the inducer's happiness or for preserving the interpersonal bond, the inducer's capacity to instill guilt will be greatly diminished. The would-be inducer's claim "See how you are hurting me" will be met with "So what?"

WHO INDUCES GUILT, AND WHEN?

At this point, it should be clear that guilt is overwhelmingly characteristic of close, communal relationships. Trying to invoke guilt in someone who is indifferent to you is bound to be a waste of time and energy. Inducing guilt is a test of relationship strength, because guilt is proportional to how much the other cares about you. You can assess the other's emotional involvement and committment by seeing how effectively you can induce guilt.

Strong evidence for the role of guilt induction in close compared to stranger relationships came from a study by Vangelisti et al. (1991, Study 2). They asked participants to rate how guilt was typically induced in them. Typicality of guilt induction correlated highly (.76) with the intimacy of the relationship. Also, participants reported that two of their main reasons for inducing guilt were to influence the partner's behavior and maintain the relationship (such as by motivating the other to devote more attention to the partner). Intimacy thus appears to increase the likelihood that individuals will try to make each other feel guilty, and the goal of this behavior is that of prolonging or maintaining the interpersonal bond.

We do not assert that people always go around trying their hardest to make their partners feel guilty. Indeed, as we show later, inducing guilt carries risks and so under many circumstances people would be wise to *avoid* making their partners feel badly. We do, however, believe that individuals realize that their partners' guilt will yield positive outcomes for the self and the relationship, and further that individuals will resort to guilt induction when other attempts to exact change prove futile.

One circumstance that gives rise to guilt induction is the presence of different standards or expectations in the relationship. Your spouse may cause you to feel guilty because you failed to remove your socks from the bedroom floor despite the fact that you spent most of your day cooking or doing laundry. In fact, Baumeister et al. (1995) found that guilty individuals were more likely than inducers to report that the inducers held high standards or expectations for their partners.

More generally, because guilt functions to strengthen the interpersonal bond, guilt induction should involve a tendency to call to the partner's attention the fact that he or she has created a disruption to the relationship. For example, people will induce guilt when their partners have inflicted pain or suffering (Baumeister et al., 1994; Tangney, 1992; Zahn-Waxler & Kochanska, 1990) or have benefitted at the other's expense (Sprecher, 1992). Baumeister et al. (1995b) found that the most frequently reported reason for inducing guilt (or being the target of guilt induction) was interpersonal neglect. This included the perception that the target was not paying one enough attention or meeting one's needs. Also, targets were more likely than inducers to report neglect spontaneously as the cause of guilt induction. Assuming that targets and inducers were equally likely to devise their narratives around themes of interpersonal neglect, this suggests that targets simply focused more than inducers on the inducer's outcomes and purported reasons for inducing guilt. This finding, however, might also indicate that targets were more likely than inducers to *recall* instances in which they neglected someone. People may feel worse about neglecting someone (an act of omission) than transgressing against someone (an act of commission) and therefore be more likely to remember instances of neglect when asked to describe a situation in which they were made to feel guilty. Conversely, people describing times when they made another feel guilty may be more likely than those writing "target" stories to include instances of overt, specific transgressions.

Regardless, the prominence of interpersonal neglect as a reason for guilt induction in both types of accounts suggests that people induce guilt mainly when events hold implications for the affectional bond. Compared to a specific transgression for which it is easier to make excuses or apologize (e.g., "I was just angry; I wasn't thinking"), neglect connotes a loss of affection for the partner. Specific transgressions (such as making a mean-spirited comment or breaking a promise) are probably more frequent than interpersonal neglect but also less detrimental to the relationship.

Research examining the determinants of relationship satisfaction offers support for this proposition. Desmarais and Lerner (1989; 1994) categorized individuals' relationships as "identity" (characterized by a merging of the self and other and strong concerns for meeting the other's needs), "unit" (characterized by concerns of mutual fairness and equity), or "nonunit" (characterized by desired to maximize individual rewards). Conceptually, "identity" relationships might be considered highest on a quantitative dimension of closeness (followed by "unit" then "nonunit"). Desmarais and Lerner (1994) found that relationship satisfaction among members of "unit" and "nonunit" relationships was associated positively with the number of positive outcomes (rewards) for the self. However, satisfaction among members of "identity" relationships depended on the partner's outcomes. These individuals were most happy when they believed they were meeting their partners' needs. This may explain why interpersonal neglect, which suggests a lack of concern for the other's happiness, emerges as the most significant source of guilt and reason for guilt induction.

People will use guilt primarily with others for whom they care deeply. Guilt may emerge as a result of differing expectations in the relationship. The main situational determinant of guilt induction is interpersonal neglect or failure to meet one's personal needs. Inducing guilt thus may be viewed primarily as a healthy and desirable interpersonal phenomenon because it alerts partners to potential problems in the relationship.

HOW TO INDUCE GUILT

There are numerous ways that individuals may make their partners feel guilty. We review a few of these techniques here, but we note that this list is not exhaustive. Regardless of the specific behaviors that go into making another feel guilty, each technique may be generally considered a variation on saying "see how you are hurting me." The main point that one must communicate when trying to induce guilt is that the partner has done something to bring one harm.

One way to induce guilt is to inflate the degree to which one has suffered. Baumeister et al. (1995b) found that inducers were significantly more likely than targets of guilt induction to report that the inducer purposefully exaggerated his or her negative outcomes in efforts to augment the other's guilt. This included admissions of lying or otherwise falsifying information. Inducers were also more likely than targets to claim that the inducer was frankly manipulative. Individuals who used guilt on their partners admitted that by distorting the extent of their harm, they could maximize their gains and capitalize on the partner's guilt experience. Intensifying the partner's guilt allowed individuals to secure maximum benefits by way of the partner's subsequent reparation.

In addition to expressing directly the suffering one has incurred as a result of the partner's neglect, transgression, or overbenefitting status, there are various techniques that individuals may use to induce guilt (Miceli, 1992). (From here on out, we use the term "transgression" to refer to any event leading to guilt.) These strategies, despite their intuitive appeal and apparent effectiveness, have received little empirical study. Because of their relevance and import for future research on the topic, however, we give them brief mention here.

First, Miceli (1992) notes that the threat of rejection and guilt are so closely linked that often people use love withdrawal to induce guilt. Demonstrating a loss of caring about the transgressing partner communicates the pain or hurt that one suffered as a result of the partner's actions. Thus, a simple exclamation "I don't know how you could do this; I don't want to be with you anymore" communicates one's victimization and in turn punishes the transgressing partner. Earlier we noted that guilt originates in the fear of losing emotional attachments. If guilt is associated systematically with thoughts of potential exclusion, then the threat of exclusion may lead to guilt, especially in the presence of a recent transgression. With this technique, then, the partner experiences not only guilt but also added anxiety over the possibility of losing the relationship (Baumeister & Tice, 1990).

A second method suggested by Miceli (1992) is that of forgiveness. To unexpectedly hear the inducer say "Don't worry about what you've done; I forgive you" leaves the partner in a particularly distressing situation. First, the inducer has succeeded in bypassing any discussion as to whether the infliction of harm took place or whether one is to blame for that harm. The transgression is considered "obvious" and not subject to debate. Second, the partner's guilt (based on the assumed suffering he or she has caused the other) is further compounded by the inducer's integrity, that is, the inducer's willingness to forgive the partner for his or her wrongdoings.

Third, Miceli (1992) notes the advantages of "noncommunicative" guilt induction, in which the inducer lets a third party know of his or her suffering with the idea that this will get back to the partner. The obvious drawback of this is that the partner may never learn of or fully realize the extent of the inducer's suffering. Even if the partner does come to acknowledge the inducer's suffering (through discussion with the third party), he or she may not take responsibility for it. However, assuming that guilt induction is successful, there are some clear advantages of this technique to the inducer. First, because there is no direct expression or complaints of suffering, the partner is unlikely to conclude that the inducer is being manipulative. Even if the partner were suspicious of the inducer's intentions, it would be costly to the relationship to accuse the inducer of intentionally "planting" the information in the third party with the hope that it gets back to the partner. Therefore, this strategy, when effective, accomplishes the goal of inducing guilt while protecting the inducer from appearing manipulative.

Fourth, people may refuse to accept reparation from those who have transgressed upon them (Miceli, 1992). As noted earlier, apologies and other reparative behaviors allow the transgressing partner to "even the score" and thus alleviate his or her guilt. Rejecting the partner's attempts to compensate for prior wrongdoings prolongs the guilt experience and places the inducer in a position to assert his or her superiority over (and make further demands of) the partner. This technique may be used in conjunction with a tendency to exaggerate one's suffering. The inducer may dismiss or devalue the partner's attempts at reparation by asserting that these attempts do little to compensate for the extreme hardship or injustice the inducer has endured. Refusing reparation may provide a valuable technique for low status individuals who chronically experience little power in the relationship. Inducing guilt elevates one's power. That power, if sustained, presents the low status individual with two advantages. The first is increased status (by virtue of being morally superior). The second is control over the other's behaviors and a greater say in mutual decisions.

Finally, and in a related vein, one may sustain another's guilt by "turning one's cheek" (Miceli, 1992). A natural response to another's transgression is to lash out, or become angry and chastise the partner. Confronting the partner helps to even the emotional score by making that partner feel bad for what he or she has done. By withholding aggressive attacks, that is, by "turning the other cheek" and ignoring the transgression, the inducer forgoes the satisfaction of evening the score but gains the benefit of prolonging the other's guilt. When the transgressing partner expects retaliation, but does not receive it, he or she may experience temporary relief (for not having to endure the aggression) but then feel an enduring sense of guilt due to the lost opportunity to repair the damage he or she has caused to the relationship. Also, like forgiveness, the decision not to retaliate but instead turn one's cheek reflects positively on the inducer's character.

There is some empirical evidence for the effectiveness of this technique. Legant and Mettee (1973) led individuals to believe they were shocking another participant as part of a learning experiment. For half the participants, the (confederate) learner retaliated by returning shocks; for the remaining half, the learner did not retaliate but instead "turned the other cheek." Also, the learner's freedom to retaliate was manipulated. Some participants believed that the learner was instructed by the experimenter to retaliate (or not to retaliate); others believed that the decision was left to the learner. Participants' liking for the learner was later assessed. The results revealed a significant crossover interaction: When participants believed the learner was free to choose her behavior, the nonretaliative learner was liked more than the retaliative learner. That is, the decision to "turn the other cheek" led participants to evaluate the confederate more positively. Conversely, when participants thought the learner was instructed as to how to respond, the nonretaliative learner was liked less than the retaliative learner. The authors speculated that participants felt guilty about shocking the confederate. When participants later realized that she was unable to even the score, they derogated her to alleviate their own sense of guilt. That is, participants used denigration as a way to escape their own negative affect.

These findings suggest that martyrlike behavior increases one's moral standing in the eyes of others. A person will be judged more positively when he or she willingly chooses to ignore a partner's poor behavior. However, the results from the Legant and Mettee (1973) study suggest that, when a person is perceived as helpless to defend against attack, the guilt may be too much to bear for the partner. Paradoxically, the partner will then resort to distancing the inducer through means of derogation or ridicule.

These five influence tactics include the essential ingredients of guilt. Their foci are to bring attention to the inducer's suffering and the cause of that suffering without appearing manipulative. These strategies make the inducer look and feel better at the expense of making the partner look and feel worse. Yet although guilt induction may succeed in bringing about short-term, positive benefits to the inducer and to the relationship, it should also have long-term costs.

COSTS OF GUILT INDUCTION

Guilt typically strengthens the bond between individuals. Put simply, guilt causes people to be better partners. Yet if guilt as an influence tool is misused (for example, if it is manipulated too frequently or invoked under the wrong circumstances), it may weaken the interpersonal bond. Inducing guilt could make something relationship-harmful out of something relationship-enhancing.

Normally, guilt is healthy for close relationships because it motivates individuals to exhibit increased concern for their partners and repair any damage they have caused. Yet it is precisely because of these robust effects that people may come to rely excessively on guilt induction to influence their partners. Excessively strong, frequent, or unjustified guilt induction yields negative outcomes for both the inducer and his or her partner and is destructive to the relationship.

One (likely unanticipated) cost of guilt induction is *metaguilt*. Metaguilt refers to the guilt one experiences from having made another feel guilty. Guilt is an aversive emotion and thus inducing guilt is a way to inflict suffering. Therefore, metaguilt should be strongest after inducing guilt in another for whom one cares strongly. Metaguilt complicates any attempts to redistribute emotional distress within the relationship because the inducer (who is motivated to feel better) feels worse by virtue of having made the partner feel badly. Baumeister et al. (1995b) found that 21% percent of guilt inducers reported feeling guilty themselves. Despite their metaguilt, however, inducers still felt better after the guilt induction. This is probably because their partners' guilt outweighed their own (leading to a partial redistribution of distress) and because inducers were successful in eliciting reparation from their partners.

It is difficult to consider the negative impact of guilt induction on the transgressing partner without also addressing the impact on the relationship. This is because the primary consequence of unresolvable or inescapable guilt is to distance the self from the person who is making you feel so bad. Also, if you conclude that your partner is manipulating your feelings for selfish reasons (as opposed to a desire to communicate genuine suffering), you will likely come to resent or devalue your partner. Baumeister et al. (1995b) found that individuals who were made to feel guilty reported high levels of resentment. This was in stark contrast to the largely absent reporting of target resentment among the guilt-inducing partners. When people induce guilt, they evidently are oblivious to the accompanying resentment they are causing.

There are three main ways in which guilt induction may become destructive to a relationship, and all three involve changes in the perceptions or behaviors of the target. The first is the perception that one's feelings and behaviors are being manipulated. The second is a tendency to derogate the inducer for making one feel so bad. The third involves the possibility that repeated guilt induction will lead one to demean the entire self as opposed to just one's behaviors. We consider each of these in turn.

Manipulation leads to a loss of trust and respect for the partner and a loss of control within the relationship. If your partner is taking advantage of your guilt, then he or she can no longer be expected to be sensitive to your feelings. Also, the belief that your partner has control over your emotional state should motivate you to disengage from the relationship. Loss of control is associated with a host of negative effects such as frustration, depression, and helplessness (e.g., Taylor & Brown, 1988). No one likes to be chronically at the mercy of another's influence. Thus, the perception that your emotions and behaviors are determined by someone other than yourself should lead you to withdraw.

We suggested earlier that the guilt induction technique of forgiveness may be recognized as manipulative, especially if it is used frequently. By forgiving the partner, the inducer attaches a negative value to the partner's "transgression" and thus deprives him or her of any control over how to define the event. This loss of control, combined with a more generalized loss of control that ensues from the perception of being manipulated, should motivate the partner to sever ties with the inducer.

The second means by which guilt becomes detrimental to a relationship is victim derogation. Baumeister et al. (1994) argued persuasively that the propensity for guilt decreases with the strength of the affectional bond. One way that an individual can avoid or eliminate his or her guilt is to sever any emotional ties with the guilt-inducing partner. Most people want to preserve their social connections (Baumeister & Leary, 1995), and so victim derogation should be used only as a last resort, for instance, when the guilty individual is prevented from alleviating his or her guilt in more positive or productive ways.

We demonstrated earlier that the primary consequence of guilt is an increased motivation to compensate or correct for prior transgressions. Reparation is, in a sense, the act of swinging the pendulum in the opposing direction in order to stabilize the amount of negative affect experienced by each partner. A guilty individual who lavishes her partner with love and respect and confesses her own remorse will restore emotional balance and equity to the relationship and thus attenuate her own guilt. To the degree that she is prevented from engaging in reparation, or to the extent that her partner dismisses this reparation as unsatisfactory, she may denigrate her partner. She may also derogate her partner if the partner is perceived as defenseless or unable to retaliate. Guilt is aversive and the inability to escape this negative state will cause a person to remove its core cause, namely, the interpersonal bond. Devaluing the victimized partner is a way to reduce the perceived importance of the relationship. If the attachment is no longer important or worth sustaining, then guilt becomes an unjustified or irrelevant emotion.

The study by Legant and Mettee (1973) (discussed earlier) found evidence for victim derogation when the victim was rendered helpless to defend against attack. Recall that when the learner in an ostensible shock experiment was purportedly instructed to either retaliate by shocking the participant or "turn her cheek," the nonretaliative learner was liked less than the retaliative learner. This was compared to when participants believed that the learner freely chose to retaliate or turn her cheek, which resulted in greater liking for the nonretaliative learner. In this study, participants who inflicted pain on the learner (and who presumably felt guilty) were not provided with an opportunity to apologize or compensate and thus had to rely on the learner's retaliative behavior to restore equity. When the learner was rendered defenseless, participants lowered their evaluations of her. These findings suggest that individuals will reduce their evaluations of another person whom they have hurt when that person's capacity to retaliate is thwarted.

Other evidence for victim derogation comes from two experiments by Katz, Glass, and Cohen (1973). These researchers examined the effects of hurting an ingroup versus outgroup member by manipulating the race of the learner in a bogus shock experiment. White participants delivered strong or weak shocks to a white or black confederate. Liking for the confederate was assessed prior to and after the ostensible delivery of shocks. Change scores indicated that liking for the learner decreased significantly when the learner was black and when the shocks were strong. The researchers maintained that participants in this condition felt most guilty about their behaviors and used victim denigration to reduce their guilt.

The researchers further suggested that these effects were due to racial ambivalence toward the victim, not uniformly negative stereotypes. Ambivalence is most likely to produce guilt because the person acknowledges having hostile or negative feelings toward another but simultaneously views those feelings as wrong or unjustified. When a racially ambivalent person harms a member of the outgroup, that person may think that he or she enjoyed it but then immediately feel guilty about having enjoyed the aggression. This hypothesis was supported in a second study by Katz et al. (1973). They found that only those participants who were high in racial ambivalence (defined by high prejudice *and* high sympathy toward members of the racial group) showed significant derogation of the black learner. This was compared to when subjects were low in racial ambivalence (i.e., low in sympathy, or high in sympathy and low in prejudice). The researchers concluded that victim denigration allowed white, racially ambivalent participants to distance themselves from their black victims, thereby justifying their aggression and alleviating their guilt.

By extrapolating from the findings of Katz et al. (1973), then, we would expect that being made to feel guilty will lead you to derogate your guilt-inducing partner when you already have some hostile feelings toward your partner. Such hostility could result from past events in which your partner angered you, or indeed from the very perception that your partner is being manipulative. Concern for the partner's suffering combined with the desire to lash out should create conflict or ambivalence, which in turn should motivate derogation rather than reparation.

Thus, individuals who want to make their partners feel guilty may unknowingly place their relationships at risk. Guilty people who are prevented from engaging in reparation will derogate and thus disengage from their inducers. Also, when inducers are perceived as weak or defenseless (thus perpetuating emotional imbalance within the relationship), they will elicit from their partners contempt or resentment rather than empathy or concern. Derogation is most likely to occur when the partner already holds some negative feelings toward the inducer.

The third instance in which guilt induction threatens the interpersonal bond is when the guilty person believes that past transgressions hold implications for the self-concept. More simply, chronic or extreme feelings of guilt may lead a person not only to regret the behavior but to derogate or demean the self. Global devaluation of the self in response to committing a transgression is typical of shame rather than guilt experiences. Guilt arises from a negative evaluation of one's behavior, whereas shame results from a negative evaluation of the self. To our knowledge, there is no research examining the developmental transition from guilt into shame. Yet it is intuitively plausible that people who are repeatedly made to feel guilty about their actions will eventually conclude that they are bad people in general.

Shame and guilt do tend to co-occur (Ferguson & Stegge, 1995). Tangney (1995) reports that the same circumstances that lead one person to feel guilty may lead another to feel ashamed. The interpersonal consequences of guilt and shame are quite different, however. Guilt motivates action tendencies toward reparation and reaffirming the relationship. Shame, conversely, motivates individuals to escape the source of their negative emotions or withdraw from the relationship. Shame is accompanied by feelings of "smallness" and inferiority. Shamed persons are preoccupied with the notion that others are evaluating them poorly, and thus their dominant motivation is to escape others' evaluations and hide (Barrett, 1995; Tangney et al., 1995). Lindsay-Hartz, de Rivera, and Mascolo (1995) found that 23% of people describing guilt experiences reported attempts to hide or escape the situation rather than make amends—behavioral tendencies which are consistent with shame. Thus, at least for some people, being made to feel guilty may also evoke feelings of shame.

Shame leads to other interpersonal behaviors in addition to withdrawal or escape. One marker of shame is the tendency to externalize responsibility for one's actions (Tangney, 1995). Instead of blaming the self, one blames the partner or finds other causes external to the self. A related consequence of shame is aggression. Whereas guilty individuals apologize or make concessions, shamed individuals lash out. Tangney, Wagner, Fletcher, and Gramzow (1992) showed that dispositional proneness to shame predicted (positively) direct and indirect, verbal and physical aggression in response to anger-provoking situations. Guilt-proneness, conversely, was negatively related to aggression. Thus, shamed individuals whose characters are perceived to be under attack will often turn their hostility outward, by externalizing blame and aggressing toward those who are judging them.

Interpersonal rejection is one guilt induction strategy that has the potential to elicit shame. The idea that one's behavior was so bad as to warrant exclusion from the partner should result in a decreased focus on the behavior and an increased focus on the self as a whole. Perceived rejection is related to feelings of low self-worth (Leary et al, 1995), and the latter is associated with shame (Tangney et al., 1995). Thus, rejection that has as its cause a specific event (transgression) may lead to shame rather than (or in addition to) guilt. Exaggeration of one's suffering may also induce shame. Miceli (1992) notes that very aggressive strategies of guilt induction (e.g., "Look at what you've done to me!") are often ineffective precisely for this reason. In response to the perception of having inflicted extreme suffering on others, partners will attempt to minimize their own blameworthiness by trivializing the transgression or criticizing and derogating the inducer. Shame responses to both rejection and exaggerated suffering are probably more frequent among low compared to high self-esteem individuals, as the former have a chronic propensity to evaluate themselves negatively and also tend to perceive low levels of acceptance in important relationships (Leary et al, 1995; Tangney et al., 1995).

Repeatedly being made to feel guilty for inequities or transgressions against a relationship partner may over time lead to a qualitative shift in the way events are interpreted, specifically, a tendency to label the self (rather than just the act) as bad. Unlike the intended emotional response of guilt, shame following "guilt induction" will result in externalization rather than internalization of blame, and aggression rather than reparation.

Thus, guilt induction can go awry—leading to destruction rather than enhancement of a relationship. If you want to induce guilt in your partner, then you should be careful to: a) avoid appearing manipulative,

b) provide your partner with an opportunity to make amends, and c) focus on what is wrong with your partner's *behavior* rather than what is wrong with your partner.

SUMMARY AND AREAS FOR FUTURE RESEARCH

Guilt is an aversive emotion that one experiences after causing harm to a close other. Causing your partner to feel guilty for his or her actions is an aversive interpersonal behavior precisely because guilt is an inherently negative feeling that most people prefer to avoid. The implications of guilt induction for the relationship, however, are typically positive. Guilt redistributes emotional distress in the relationship; the inducer feels better by virtue of making his or her partner feel worse. Guilt also motivates the transgressing partner to express concern and affection through use of apologies and reparation.

The capacity or tendency for guilt increases with the intimacy of the relationship, suggesting that guilt originates in the fear of losing important attachments. Put this way, guilt arises from the knowledge that one has created a disruption to the interpersonal bond, and guilty individuals will work hard to make amends and reaffirm the relationship.

Effectively inducing guilt does not depend on power or status but instead operates on the degree of emotional connection between individuals. When inducing guilt to get your way, you are counting on your partner's emotional investment in the relationship. In close relationships, guilt allows less powerful individuals to gain control over their partners' feelings and actions. Relatively powerless people may use guilt to elevate their own status and to bind their partners to the relationship.

The main goal in inducing guilt is to bring your partner's attention to the pain or suffering he or she has caused you. This may be accomplished in several ways, including exaggerating your suffering, preemptively "forgiving" your partner, turning your cheek (i.e., ignoring the transgression), using "noncommunicative" strategies (i.e., conveying your suffering to a third party), threatening to leave your partner, and refusing reparation.

Trying to make your partner feel guilty in efforts to enhance the quality of the relationship may backfire. There are three main paths to relationship destruction following the induction of guilt. The first is when your partner concludes that you are not truly suffering but rather are being manipulative. If your partner perceives that you are manipulating his or her emotions and behaviors, your partner will lose respect for you and experience a loss of control in the relationship—or withdraw. The second is when your partner derogates you. This occurs when you are perceived as defenseless or when your guilty partner is somehow prevented from engaging in reparation. By derogating you, your partner can distance himself or herself from you emotionally and consequently devalue the relationship—thereby alleviating any guilt. The third means to relationship destruction is the transformation of guilt into shame. If you frequently make your partner feel guilty or exaggerate the amount of suffering you have incurred, your partner may eventually conclude that he or she is a bad or unworthy person. Shame will lead to defensive withdrawal, externalization of blame, and aggression toward the source of the negative emotions, namely, you.

We conclude by noting the need for future research on guilt induction. Two main areas deserve further attention. First, there is little empirical work examining the various ways that people induce guilt in others. For instance, future research might examine the effectiveness of the guilt induction strategies outlined by Miceli (1992). Which strategies are most likely to be perceived as manipulative, and which are most successful in instilling guilt? Also, what circumstances give rise to guilt induction, and what types of people are most susceptible or responsive to this influence tactic? We suggested earlier that low status individuals will use indirect or "adoptive" strategies (such as forgiveness and "turning one's cheek") to elevate their moral superiority, and thus power in the relationship. We also speculated that interpersonal rejection should be least effective with targets low in self-esteem. Other individual differences may similarly moderate the impact of direct and indirect guilt induction techniques on subsequent guilt and reparative behaviors.

Second, what circumstances lead people to use guilt induction as an influence tactic more often than others? Put another way, what kinds of people are most likely to make their partners feel guilty? Two personality types may predict individuals' tendencies to induce guilt. The first is guilt-proneness. Tangney and colleagues (see Tangney, 1990; Tangney et al., 1995; Tangney, Wagner, & Gramzow, 1992) have developed measures that assess individuals' dispositional tendencies to respond to daily events with guilt versus shame. It is plausible that individuals dispositionally prone to experience guilt will be most familiar with its aversive nature and its impact on behavior. Thus, these individuals may be especially likely to rely on guilt induction as a method for achieving desirable outcomes within the relationship. There is also reason to expect the exact opposite finding, however. Individuals high in guilt-proneness may be most susceptible to "metaguilt," or the guilt that results from making a close other feel guilty. A propensity toward metaguilt would discourage rather than encourage guilt-prone individuals from making their partners feel bad.

Another personality variable that may predict the tendency to induce guilt is the capacity for empathy (Davis, 1983). Unempathic individuals are relatively incapable of experiencing vicariously another's pain or suffering, and indeed are less likely than empathic individuals to be guilt-prone (Tangney, 1991; 1995). Lack of concern for the partner's emotional outcomes combined with the low likelihood of metaguilt should make the unempathic person especially inclined toward using guilt induction for exploitative reasons—that is, to manipulate the partner and to maximize personal rewards in the relationship.

In the final analysis, guilt is a common emotion that holds great power for strengthening interpersonal bonds. Judicious induction of guilt may help it achieve that potential. Like any tool, however, guilt may be misused, and excessive or improper induction of guilt may backfire and harm the relationship. Making people feel guilty is one of the most important and theoretically interesting ways that relationship partners exert control over each other's emotional states and behavior.

REFERENCES

Aron, A., Aron, E.N., Tudor, M. & Nelson, G. (1991). Close relationships as including other in the self. *Journal of Personality and Social Psychology, 60,* 241–253.

Attridge, M., & Berscheid, E. (1994). Entitlement in romantic relationships in the United States: A social-exchange perspective. In M.J. Lerner & G. Mikula (Eds.), *Entitlement and the affectional bond: Justice in close relationships* (pp. 117–148). New York: Plenum.

Barrett, K.C. (1995). A functionalist approach to shame and guilt. In J.P. Tangney & K.W. Fischer (Eds.), *Self-conscious emotions: The psychology of shame, guilt, embarrassment, and pride* (pp. 25–63). New York: Guilford.

Barrett, K.C., & Campos, J.J. (1987). Perspectives on emotional development: II. A functionalist approach to emotions. In J. Osofsky (Ed.), *Handbook of infant development* (pp. 555–578). New York: Wiley.

Baumeister, R. F., & Leary, M. R. (1995). The need to belong: Desire for interpersonal attachments as a fundamental human motivation. *Psychological Bulletin, 117,* 497–529.

Baumeister, R.F., Reis, H.T., & Delespaul, P.A.E.G. (1995). Subjective and experiential correlates of guilt in daily life. *Personality and Social Psychology Bulletin, 21,* 1256–1268.

Baumeister, R.F., Sommer, K.L., & Cicora, K.F. (in press). Inequity and iniquity in marriage. *Social Justice Research.*

Baumeister, R.F., Stillwell, A.M., & Heatherton, T.F. (1994). Guilt: An interpersonal approach. *Psychological Bulletin, 115,* 243–267.

Baumeister, R.F., Stillwell, A.M., & Heatherton, T.F. (1995a). Interpersonal aspects of guilt: Evidence from narrative studies. In J.P. Tangney & K.W. Fischer (Eds.), *Self-conscious emotions: The psychology of shame, guilt, embarrassment, and pride* (pp. 255–342). New York: Guilford.

Baumeister, R.F., Stillwell, A.M., & Heatherton, T.F. (1995b). Personal narratives about guilt: Role in action control and interpersonal relationships. *Basic and Applied Social Psychology, 17,* 173–198.

Baumeister, R.F., Stillwell, A., & Wotman, S.R. (1990). Victim and perpetrator accounts of interpersonal conflict: Autobiographical narratives about anger. *Journal of Personality and Social Psychology, 59,* 994–1005.

Baumeister, R.F. & Tice, D.M. (1990). Anxiety and social exclusion. *Journal of Social and Clinical Psychology, 9,* 165–195

Bowlby, J. (1969). *Attachment and loss. Vol 1: Attachment.* New York: Basic Books.

Bowlby, J. (1973). *Attachment and loss. Vol 2: Separation anxiety and anger.* New York: Basic Books.

Buss, A. (1980). *Self-consciousness and social anxiety.* San Francisco: Freeman.

Clark, M.S. (1984). Record keeping in two types of relationships. *Journal of Personality and Social Psychology, 47,* 549–557.

Clark, M.S., & Chrisman, K. (1994). Resource allocation in intimate relationships: Trying to make sense of a confusing literature. In M.J. Lerner & G. Mikula (Eds.), *Entitlement and the affectional bond: Justice in close relationships* (pp. 65–88). New York: Plenum.

Cunningham, M.R., Steinberg, J., & Grev, R. (1980). Wanting to and having to help: Separate motivations for positive mood and guilt-induced helping. *Journal of Personality and Social Psychology, 38,* 181–192.

Davis, M.H. (1983). Measuring individual differences in empathy: Evidence for a multidimensional approach. *Journal of Personality and Social Psychology, 44,* 113–126.

Desmarais, S., & Lerner, M.J. (1989). A new look at equity and outcomes as determinants of satisfaction in close personal relationships. *Social Justice Research, 3,* 105–119.

Desmarais, S., & Lerner, M.J. (1994). Entitlement in close relationships: A justice-motive analysis. In M.J. Lerner & G. Mikula (Eds.), *Entitlement and the affectional bond: Justice in close relationships* (pp. 43–63). New York: Plenum.

Ferguson, T.J., & Stegge, H. (1995). Emotional states and traits in children: The case of guilt and shame. In J.P. Tangney & K.W. Fischer (Eds.), *Self-conscious emotions: The psychology of shame, guilt, embarrassment, and pride* (pp. 174–197). New York: Guilford.

Hochschild, A. (1989). *The second shift.* New York: Viking.

Hoffman, M.L. (1981). Is altruism part of human nature? *Journal of Personality and Social Psychology, 40,* 121–137.

Hoffman, M.L. (1982). Development of prosocial motivation: Empathy and guilt. In N. Eisenberg (Ed.), *Development of prosocial behavior* (pp. 281–313). New York: Academic Press.

Jones, W.H., Kugler, K., & Adams, P. (1995). You always hurt the one you love: Guilt and transgressions against relationship partners. In J.P. Tangney & K.W. Fischer (Eds.), *Self-conscious emotions: The psychology of shame, guilt, embarrassment, and pride* (pp. 301–321). New York: Guilford.

Josephs, R.A., Markus, H.R., & Tafarrodi, R.W. (1992). Gender and self-esteem. *Journal of Personality and Social Psychology, 63,* 391–402.

Katz, I., Glass, D.C., & Cohen, S. (1973). Ambivalence, guilt, and the scapegoating of minority group victims. *Journal of Experimental Social Psycholoyg, 9,* 423–436.

Leary, M.R., Tambor, E.S., Terdal, S K., & Downs, D.L. (1995). Self-esteem as an interpersonal monitor: The sociometer hypothesis. *Journal of Personality and Social Psychology, 68,* 518–530.

Legant, P., & Mettee, D.R. (1973). Turning the other cheek versus getting even: Vengeance, equity and attraction. *Journal of Personality and Social Psychology, 25,* 243–253.

Leith, K.P., & Baumeister, R.F. (in press). Empathy, shame, guilt, and narratives of interpersonal conflicts: Guilt-prone people are better at perspective taking. *Journal of Personality.*

Lindsay-Hartz, J., de Rivera, J., & Mascolo, M.F. (1995). Differentiating guilt and shame and their effects on motivation. In J.P. Tangney & K.W. Fischer (Eds.), *Self-conscious emotions: The psychology of shame, guilt, embarrassment, and pride* (pp. 274–300). New York: Guilford.

Mascolo, M.F., & Fischer, K.W. (1995). Developmental transformations in appraisals of pride, shame, and guilt. In J.P. Tangney & K.W. Fischer (Eds.), *Self-conscious emotions: The psychology of shame, guilt, embarrassment, and pride* (pp. 64–113). New York: Guilford.

Miceli, M. (1992). How to make someone feel guilty: Strategies of guilt inducement and their goals. *Journal for the Theory of Social Behaviour, 22,* 81–104.

Sprecher, S. (1992). How men and women expect to feel and behave in response to inequity in close relationships. *Social Psychology Quarterly, 55,* 57–69.

Steil, J.M. (1995). Equality and entitlement in marriage: Benefits and barriers. In M.J. Lerner & G. Mikula (Eds.) *Entitlement and the affectional bond: Justice in close relationships* (pp. 229–258). New York: Plenum.

Tangney, J.P. (1990). Assessing individual differences in proneness to shame and guilt: Development of the Self-Conscious Affect and Attribution Inventory. *Journal of Personality and Social Psychology, 59,* 102–111,

Tangney, J.P. (1991). Moral affect: The good, the bad, and the ugly. *Journal of Personality and Social Psychology, 61,* 598–607.

Tangney, J. P. (1992). Situational determinants of shame and guilt in young adulthood. *Personality and Social Psychology Bulletin, 18,* 199–206.

Tangney, J.P. (1995). Shame and guilt in interpersonal relationships. In J.P. Tangney & K.W. Fischer (Eds.), *Self-conscious emotions: The psychology of shame, guilt, embarrassment, and pride* (pp. 114–142). New York: Guilford.

Tangney, J.P., Burggraf, S.A., & Wagner, P.E. (1995). Shame-proneness, guilt-proneness, and psychological symptoms. In J.P. Tangney & K.W. Fischer (Eds.), *Self-conscious emotions: The psychology of shame, guilt, embarrassment, and pride* (pp. 343–367). New York: Guilford.

Tangney, J.P. & Fischer, K.W. (Eds.) (1995). *Self-conscious emotions: The psychology of shame, guilt, embarrassment, and pride.* New York: Guilford.

Tangney, J.P., Wagner, P.E., Fletcher, C., & Gramzow, R. (1992). Shamed into anger? The relation of shame and guilt to anger and self-reported aggression. *Journal of Personality and Social Psychology, 62,* 669–675.

Tangney, J.P., Wagner, P.E., & Gramzow, R. (1992). Proneness to shame, proneness to guilt, and psychopathology. *Journal of Abnormal Psychology, 103,* 469–478.

Taylor, S.E., & Brown, J.D. (1988). Illusion and well-being: A social psychological perspective on mental health. *Psychological Bulletin, 103,* 193–210.

Vangelisti, A.L., Daly, J.A., & Rudnick, J.R. (1991). Making people feel guilty in conversations: Techniques and correlates. *Human Communication Research, 18,* 3–39.

VanYperen, N.W., & Buunk, B.P. (1994). Social comparison and social exchange in marital relationships. In M.J. Lerner & G. Mikula (Eds.), *Entitlement and the affectional bond: Justice in close relationships* (pp. 89–115). New York: Plenum.

Zahn-Waxler, C., Kochanska, G. (1990). The origins of guilt. In R.A. Thompson (Ed.), *The Nebraska symposium on motivation 1988: Socioemotional development* (Vol. 36, pp. 182–258). Lincoln: University of Nebraska Press.

Zahn-Waxler, C., Radke-Yarrow, M., Wagner, E., & Chapman, M. (1992). Development of concern for others. *Developmental Psychology, 28,* 126–136.

Zahn-Waxler, C., & Robinson, J. (1995). Empathy and guilt: Early origins of feelings of responsibility. In J.P. Tangney & K.W. Fischer (Eds.), *Self-conscious emotions: The psychology of shame, guilt, embarrassment, and pride* (pp. 143–173). New York: Guilford.

CHAPTER 4

WHY WOULD ANYONE WANT TO INTENTIONALLY EMBARRASS ME?

WILLIAM F. SHARKEY

INTRODUCTION

Welcome to the world of intentional embarrassment. During our lives, you and I have experienced a variety of embarrassing situations. Maybe we dropped a drink on someone. Maybe we tripped over that demon crack in the sidewalk. Maybe we unknowingly walked in on someone who was using the bathroom. Or, maybe we felt empathic embarrassment when our best friend, sibling, child performed poorly on stage. Each of the above situations were more than likely accidental occurrences. However, during our lives, we may have been the recipient of an *intentional* act performed to cause us embarrassment. At other times, we may have been the intentional embarrassor of a deserving, or not so deserving, individual as exemplified by self-proclaimed embarrassors below (from Sharkey, 1990a):

> I work as a creative consultant for an advertising firm and a manipulative coworker made a habit of stealing our (the creative team's) ideas.

WILLIAM F. SHARKEY • University of Hawaii at Manoa, 2560 Campus Road, George Hall 326, Honolulu, Hawaii 96822. sharkey@hawaii.edu; http://www2.hawaii.edu/~sharkey/

Aversive Interpersonal Behaviors, edited by Kowalski
Plenum Press, New York, 1997

> When wise to this situation, we confronted the boss with our problem and asked him to question the person in question about his so-called ideas—releasing the "lies." After his spiel, the boss called us in and the man was caught in his lies. He was not fired but *very* embarrassed and reprimanded, including a demotion.

> I would spontaneously be showing how much I enjoyed something in a public event by dancing, finger snapping, clapping, etc. My younger daughter would be embarrassed and ask me to stop—and I would always increase my activity.

> My sister's bridal shower was one that had your ordinary bridal shower gifts, except for mine of course...After the tupperware bowls and third set of measuring cups she finally got to mine. The wrapping paper was a clever disguise for what was really in there. As she opened it up her eyes grew larger and larger with her face flashing bright red. It was a very see-through "Teddy" and an inflateable[sic] nude man.

> I was sitting at a stoplight one day when up beside me pulled a gentleman (in his mid-forties, balding) in a white corvette. When he pulled up beside me, he struck me as a person trying to put on airs, trying to be sophisticated, suave, Mr. Macho. He began flirting with me by winking, etc. I was so amused by his behavior and the obviousness of the situation that I decided to be as crude as he was in trying to be suave. So I stuck my finger up my nose, pretending to pick my nose and looked right at him. He *quickly* turned away, losing all composure.

Intentional embarrassment is the focus of this chapter on aversive interpersonal behaviors. In what follows, I will present studies that help us more fully understand this phenomenon, the intentional use of behaviors to cause another to feel embarrassed. But first, a quick look at the emotion of embarrassment itself will set the stage for understanding why anyone would intentionally embarrass another individual.

Embarrassment is a *short-lived emotional/psychological response of social chagrin (i.e., anxiety or fear due to negative sanctioning or lower evaluations from others) or uneasiness that occurs as a result of a discrepancy between one's idealized role-identity and one's presented role-identity and the uncertainty that follows an incident*. This emotion has been a part of interpersonal relationships since people became aware of themselves in the eyes of others. Judeo-Christian literature suggests that, after Adam and Eve ate of the forbidden fruit, God made them aware of their nakedness, and they then covered themselves with fig leaves. Thus, we have the beginning of embarrassment for humans. All people universally experience embarrassment beginning somewhere between two to five years of age (Buss, Iscoe, & Buss, 1979). It is an emotion most individuals try to avoid through protective means. Many consider it a taboo emotion because it represents one's degree of social incompetence. It disrupts the normal, expected flow of conversation (Goffman, 1967). "To embarrass is, literally, to bar or stop" (Gross & Stone, 1964, p. 3). Consequently, people view embarrassment as an aversive social emotion because it is a threat to interaction.

Most individuals would maintain that the act of intentionally causing someone to experience embarrassment is just as aversive or more aversive than the emotion itself. Nevertheless, even though most people actively avoid embarrassment, its behavioral displays, and the intentional use of behaviors to cause embarrassment in another, embarrassment and the threat of embarrassment may serve a positive function for individuals, relationships, groups, and even societies. Individuals and groups need the threat of embarrassment to insure social and interactional conformity (Armstrong, 1974; Harré, 1990). Indeed, the threat of and aversion to embarrassment helps keep people from displaying inappropriate behaviors (Edelmann, 1987). In fact, we may view embarrassment as a fusing mechanism for maintaining an agreed upon definition of interactants' social reality. The purpose of this chapter is to address a number of questions dealing with intentional embarrassment and to provide a clearer understanding of this so called "aversive" form of interpersonal behavior. Why do people embarrass others? How do embarrassors embarrass others? And what are the consequences of embarrassing others? The answers to these questions will, hopefully, show that, although the experience of embarrassment is undesirable, the intentional creation of embarrassment in another has the potential to create positive as well as negative outcomes for all individuals and relationships involved.

THE BEGINNINGS

Researchers have attempted to untangle the development (Buss et al., 1979; Sattler, 1965; Seidner, Stipek, & Feshbach, 1988), the causes (Buss, 1980; Gross & Stone, 1964; Weinberg, 1968), the influential variables (Petronio, 1984; Sattler, 1965; Sharkey & Stafford, 1990), and the consequences of embarrassment (Apsler, 1975; Druian & DePaulo, 1977; Goffman, 1967). Others have focused on an embarrassee's physiological reaction to embarrassment (Buck & Parke, 1972; Buck, Parke, & Buck, 1970), the effect of one's embarrassment on others (Edelmann, 1982; Sharkey & Stafford, 1990), and how people recover from embarrassment when they are unable to protect themselves from its occurrence (Cupach & Metts, 1990; Sharkey & Stafford, 1990). Still others have focused on individuals' susceptibility to embarrassment (Miller, 1995; Modigliani, 1966; Sharkey & Singelis, 1995). However, with all the literature dealing with this phenomenon, most theorists and researchers have viewed embarrassment as (a) an unintentional occurrence in which an individual performs unwanted behavior or another person unintentionally performs a behavior that causes a target to feel embarrassment (Metts & Cupach, 1989) or (b) an empathic response to another's embarrassment (Miller, 1987). Recently, however, a number of projects have begun an intriguing look at how and why individuals intentionally embarrass others. Unfortunately, very few studies on intentional embarrassment are published (i.e., Bradford & Petronio, in press; Gross & Stone, 1964; Sharkey, 1991, 1992, 1993); many of the studies are in the form of conference papers (Bradford, 1994; Petronio & Snider, 1990, 1992; Sharkey, 1995; Sharkey, Diggs, & Kim, 1993; Sharkey & Waldron, 1990), dissertations (Bradford, 1993; Sharkey, 1990b) or Master's theses (Chapman, 1993; Snider, 1992). Even so, much has been learned from these studies.

The study of intentional embarrassment provides clues as to the norms and rules underlying individuals' behaviors during interaction. Moreover, the research provides information about variables that influence the choice of communicative tactics and strategies and, in doing so, enhances our understanding of emotions overall and the dynamics of relational communication. More specifically, the study of intentional embarrassment leads us to a better understanding of how emotions are orchestrated in relationship processes (Bradford, 1994; Sharkey, 1993).

In the case of Adam and Eve above, we could argue that God was the first to employ intentional embarrassment to achieve a goal of negatively sanctioning their actions by making them aware of their own and each other's "private" body. Nevertheless, Darwin (1872/1965) appears to be the first researcher to discuss intentional embarrassment indirectly by claiming that disapprobation and approbation may lead to blushing, which Buss (1980; cf. Edelmann, 1987) maintained is the hallmark of embarrassment. Goffman (1953), however, appears to be the first individual to discuss the use of deliberate embarrassment directly. He stated that practical jokes, social games, and embarrassing stories play a significant role in people's social life. He elaborated on this idea later claiming that individuals' self-presentation (or face) may be threatened by oneself or by another unintentionally *or* intentionally (Goffman, 1967, 1973). Goffman's work has acted as a springboard from which most of the research on intentional, as well as unintentional, embarrassment has proceeded. Nevertheless, before moving into a discussion of research on intentional embarrassment, I would like first to show the prevalence of this phenomenon. Just how often do people intentionally embarrass others?

How Often Do People Embarrass Others?

It would appear that the use of intentional embarrassment is a rare occurrence (Miller, 1996). Due to the aversive and infectious nature of embarrassment and the uncertain consequences, it may appear that many people would want to avoid intentionally embarrassing someone. If we look at our own lives, we may be hard pressed to think of a number of times when we intentionally embarrassed another. In fact, in a study of intentional embarrassment in a variety of workplaces, Sharkey and Waldron (1990) found that only 7% of 228 superiors stated that they had ever embarrassed a subordinate and only 18% of 555 respondents reported ever being intentionally embarrassed by a superior. Researchers have even discovered that some individuals claimed that they had *never* intentionally embarrassed others. For example, with a sample of 1,134 college students and non-student adults over the age of 30, Sharkey (1992) found that approximately 3% of the respondents claimed that they had never intentionally embarrassed another. Bradford (1993, 1994) found that 9.5% of the 126 adolescents sampled stated that they never intentionally embarrassed a friend. Sharkey, Tamashiro, Igawa, and Muranaka's (1996) data show that approximately 1% of 614 individuals did not remember ever intentionally embarrassing another person. As a result, it seems that some people cannot remember intentionally embarrassing anyone. Others may feel that intentionally embarrassing another is not something they would care to do—or admit to doing. Interestingly, L. Bradford (personal communication, May 28, 1996) informed me that one of her respondents not only stated that she never intentionally embarrassed another person, but she also questioned Bradford's research ethics for even asking about such an activity!

Still, the research shows that most people can remember intentionally embarrassing someone at some point during their lives, but how often do they use embarrassment as a means to achieve their goals? Berger (1990) argued that intentional embarrassment is probably not a very frequent occurrence. Sharkey (1991) specifically asked respondents how often they had intentionally embarrassed others in the last six months. He found that, of 1,116 participants who provided a situation in which they had intentionally embarrassed a target, 24.5% indicated that they had not intentionally embarrassed anyone in the last six months. However, 53.2% said that they had intentionally embarrassed someone 1 to 5 times in the last six months, 10.3% said that they had intentionally embarrassed someone 6 to 10 times, 2.8% said 11 to 15 times, 2.5% said 16 to 20 times, and 6.7% reported that they embarrassed others more than 20 times during the last six months. These findings suggest that the frequency of use may be very individualistic. Some people totally avoid its use whereas others may thrive on it; some are even paid to embarrass others. Comedians, such as Don Rickles, are hired to intentionally embarrass people in an audience. During the Middle Ages, royalty recruited court jesters to embarrass and poke fun at those of nobility—although some went a bit too far and found themselves at the guillotine (Gross, 1984). The frequency of use may be related to relationship rules. This is supported by the fact that intentional embarrassment is not used to any great extent in the workplace between superiors and subordinates (Sharkey & Waldron, 1990) but is found more frequently in friendships (Bradford, 1994; Sharkey, 1993). That is, within some relationships, people may prohibit the use of embarrassment, whereas in others, people may expect its use and even encourage its use. Further research is needed to explain why some people employ intentional embarrassment more than others and how one's relationship plays a role. Still, it appears that most individuals use embarrassment to achieve their goals at one time or another. This leads us to the questions why and how people intentionally embarrass others and what outcomes result from such behaviors?

Intentional embarrassment can be more fully understood by mapping its process. Petronio and Snider (1990; see also Bradford & Petronio, in press), utilizing Berger's (1995) plan-based approach to strategic communication, developed the Planned Strategic Embarrassment Model (PSEM) to help explain what is entailed in the process of intentionally embarrassing a target and the possible outcomes/consequences of doing so. They state that there are roughly three stages in the process: (a) the establishment of one's goals, (b) the creation of a plan of action, and (c) the outcomes/consequences of one's plan. I will begin by asking the question, "Why do people intentionally embarrass others?"

THE ESTABLISHMENT OF ONE'S GOALS

WHY DO PEOPLE INTENTIONALLY EMBARRASS OTHERS?

The first stage of the PSEM focuses on the goals embarrassors want to achieve. Generally, embarrassors focus on a minimum of three goals: meta-goals, first-order goals, and second-order goals (see Dillard, 1990, and Berger, 1995, for a more in-depth discussion of goals).

The first type of goal found in the first stage of the PSEM is called meta-goals. Meta-goals represent the basic underlying objectives of every plan. At a minimum, we can see two meta-goals attempted by anyone devising a plan of action: (a) the degree of efficiency and (b) the degree of social appropriateness (Berger, 1995). *Efficiency* infers that people seek to create plans that will be realized with the least amount of time and effort expended to reach their goals. On the other hand, *appropriateness* refers to people's concern with producing plans that are acceptable to social others. At times, these two goals may conflict with each other. Petronio and Snider (1990) suggest that this is precisely what usually occurs when one plans to embarrass a target intentionally. The embarrassor favors efficiency over appropriateness (i.e., high efficiency, low social appropriateness). Thus, this is where the aversive nature of intentional embarrassment is derived. For example, suppose a number of friends are sitting around the table listening to one tell of a wonderful first date. Also suppose that this person begins to monopolize the conversation. One friend may intentionally embarrass this person to get the person to share the floor with others by saying, "Do your parents know you talk this much?" The plan to open the floor for others by using embarrassment may have been efficiently planned and very effective in achieving the embarrassor's goal. However, the target may become hostile toward the embarrassor and others may view the embarrassor's behavior as inappropriate for this situation and ask for some type of apology. Thus, the embarrassor sacrificed appropriateness for efficiency.

Still, embarrassors do not always favor efficiency over appropriateness; in fact, embarrassors may emphasize both (i.e., high efficiency, high social appropriateness) (Braithwaite, 1995; Petronio & Snider, 1992; Sharkey, 1995). Take, for example, some comedic performances and celebrity roasts. An exemplar may be the performances by Don Rickles. Rickles plans his act in a relatively efficient manner *and* in a most socially appropriate way. All who attend expect that he *will* embarrass people in the audience. That is his trademark. Other contexts may also encourage people to embarrass others intentionally. In fact, intentional embarrassment is ritualized in some contexts where "the *context* dictates the appropriateness of embarrassment" (Braithwaite, 1995, p. 155). Many initiation ceremonies require acting members to intentionally embarrass new or prospective members (e.g., fraternities, armed forces, scouting troops). Braithwaite (1995), who looked at the use of intentional embarrassment at "coed" wedding and baby showers, showed that women embarrass men to socialize them into the shower culture and to teach them appropriate shower behaviors. In still other contexts, such as birthday and bachelor and bachelorette parties, all attendees expect that the "celebrity" will be the target of many embarrassments throughout the celebration. In this light, we can see that for socialization and solidarity reasons, at least, embarrassors may achieve both meta-goals of efficiency and appropriateness. Indeed, some of these situations may actually emphasize social appropriateness at the expense of efficiency. For example, an individual may take much time to plan the perfect embarrassing situation for the person celebrating a birthday or for the new organizational recruit. Thus, we have low efficiency and high social appropriateness.

A final possibility is that embarrassors will emphasize neither meta-goal (i.e., low efficiency, low social appropriateness). A prime example may be revenge—as opposed to friendly retaliation for a previous embarrassment. An embarrassor may create an extensive plan that takes much time and deliberation (low efficiency) that, in the end, will violate what would be considered socially appropriate. So, the embarrassor fails to achieve both efficiency and social appropriateness. As can be seen, intentional embarrassment is not necessarily socially inappropriate behavior that is hastily enacted. Although each embarrassor achieves a level of social appropriateness and efficiency, meta-goals are relatively unconsciously pursued. Goals that are more consciously attended to and are more immediate are a person's first-order goals.

The second type of goal found in the first stage of the PSEM is first-order goals. Berger (1995) suggests that we pursue multiple goals simultaneously and one's goals are constantly changing. Additionally, what is an implicit goal at one point in time may be explicit in the next or vice versa. At any particular time, a person may only be aware of a subset of these goals. Using the characteristics of explicitness and immediateness, Bradford and Petronio (in press) define one's first- and second-order goals. First-order goals help to guide the planning process. They drive the communicative episode and tend to be more explicit and immediate than other goals. If an individual wants to get her or his significant other jealous, jealousy would be this person's first-order goal. If parents want their children to clean up their rooms, this would be the parents' first-order goal. For embarrassors, we would expect that their first-order goal is the embarrassment of another person (Bradford & Petronio, in press; Petronio & Snider, 1992), although, as will be seen, this is not always the case.

In general, individuals' first-order goals are affected by a multitude of variables. For embarrassors, their first-order goal of embarrassing a target is influenced by the relationship between the two parties and the biological sex of the people involved. That is, researchers have discovered that the desired end state of embarrassing a target is partially dependent on the definition of the interactors' relationship and each person's sex. For example, friends and intimate partners appear to employ intentional embarrassment more than any other relationship type, and embarrassors tend to embarrass targets of the same sex (Bradford, 1993, 1994; Sharkey, 1993). Also, using a Likert scale, Bradford (1993, 1994) asked embarrassors to indicate the degree of closeness they felt toward their target. The results indicate support for the above findings by indicating that embarrassors tend to embarrass people to whom they feel the closest, although females reported embarrassing very close friends more that males. Each of the above findings could be due to the fact that people tend to have more same sex friends. There are more opportunities for friends to embarrass each other (Sharkey, 1993). Embarrassors may be more aware of what triggers embarrassment in friends, whom they must know more intimately than others. Additionally, embarrassors are probably more aware of what triggers embarrassment in members of their own sex. Hence, first-order goals are those that individuals consciously pursue; those that are explicit and more immediate. Although first-order goals appear to be self-contained, another set of goals, second-order goals, help shape the planning of the first-order goals.

Second-order goals are the third type of goal found in the first stage of the PSEM. Second-order goals are those that drive the first-order goal. They are usually implicit, though they may be just as immediate and explicit as the first-order goal. For embarrassors, "these goals represent the impetus behind the need to embarrass and have an effect on the actual tactics selected to embarrass a person" (Petronio & Snider, 1992, p. 6). Using Gross and Stone's (1964) seminal work, researchers have helped us understand more fully these second-order goals. Gross and Stone (1964) and Sharkey (1992; Sharkey & Waldron, 1990) have identified a number of second-order goals that people attempt to achieve using embarrassment. Sharkey relied on the self-report of people who claimed to have intentionally embarrassed a target or who claimed to be recipients of intentional embarrassment. Content analysis of the data revealed the following second-order goals: (a) to socialize individuals into a group, (b) to negatively sanction an individual's behaviors, (c) to establish and/or maintain power, (d) to discredit another, (e) to show solidarity, and (f) to achieve self-satisfaction. Although some of these goals were combined for research purposes, this list covers all the goals reported by embarrassors and targets in these studies. What is interesting, though, is that embarrassors and targets view the second-order goals differently from each other. That is, they each perceive the embarrassors' intent differently. The following discussion will first provide the embarrassors' perspective of their second-order goals followed by the targets' perspective of embarrassors' second-order goals.

The Embarrassors' Perspective

The first of these second-order goals is to socialize individuals into various groups. Society, for example, is a macro group into which individuals are socialized. Because embarrassment is inevitable during one's life, childhood is the time when one needs to learn how to handle embarrassing situations—how to restore or redefine one's presented identity and how to maintain or recover one's poise when threatened. Through teasing, one is taught what is expected in terms of handling oneself in such situations. One learns through personal experience, not only how to handle an embarrassing situation, but also how to create such a situation for others. For example, children at school may become the center of attention when their friends remove their chairs before they can sit; the children thus fall to the ground. By experiencing this type of embarrassing situation, children are, in effect, learning through experience how to handle such a situation in the future. They learn what causes them embarrassment and what behaviors will "get them out of a jam." They also learn what to avoid so that others will have a more difficult time embarrassing them. In essence, Gross and Stone (1964) argue that embarrassment is used to test people's ability to remain poised or to regain their poise and to protect or to reestablish their social identity (i.e., face). They also point out that this testing continues into adulthood with the use of insults, teasing, "drinking each other under the table," and "playing the dozens." As mentioned previously, adults may use embarrassment as a way to allow individuals entree into a group. Embarrassors may be encouraged to use embarrassment because of positive reinforcement from other group members, and they may gain friends and/or status within the group for socializing a target into the group (Braithwaite, 1995; Sharkey, 1992). One embarrassor in Sharkey's (1990a) study claimed that she embarrassed a fellow Air Force Cadet because "[this fellow Cadet] was a new member of the group & it was an initiation."

Second, one may intentionally embarrass others to negatively sanction their actions. Here an embarrassor places the target in an embarrassing position to change the target's behavior. For example, Martin (1987) showed that teachers' practice of placing students in a corner for misbehaving is a prime example of the use of embarrassment to change one's behaviors. Some embarrassors in Sharkey's (1990a) study offered the following reasons for embarrassing a target that emphasize the negative sanctioning of behaviors: "I did this in order to stop her from inferring that we were the same age." "[I wanted] to get her to lighten up a little." "My goal was to get her to shut up." Grasmick, Bursik, and Kinsey (1991) provide another example. They claim that government public policies, such as the 1987 Oklahoma Anti-Littering Campaign, may be written in a way that increases the possibility of embarrassment for violators of community rules and laws. Using deterrence theory, they claim that the state can reduce the number of law violators by threatening a violator with legal sanctions. However, the state could also use moral appeals that people whose opinions potential violators value endorse. The potential violators then run the risk, not only of legal sanctions, but also of being embarrassed in front of the people they care about. In the 1987 Oklahoma Anti-Littering Campaign, the state appealed to the citizens' conscience and sense of community spirit as a way to create a threat of embarrassment for those who littered. They established the "Adopt-a-Highway" program that included placing signs along the adopted highways showing which neighborhood community groups were volunteering their time and efforts to keep the stretch of road free of litter. They also created an anti-litter media campaign slogan, "Don't Lay that Trash on Oklahoma," which was incorporated into a song and printed on trash bags and bumper stickers for vehicles. The song stressed the citizens' moral obligation to keep Oklahoma litter free. The goal of the state was intentionally to create a situation in which citizens would think twice about littering because of the fear of embarrassment. In each of these examples, the embarrassor is, in effect, attempting to create a situation in which the costs for continuing a particular behavior far outweigh the costs of being placed in an aversive situation.

A third goal one may have in intentionally embarrassing another is to establish and/or maintain power and control over others. Embarrassors attempt to gain or maintain their status position in relation to the target. Through embarrassment, individuals may create a situation in which the target will think twice about questioning one's status. The following embarrassors provided these examples of power plays: "By embarrassing my sister, I was trying to make myself look better. I wanted my family to think I was better, more intelligent than my sister." "I was trying to let the person know that I do know what I'm talking about and that he should listen to me" (Sharkey, 1990a).

Fourth, one may use embarrassment to discredit another person. Embarrassors, in essence, attempt to strip targets of their presented roles. They try to "bring targets down a notch." It is not necessarily the case that the embarrassor is also trying to gain power. This may happen, but the primary goal is simply to teach the target a lesson or to transform the targets' presented role/image into another. Social degradation ceremonies are one type of discrediting (see Garfinkel, 1956). Wolchover (1988) discussed how defense attorneys intentionally use police officers' past embarrassments to discredit their present testimonies and show that the officers are not who they purport themselves to be (i.e., honest and trustworthy witnesses). In this way, defense attorneys lead the jury to question the credibility of the officers. Some reasons given by embarrassors in Sharkey's (1990a) study included: "Our goal was to give him a lesson in honesty." "He needed to be brought down off his high horse and shown not every woman was dying to be his slave." "We wanted to bring this kid back down to earth. He had an attitude all season long that he was the best so we wanted to point out a major flaw."

Fifth, one can use embarrassment to achieve solidarity. Embarrassment may be a means through which a relationship can avoid atrophy. It adds a degree of excitement and novelty to a relationship and functions as a form of relational play used to create and sustain a level of intimacy and togetherness (Braithwaite, 1995; Cupach & Metts, 1994). Other embarrassors in Sharkey's (1990a) study reported the following solidarity reasons for embarrassing a target: "I wanted him to know that I care." "[I wanted to] put a little excitement into the night." "[I wanted] to make my friend have a memorable birthday." "[I did it] for fun, we do these things to each other a lot."

Finally, people embarrass others for self-satisfaction. Harré (1990) stated that the embarrassment of others can be fun. In their study of embarrassment in the workplace, Sharkey and Waldron (1990) found that one superior claimed that he just enjoyed embarrassing others. Embarrassors from another study by Sharkey (1990a) claimed the following reasons for embarrassing a target: "I thought it was funny," "I just wanted to see her blush," and "I get a kick out of watching her squirm." With each of these examples, one can see that the focus is on the self rather than on the relationship, i.e., "I." In these cases, the embarrassor is embarrassing the target for self-satisfaction and personal pleasure. There may be other latent second-order goals that the embarrassor was attempting to achieve in these situations (e.g., power and control over others, to show solidarity, discredit the target). The data do not provide sufficient information to make this determination.

Embarrassors do not employ these second-order goals equally in the attainment of first-order goals. Sharkey and his colleagues (1991, 1992; Sharkey, Tamashiro et al., 1996; Sharkey & Waldron, 1990) found that, of these goals, embarrassors reported using embarrassment as a way to show solidarity more than any other second-order goal. This was followed by the goal of negatively sanctioning another's behavior. Attribution theory explains these results by proposing that embarrassors tend to disclaim any dispositional reasons for their acts and instead egotistically report positive aims (i.e., solidarity) or blame environmental factors (e.g., the target's inappropriate behaviors). Just as a side note, Braithwaite (1991, 1995), acting as an observer/participant, concurred that, at least within the context of "coed" baby and wedding showers, female embarrassors tend to employ embarrassment to show togetherness and intimacy with the men (i.e., solidarity) and to socialize them by correcting their inappropriate shower behaviors. Continuing with our discussion, attribution theory, then, argues that targets or victims should attribute responsibility to the embarrassor more so than to the environment or themselves. Even though embarrassors state that they tend to embarrass for "positive" reasons, targets tend to have a different view of embarrassors' intentions.

The Target's Perspective

Researchers have also looked at the second-order goals of embarrassors from the target's perspective (Martin, 1987; McPherson & Kearney,

1992; Petronio, Olson, & Dollar, 1988, 1989; Sharkey et al., 1993; Sharkey, Kulp, Carpenter, Lee, & Rodillias, 1996). Martin's (1987) and Petronio et al.'s (1988) research represent the first attempts to detect targets' perceptions of embarrassors' second-order goals. Their research did not focus on intentional embarrassment. Nevertheless, their results indicated that targets did attribute intentionality to many of their embarrassors' acts. For example, some students in Martin's (1987) study reported that teachers intentionally embarrassed them to negatively sanction their behaviors, to "pick on" them, or to "destroy students." Petronio et al.'s (1988) work on romantic partners clearly showed that targets reported being intentionally embarrassed by a partner to control the relationship, to impress others at the partner's expense, to violate a norm of the relationship, and to retaliate against the partner.

Sharkey and Waldron's (1990) workplace study was the first to focus specifically on intentional embarrassment from the perspective of the target. In this study, subordinates were asked to describe an incident in which they believed a supervisor intentionally embarrassed them. The majority of subordinates maintained their superiors intentionally embarrassed them to establish or maintain power. This was closely followed by the goal of "personality" (i.e., self-satisfaction), solidarity, negative sanctioning of behavior, and discrediting. Here we see the victims claiming that the embarrassors were self-focused. That is, targets attributed the embarrassing act to the superiors' personalities—wanting to get ahead or self-satisfaction. However, it should be noted that this project was exploratory and the sample was small. So, the results should be accepted cautiously. Also, the context may have played a large part in the reports—clear status differences. Based on the above-mentioned studies, it appears that the prediction offered by attribution theory is supported. However, one study appears to cast doubt on these claims.

In questioning 514 targets, Sharkey et al. (1993) found that, despite the context in which embarrassment occurred, targets' reports were very similar to those of embarrassors. The goal of solidarity was the most widely reported goal followed by negatively sanctioning behaviors, self-satisfaction, and power. Sharkey et al. (1993) decided to combine and compare the targets' responses with Sharkey's (1992) embarrassors' responses. They learned that targets were more likely than embarrassors to claim that the embarrassor was attempting the goal of self-satisfaction, whereas embarrassors were more likely to report solidarity and negatively sanctioning of the target's behavior. Here then the argument is supported that targets tend to attribute the responsibility to the perpetrator of the act rather than to themselves (i.e., negatively sanctioning the target's behavior) or to prosocial goals such as solidarity. Overall, it appears that embarrassors claim that their second-order goals are positively valenced. They embarrass targets to achieve solidarity or to inform the target that she or he is violating some norm or rule, thereby helping targets conform to what is expected. Targets appear to emphasize more negatively valenced second-order goals such as power and self-satisfaction.

Goal Valence

Until now, the focus has been on the types of second-order goals and embarrassors' and targets' perspectives without concern for the valence of these goals. This is a new and promising area of research which should help us understand more fully the role second-order goals play in planning to embarrass a target. Rather than focusing on the second-order goals themselves, Petronio and her colleagues (Bradford & Petronio, in press; Petronio & Snider, 1990, 1992) suggest that second-order goals may be divided into those goals that have either a positive valence or a negative valence. For example, they suggest that revenge and retaliation are negatively valenced goals. However, Sharkey (1992, 1993) reported that revenge and retaliation may be positively or negatively valenced. There is a difference between the two friends who define part of their relationship on the ability to outdo the other's embarrassments and the ex-lover who wishes to totally humiliate her or his ex-partner. This difference may be justified if we measure the positive or negative valence of a second-order goal by the intensity of embarrassment desired and the amount of helpful face work from the embarrassor after the embarrassment (Bradford & Petronio, in press). In other words, if embarrassors want targets to suffer and they do not help the targets alleviate the embarrassment felt, embarrassors' goals most likely have a negative valence. Just the reverse would be true for positively valenced goals. Unfortunately, we do not possess the tools capable of probing the true intentions of the embarrassor as of yet. Indeed, future research will most likely find that embarrassors and targets will also differ in terms of their attributions of positive or negative valence to the intent of embarrassors second-order goals.

Variables Associated with an Embarrassor's Second-Order Goals

Research to date has identified two variables that appear to be associated with an embarrassor's choice of second-order goals, the relationship between the parties and the biological sex of the parties. Sharkey (1993) found that friends, intimate partners and subordinates tend to employ intentional embarrassment to achieve the second-order goal of solidarity more than any other goal and that friends are unlikely to use embarrassment to gain power. Superiors, on the other hand, tend to use embarrassment to negatively sanction the behaviors of subordinates or to show solidarity (Sharkey, 1993; Sharkey & Waldron, 1990).

The biological sex of the people involved is associated with an embarrassor's second-order goals as well. Although both males and females appear to use embarrassment to show solidarity with a target, males use embarrassment more than females to establish and maintain power, and females more than males use embarrassment to negatively sanction a target's behaviors. Male targets tend to be the recipients of negatively sanctioned goals whereas females tend to be the recipients of power goals (Sharkey, 1993). We can see that the cited research is beginning to paint a picture of why embarrassors embarrass targets, how embarrassors and targets differ in their perceptions of the goals attempted, and how variables such as the relationship between the participants and the participants' sex are associated with an embarrassor's choice of first- and second-order goals.

One final note on the second-order goals of embarrassors. The goals of solidarity, power, negative sanctioning of behaviors, discrediting a target and self-satisfaction are all second-order goals according to the PSEM. This brings up an interesting question that needs to be considered. Could the goal of embarrassment *and* these second-order goals in reality both be first-order goals? Suppose I wish to discredit a coworker—my first-order goal. It is immediate and explicit. I also decide that the best way to discredit this person is to embarrass her or him during a company meeting. This is also a first-order goal. It is immediate and explicit. From here, I plan how to go about accomplishing these goals. This is one question that seems problematic for the model. Retaining Berger's (1995) classification of implicit and explicit goals, discussed earlier, may be more beneficial. Take the degree of embarrassment one wishes to create in a target. For some embarrassors, this may be a first-order goal, but for others it may be a second-order goal depending on how implicit or explicit and how immediate the goal is. Labeling any goal a first-order or second-order goal gives the impression that one prioritizes goals and that a goal is one type of goal or the other. It fails to take into account the process of goal planning; it does not seem to capture the fluctuating nature of one's goals as well as describing them using terms of degrees of explicitness and immediateness.

In sum, embarrassors attempt multiple goals in the planning of the embarrassment of a target. They are concerned, to some degree, about the extent to which they wish to be efficient and socially appropriate, their meta-goals. Embarrassors attempt to cause a target to become embarrassed to some degree, their first-order goal. They are also, consciously or unconsciously, attempting a number of second-order goals: socializing individuals into a group, negatively sanctioning an individual's behaviors, establishing and/or maintaining power in a relationship, discrediting a target, showing solidarity, or achieving self-satisfaction. The embarrassor's relationship with a target and the sex of each party are associated with the development of an embarrassor's first- and second-order goals. Next, I will turn to the establishment of the plan of action. That is, what does an embarrassor do to embarrass a target?

THE PLANNING OF ACTIONS

According to the PSEM, after one selects the goals toward which one wishes to strive, embarrassors devise a *plan*. "A plan specifies the actions that are necessary for the attainment of a goal or several goals" (Berger, 1988, p. 96). The process by which embarrassors devise action sequences, anticipate possible outcomes, adjust actions based on anticipated outcomes, and enact their plans through action is termed *planning*. The planning process and one's plan(s) are constructed based on one's own experiences of embarrassing others, unused plans, direct instructions from others, and watching others construct and carry out embarrassment plans (Berger, 1995; Petronio & Snider, 1992). A number of contributing factors also influence the plan, some of which are the "plan tempo," an embarrassor's experiences, the context, the definition of the relationship, one's skill level, and the amount of information the embarrassor has about the target (Petronio & Snider, 1992). For example, Sharkey (1995) argued that, for embarrassors to increase the success of their plan, they must have a clear understanding of the target's *self-identity frame*. The self-identity frame affects the degree to which a target will experience embarrassment when his or her presented role-identity is questioned and what type of violation is needed to create embarrassment. The self-identity frame consists of "(1) the strength of one's idealized role-identity (as bounded and separate) going into the interaction, (2) the sensitivity to others' evaluations as the interaction unfolds, and (3) the degree to which one's identity is entwined with and dependent on others" (Sharkey & Singelis, 1995, p. 924). The self-identity frame affects the degree to which a person will experience embarrassment when her or his presented role-identity is questioned or when her or his poise is threatened. Having knowledge about a target's self-identity frame will help an embarrassor choose which tactic/strategy would be needed to create embarrassment in the target. Thus, the planning of actions can be a very complex procedure. For a more detailed discussion of the planning process and what is entailed see Bradford and Petronio (in press). The purpose of this discussion is to focus on the tactics/strategies embarrassors use to carry out their plans.

How Do Embarrassors Embarrass Others?

Based on research conducted by Sharkey and his colleagues (1990b, 1992; Sharkey & Stafford, 1990; Sharkey & Waldron, 1990) and Cupach and Metts (1990), there are a number of tactics/strategies that embarrassors have at their disposal to embarrass a target: Recognition/Praise, Criticism/Correction, Teasing, Cause to Look Unpoised, Violation of Privacy, and Association.

First, Recognition/Praise refers to behavior that honors or singles out a target to show appreciation. One may recognize someone by asking her or him to stand in a meeting to receive a round of applause for a job well done. Or one may be recognized by seeing her or his name flash across the sky with the message happy birthday attached. One may praise another though compliments such as telling the target, in front of fellow workers or friends, how fantastic he or she looks. L. Buss (1978, as cited in A. Buss, 1980) claimed that what makes praise embarrassing is the discrepancy between one's own self-evaluation and the degree of praise. Yet praise is only embarrassing when the degree of praise is higher than one's own self-evaluation. The target is both pleased and uncomfortable due to the possible fear of immodest thoughts and feelings (Buss, 1980).

Second, Criticism/Correction refers to behavior used to blame, judge or denounce a target's behaviors. This would include such actions as reprimanding a subordinate in front of a client or fellow worker, public degradations, and so on. The embarrassor's aim is to show that the target is wrong for whatever behavior is being displayed. The embarrassor is in effect passing a moral judgment upon the target.

Third, Teasing refers to behavior used to make fun of another. It also refers to practical jokes. What is interesting about teasing is that it is a paradoxical form of communication. It is both irritating and playful (Pawluk, 1989). Teasing is the most recognizable form of intentional embarrassment. It may include playful jibes, friendly antagonism, permitted disrespect, and so on (Pawluk, 1989). Children are notorious for making fun of each other and for playing practical jokes on one another.

Fourth, Causing a Target to Look Unpoised refers to behavior used to cause a target to appear awkward and/or ungraceful. It refers to a person's inability to control himself or herself or the situation (Gross & Stone, 1964). In the cafeteria, embarrassors may try to make targets laugh while they are drinking because they would usually expel the beverage through the nose. This is quite an awkward and embarrassing situation to be placed in. Tripping someone, pulling a person's chair out from under her or him as this person is beginning to sit, and so on are all ways to make a person lose poise.

Fifth, Violation of One's Privacy refers to behavior used to reveal things that one would rather not have revealed. This would include revealing private information as well as revealing a person's private clothing, objects, spaces, territories, and body areas. Walking in on someone while the person is using the toilet, "de-panting" someone, showing children's significant others pictures of them in the tub when they were one year old, or divulging a story about a friend that was not to be divulged all constitute violations of privacy.

The last tactic/strategy embarrassors use to intentionally embarrass a target is Association. Association refers to behavior used to associate a person with someone or something who "is enacting untoward behavior and assumes that negative attributions will be generalized to him or her from those actions" (Cupach & Metts, 1990, p. 346). For example, a person may present a very poor report at a board meeting and then thank the person sitting next to him or her for doing most of the work on the project. Here, the person sitting is embarrassed by being associated with the poor presentation. In another context, individuals may act in an unusual way which may call attention to the person they are with. For example, a person may act in a loud and silly manner while sitting with a significant other in an exclusive restaurant. The significant other may feel that negative attributions from the patrons will be generalized toward him or her because of the other's unusual behavior.

Researchers have found that not all tactics/strategies are used with the same frequency and that some tactic/strategies are used more within certain relationships than within others. Sharkey (1992) found that a violation of privacy was the most commonly reported tactic/strategy employed to embarrass a target. In fact, friends, parents, and siblings appear to use this tactic/strategy more than any other tactic/strategy. Adult children, on the other hand, tend to use recognition/praise with their parents and, in the workplace, superiors use criticism or teasing with subordinates (Sharkey, 1993; Sharkey & Waldron, 1990).

The sex of embarrassor and target also seems to play a role in the planning of embarrassment tactics/strategies. For example, Sharkey (1993) discovered that males more than females tend to report causing the target to appear unpoised or association, whereas females tend to report using recognition/praise more than men to intentionally embarrass others.

Researchers have also hypothesized ethnic background and culture to be factors influencing tactic/strategy choice. Only one researcher thus far has looked at this possibility with regard to intentional embarrassment. Bradford (1993, 1994) surveyed a number of Hispanic and non-Hispanic adolescents but found no association between ethnic background and tactic/strategy choice. She suggested that one reason for not finding an association may be the fact that the Hispanic sample may have become acculturated to their non-Hispanic (United States) friends' norms. I would argue that one's ethnic background may be less a factor in choosing a tactic/strategy than an emphasis on one's independent or interdependent self-construal (see Sharkey & Singelis, 1995; Singelis & Sharkey, 1995). People who emphasize their independent self-construal are less interested in the target's ability to handle an embarrassing situation than people who emphasize their interdependent self-construal. It may be that those with highly developed independent self-construals may employ many of the above-mentioned tactics whereas those with highly developed interdependent self-construals may only choose those tactics/strategies that they feel targets will perceive as having a positive valence. Due to the increase in cross-cultural interactions around the globe, future studies using individuals' self-construals, rather than their ethnic or cultural identity, may lead researchers on a more productive path to understanding embarrassors' tactic/strategy choices.

Finally, what tactics/strategies an embarrassor plans to use may be associated with the embarrassor's goals. Sharkey and his colleagues (Sharkey, 1991, 1992, Sharkey & Waldron, 1990) have shown that an association exists between an embarrassor's second-order goal and the tactic/strategy chosen to achieve the goal. In Sharkey and Waldron's (1990) study of superiors and subordinates in the workplace, they found that there was a tendency for superiors to use teasing to achieve solidarity and criticism to negatively sanction subordinates' behavior. Further support was found for the association between one's goals and tactic/strategy choice. Using a large sample of college students and non-college adults, Sharkey (1992; Sharkey, Tamashiro, et al., 1996) found that embarrassors who want to achieve the goal of solidarity not only use the tactic/strategy of teasing, but they also use recognition/praise and violations of privacy. The violation of privacy as a means to show solidarity came as a surprise. Because the majority of intentional embarrassment situations occur between friends and romantic partners, individuals may perceive that this is an acceptable behavior because both parties expect that positively valued behaviors will either accompany or follow the privacy violation. These positively valenced actions will then compensate for the violation (Sharkey, 1993). It may also be the case that the relationship history has defined this type of behavior as acceptable—so long as it is not a frequent occurrence (see Petronio et al., 1989). Additionally, embarrassors who wish to negatively sanction a target's behaviors or establish and maintain power tend to choose the tactic/strategy of criticism (Sharkey, 1992; Sharkey, Tamashiro, et al., 1996). So, it appears that embarrassors' goals help in the planning and selection of tactics/strategies to achieve those goals. However, Petronio and Snider (1992) did not find an association between embarrassors' goals and tactics/strategies chosen. This is not surprising.

Sharkey's (1990b, 1992) goal classification was based on what embarrassors claimed were their goals. Petronio and Snider's (1992) classification was based on whether an embarrassor used face-saving strategies after the embarrassment (i.e., positive valenced tactics) or continued face threatening strategies (i.e., negative valenced tactics). I would agree that goals and tactics may be positively or negatively valenced. Nevertheless, embarrassors, targets, and observers will most likely perceive a positive or negative goal valence or tactic valence differently.

In sum, embarrassors employ a number of tactics/strategies to embarrass others. They tend to recognize/praise a target, criticize a target, tease a target, cause a target to look unpoised, violate a target's privacy, or associate a target with someone or something performing an untoward act. The research suggests that a number of factors affect an embarrassor's tactic/strategy selection. These factors, including the definition of the relationship between the embarrassor and the target and the sex of the two individuals, play a part in the planning process. Although ethnic background was not associated with tactic/strategy choice, future research may show how self-construals play a role in the selection process. Future research should also continue to see how the "plan tempo," an embarrassor's experiences, other contextual variables, one's skill level, and the amount of information the embarrassor has about the target will affect an embarrassor's plan for embarrassing a target. Next, I would like to move on to the final stage of the PSEM, the outcomes/consequences of one's plan.

THE OUTCOMES/CONSEQUENCES OF ONE'S PLAN

WHAT ARE THE CONSEQUENCES OF EMBARRASSING OTHERS?

The last step in the PSEM is the outcomes or consequences of intentional embarrassment. There are obvious consequences to the embarrassment episode as discussed in the introduction of this chapter. However, these consequences, both positive and negative, are generally short-lived and tend to dissipate with time (Sharkey, 1991). Despite intentionality, embarrassment disrupts the flow of the interaction. Interaction is sidetracked and is forced to focus instead on remediating the disruption caused by the embarrassment. Over and beyond the effect of embarrassment on the interaction episode, there are also consequences beyond the emotion of embarrassment for the target. Research on embarrassment from the target's perspective, again regardless of intent, has shown that, when embarrassed by an embarrassor, targets report experiencing various personal and relational consequences. For example, student targets reported developing a dislike for teachers, becoming "mad" and afraid of teachers' actions, and developing a negative self-concept (Martin, 1987). They also stated that teachers' actions negatively affected their learning and, moreover, led some of them to truancy and some even thought about quitting school. On the other hand, some students stated that the embarrassment and fear of embarrassment led them to study more. In a study of romantic partners, frequent other-generated-embarrassment negatively affected the relationship and satisfaction with relational communication (Petronio et al., 1988, 1989). Another consequence of embarrassment for some targets is that they are forced into a situation in which they must try to regain their presented image or regain their poise. That is, targets must engage in face-work.

Much research has looked at remedial strategies that targets employ to return interaction to its homeostatic state (for a review of this research see Cupach & Metts, 1990, 1994; Edelmann, 1987; Miller, 1996; Tracy, 1990). People who are embarrassed may physically remediate (i.e., fix the problem), apologize, account (i.e., justify or provide an excuse), describe the action, employ humor, escape the encounter, display objective symptoms (e.g., blushing, laughing, exclamations), or try to conceal their embarrassment (Cupach & Metts, 1994; Sharkey & Stafford, 1990). Some of this research has shown that the person responsible for embarrassment is associated with embarrassed individuals' use of face-work (Sharkey & Stafford, 1990). This is relevant here because, by its very nature, intentional embarrassment is usually caused by another individual, although at times individuals may purposefully embarrass themselves. What was discovered is that, regardless of intentionality, when one person is responsible for another's embarrassment, the target tends to respond to the embarrassor with hostility (Miller, 1996). Indeed, the embarrassor now has to deal with the target's negative response and any relational consequences that follow. Overall, the consequences of intentional embarrassment affect more than just the target. In fact, Bradford and Petronio (in press) argue that the outcomes of intentional embarrassment affect not only the target but also the embarrassor, the relationship between the two, and any observers present.

The Targets (Embarrassees)

When individuals intentionally embarrass a target, there are both desired and undesired consequences for the target. Some possible consequences to the target include the perception of appearing incompetent and less attractive to others (Bradford, 1994). A target may experience lower social self-esteem (Apsler, 1975) and psychological discomfort (Grasmick et al., 1991). If a supervisor embarrassed a subordinate, the subordinate may quit the job (Sharkey & Waldron, 1990). Targets may also change their view of the embarrassors. For example, suppose a target has a very positive view of the embarrassor before the embarrassing incident. If the embarrassing act violates a major relationship rule, the target may develop a more negative opinion of the embarrassor.

From the embarrassors' perspective, embarrassors report that targets respond with objective symptoms (e.g., blushing) and hostility more than any other response. Some embarrassors report that targets retaliate in a positive or negative fashion or engage in protective measures to prevent similar situations from happening in the future. Embarrassors also claim that, if they criticize targets, targets tend to respond by trying to conceal the embarrassment or they account for their own behavior (i.e., justify or excuse) (Sharkey, 1991, 1992; Sharkey & Waldron, 1990).

Targets do not see their responses in the same way as embarrassors. However, the results are not consistent. For example, targets reported that they tend to respond with objective symptoms, concealment, accounts, escape, and remediation more than any other response. In fact, they claimed that hostility was *not* a response that they would tend to choose (Sharkey et al., 1993). This result can be compared to Sharkey and Waldron's (1990) study that showed that, within the workplace, subordinates reported responding with aggression more than any other response. From an observer's perspective, using a participant/observation naturalistic method, Braithwaite (1995) reported that male targets attending "coed" wedding and baby showers did not, at any time, respond to the embarrassors with aggression. In fact, the most identified responses included avoidance and humor. In addition, Snider (1992) had participants engage in one of three potentially embarrassing situations in a laboratory setting. In one of the situations, a friend, acting as a confederate, intentionally violated the participant's privacy by revealing some private information. He found that none of the targets responded with hostility.

Based on the above findings, it appears that the context plays an important part in target responses. Despite the context, targets respond with hostility more than any other response (Sharkey, 1992). However, when researchers focus on a particular context, the context seems to have an impact on targets' responses. The work setting and the shower setting have their own norms and regulations that constrain certain behaviors and encourage others. That is, the context informs interactors of expected meta-goals, that is, what behavior is socially appropriate. In turn, this will affect the meta-goal of efficiency. The workplace is filled with situations in which a superior must correct a subordinate's behaviors. Hence, we should find more criticisms to negatively sanction inappropriate behaviors in this context and more targets responding with anger/hostility. However, because there is not such a clear-cut power differential at showers, this context would be more prone to teasing to achieve solidarity ends, resulting in less hostility. The context allows for and, at many showers, requires the intentional embarrassment of the celebrity.

Looking to embarrassment in the laboratory context is also beneficial because it provides valuable information about targets' responses. Although not focused specifically on intentional embarrassment, researchers have intentionally created embarrassing situations for their participants using various tactics (e.g., having them suck on a pacifier, sing the Star-Spangled Banner, spill coffee into a confederate's camera bag) to see how targets would respond to such situations. Some found that embarrassment led to increased compliance to help others (Apsler, 1975; Cann & Blackwelder, 1984; cf. Foss & Crenshaw, 1978), face-saving behaviors (e.g., humor, escape, remediation, accounts, descriptions of the event, and apologies) (Fink & Walker, 1977; Garland & Brown, 1972; Gonzales, Pederson, Manning, & Wetter, 1990), sacrificing tangible rewards (Brown, 1970; Brown & Garland, 1971), changes in nonverbal behaviors (e.g., decreased eye contact, increased smiling, speech disturbances) (Edelmann & Hampson, 1979, 1981), and physiological changes (e.g., increased skin conductance and deceleration of heart rate) (Buck et al., 1970). Though experimenters were intentionally creating situations where targets would experience embarrassment, some conditions made it difficult for targets to identify the actual embarrassor (e.g., Edelmann & Hampson, 1981). In other contrived situations, the context was intentionally set up to have the target believe that she or he was responsible for the situation (e.g., Gonzales et al., 1990). Some possible reasons for why targets did not respond with hostility in these situations may include: targets were unclear about who was responsible for their embarrassment; they were led to believe that they were the cause of the situation; or maybe the researcher's "social position" affected the targets' perception of the situation (i.e., you do not become hostile with a researcher). This points to the fact that embarrassors can create situations in which targets are uncertain about whom to hold responsible for the situation or are led to believe that they were responsible for the situation. How targets interpret the embarrassing situations, which includes the assignment of responsibility, plays a large part in the targets' outcomes/consequences. Outside the laboratory context, embarrassors may create such situations to avoid any type of negative consequence for themselves and/or to alleviate any perceived responsibility for creating the situation. Indeed, the context seems a prime area for future research to discover more about how various contexts affect targets' consequences. It also seems that future research should look at how embarrassors are able to manipulate a situation in such a way so that they can appear uninvolved or unresponsible for the situation. This would be considered another first-order goal for the embarrassor, "How can I intentionally embarrass this target without being held responsible for the embarrassment?"

Another area worthy of study is the process of embarrassment (i.e., the unfolding of the embarrassment event) and its effect on targets' outcomes/responses. Snider (1992) has embarked on an interesting line of research that focuses on the temporal nature of intentional embarrassment and how its chronology affects a target's behavior. His research promotes the idea that targets will proactively engage in behaviors to keep embarrassors from proceeding with their plans. If the potential target is unsuccessful, then targets will enact other behaviors concurrent with the execution of the embarrassors' plans, again to keep embarrassors from achieving their first-order goals or to reduce the threat. Finally, if embarrassors are successful, targets engage in face-saving behaviors reactively to help regain their poise or presented identities. This is a promising line of research in that it views intentional embarrassment as a relational creation; it is a process that unfolds over time. Continued research should help us understand the intentional embarrassment process more fully.

Still another fruitful area of research is concerned with the positive or negative valence of an embarrassor's goal. Petronio and Snider (1990, 1992; Bradford & Petronio, in press) implicitly claim that embarrassors' positive or negative goal valence has an effect upon targets' outcomes. They state that positive valenced goals (e.g., socialization) tend to be thought out and planned more fully than negative valenced goals (e.g., establishing or maintaining power) and embarrassors' goal valence affects how they will interact with the target after the embarrassment (i.e., help the target save face or continue to threaten the target's face even more). However, regardless of an embarrassor's desire for a benevolent or a malevolent outcome for the target, the target may not recognize the intent. It is not the embarrassors' positive or negative perception or intention of their goals that lead to various consequences for targets but the targets' perceptions of the embarrassors' goals. Obviously embarrassors could increase the possibility that the target will agree with the valence intended by engaging in face-saving behaviors or continued face-threatening behaviors (Petronio & Snider, 1992). As we can see, when people intentionally embarrass others, there are many possible consequences for the target. Indeed, as alluded to above, there are also consequences for the embarrassor.

The Embarrassor

The consequences for embarrassors may depend on how successful they are at achieving their first-order goal of embarrassing the target. What happens to embarrassors who fail at their first-order goal? The flubbed attempt may embarrass them. Targets may respond with unwanted and/or unanticipated behaviors such as verbal and/or physical hostility. Embarrassors could lose the trust of the target and may find that the targets now dislike them. Superiors may lose workers and teachers may find that students now avoid them or dislike them (Bradford, 1994; Martin, 1987; Sharkey, 1992, 1995; Sharkey & Waldron, 1990). Obviously, the most important outcome for the embarrassor is the achievement of her or his second-order goals (e.g., power, solidarity, self-satisfaction), but there may be unwelcome consequences. Because embarrassment is contagious, the situation may embarrass embarrassors or unintended others may become embarrassed. If this is the case, then embarrassors must engage in face-work to restore their own identities or poise or help the unintended others to regain their face. Another consequence for embarrassors is wanting to or having to help targets save face. One basic axiom of interaction is that fellow interactants should help those in trouble save face (Cupach & Metts, 1994). So, embarrassors may try to help targets restore their face. In fact, as stated earlier, embarrassors who are interested in achieving a positively valenced goal tend to help targets regroup (Petronio & Snider, 1992). One factor that appears to influence whether an embarrassor will help the target recover is the embarrassor's biological gender. Bradford (1994) found that female embarrassors tend to help targets recover from embarrassments more than males. She argued that this could be because women are generally more relationship oriented than men. She also found that male embarrassors reported that they felt more positive emotions or were unconcerned after embarrassing a target than female embarrassors. Bradford argued that females may report more negative emotions or concern because they tend to embarrass individuals they consider relationally closer than do males, and females may fear the embarrassment's relational effect more so than males. Additionally, the targets' emotional responses and face-saving efforts may mediate embarrassors' emotional response. For example, embarrassors felt more positive about the situation when they perceived that targets engaged in more assertive face-saving efforts and when the targets appeared to feel positive about the embarrassing situation. Braithwaite (1995) also supported this in her study of men attending baby and wedding showers. She interviewed the men (the targets) and the women (the embarrassors) after the showers and found that men did not report any negative experiences occurring during the showers. She also found that both embarrassors and targets stated that they had positive feelings about the showers. This may suggest that, because participants expect embarrassment in this type of situation and because all come to such an occasion with an understanding that embarrassments will occur "in-good-fun" (i.e., they are socially appropriate), men and women interpret embarrassment positively and respond in positive ways to the embarrassment. Therefore, the outcome/consequences to embarrassors (the women) were generally positive.

The embarrassment situation may also have consequences for the future behavior of the embarrassor. Sharkey (1991) found that embarrassors will use past intentional embarrassments to "rib" targets in the future. We can also imagine that, depending on the outcomes of an embarrassment situation, an embarrassor may decide that this type of behavior is not acceptable or appropriate or just the inverse. Consequently, the embarrassor may later either avoid this type of behavior or increase the behavior in certain relationships. We can see that the outcomes/consequences of intentional embarrassment episodes are not reserved solely for the target. The embarrassor must also accept and deal with the consequences of her or his acts. Because the consequences of intentional embarrassment affect both targets and embarrassors, the consequences may also affect their shared relationship.

The Relationships

Embarrassors claim that short-term relational consequences of intentional embarrassment tend to be negative, but these negative consequences tend to dissipate over time (Sharkey, 1991). Even so, many of these embarrassors claimed that the intentional embarrassment positively affected their relationship. In fact, intentional embarrassment, in many instances, may be viewed as a relationship maintenance strategy. Sharkey (1992) argues that, with some relationships, embarrassment helps to show a degree of solidarity and is a way to avoid boredom in a relationship. As Duck (1988) points out, it is novelty and challenge that help relationships maintain themselves. Even though intentional embarrassment is one identifying feature of some people's relationships, for others, it is a taboo. Two of Bradford's (1993) participants exemplify this dichotomy:

> Person 1: "My friends and I embarrass each other alot [sic]. It's only for fun."
>
> Person 2: "Im [sic] ther [sic] friend and friends aren't suppost [sic] to harm or hurt here [sic] friends feelings."

Although embarrassment may be acceptable in a relationship, and although most embarrassment episodes dissipate over time, it is a risky enterprise (Miller, 1996), and it is possible to overdo it. Embarrassments may have a detrimental effect on the relationship. Petronio et al. (1988, 1989) discovered that frequent privacy violations in romantic relationships lead to lower reported relational quality and satisfaction with relational communication. I would argue that, because intentional embarrassment is such a complex phenomenon, relational consequences will probably be dependent on a multitude of variables. For example, the context, the definition of the relationship, the closeness of the relationship, the intent and subsequent actions of the embarrassor, the target's perception of the embarrassor's intent and subsequent responses, and the degree of embarrassment attempted and experienced may affect relational consequences. Future research will need to consider these and other variables to gain a clearer understanding of how the use of embarrassment affects the interactants' relationship.

So far we have discussed some consequences for the embarrassor, the target, and the relationship itself. There could be consequences for others not directly involved in the embarrassment event as well.

Observers

Outsiders may be affected as the embarrassing events unfold. Most obviously, because embarrassment is contagious, it is possible that, regardless of intent, others observing the embarrassing situation will want to help return the interaction to an acceptable flow. In such cases, it is highly possible that the observers will attempt to help the target recover from the embarrassment by pretending that nothing has happened or help remediate the situation (see Cupach & Metts, 1990; Sharkey & Stafford, 1990). In addition, observers may respond by denouncing the embarrassor for her or his acts. On the other hand, if observers feel that the embarrassor was justified in intentionally embarrassing the target, they may actually encourage or participate in the continued embarrassment of the target (Cupach & Metts, 1990). Assume person A has a habit of taking credit for coworker B's projects. Further assume that fellow workers are witnesses to these thefts and feel person A is "out-of-line." One day, person A has to give a presentation to the organization. Person B, the fellow workers, and management are all present. During the presentation, person A again takes credit for person B's project. Person B then questions person A in more detail about the project and the project's history thereby intentionally discrediting person A. Because the fellow workers believe that person B was justified in embarrassing person A, they may help exacerbate the embarrassment by not helping person A recover; they may also ask questions to further discredit person A and so on.

The consequences to others may also be part of embarrassors' plans. Embarrassors may intentionally embarrass a target to affect the behaviors of others. One may especially see this when an embarrassor wants to discredit a target. One possible goal of a degradation ceremony is to bring others closer together with the embarrassor (this could have been part of person B's goals in the above example). Garfinkel (1956) claims that public denunciation may reinforce group solidarity by destroying and reconstituting the "target's" presented image. Wolchover's (1988) study of defense attorneys' use of past police officer embarrassments is such an example. The point is to get the jury to view this witness as uncredible and to distance themselves from the witness. There is another possible consequence for others. We can see this in political campaigns when opponents "mud sling." The purpose is to embarrass one's opponent to cause the voters to distance themselves from the target and rally behind the embarrassor. Finally, Martin (1987) discusses how being a "teacher's pet" may affect this student's relationship with other students. Some teachers may continually embarrass a student by praising and giving recognition to him or her. This may cause other students to avoid the "suck-up."

The overview of consequences of embarrassment should show that the fallout from an intentional embarrassment episode is numerous. Embarrassors' acts not only affect the targets, but they also affect the embarrassors themselves, their relationship with the targets, and other parties. One final question remains: how successful are embarrassors at achieving their goals?

How Successful are Embarrassors at Achieving Their Goals?

Although embarrassment is not employed with great frequency, it appears that embarrassors feel they are quite successful in achieving their goals. Sharkey (1992) reported that 92% of 1,040 embarrassors stated that they achieved their goals using embarrassment. Sharkey et al. (1993) also discovered that targets concurred that embarrassors overwhelmingly achieved their goals (83% of 894 respondents). Also, Sharkey, Tamashiro, et al. (1996) support this finding with 89.1% of 514 embarrassors reporting that they achieved their goals. However, more embarrassors reported achieving their goal than did targets (Sharkey et al., 1993). These findings may be an artifact of retrospective questionnaire studies. Embarrassors may only report those instances when they feel they were successful and distance themselves from their failures. Even so, the majority of targets reported that embarrassors were successful. This could be because successful attempts at embarrassment are very salient in a target's mind. Further research may shed light on just how victorious embarrassors truly are.

Sharkey (1992) also discovered an association between the achievement of one's goal and the goal attempted. Not surprisingly, embarrassors claimed that they achieved their goals when attempting solidarity and had the least success when attempting to establish or maintain power. As for the tactic/strategy used, Sharkey found that embarrassors claimed that they did not achieve their goals more than expected when they used teasing. This could be due to the uncertain meaning behind teasing. Pawluk (1989) explains that teasing is an annoying and irritating behavior that is supposed to induce liking. A receiver of the tease may not understand the intent behind the tease. If the target interprets a tease as ridicule instead of teasing, this may result in embarrassors not achieving their goal, for example, of solidarity. What is very interesting is that embarrassors and targets, at least in friendship relationships, are very adept at perceiving embarrassors' intent (Sharkey, Kulp, et al., 1996).

Sharkey, Kulp, et al. (1996) asked friendship dyads to recall a situation in which one of the friends was embarrassed because of something her or his friend did or said. They found that embarrassors and targets were able, with great accuracy, to agree on the intent or non-intent of the embarrassors. Sharkey, Kulp, et al. argue that this may be a reflection of the fact that friends may possess certain qualities that are not present in other relationships or that they may understand more fully the idiosyncratic, relational rules for behavior that the two have developed for their relationship which allow them to "mind read" each other. Another possibility it is that the communication during and/or after the event may give some indication of the intent of the embarrassor. This is an area worthy of further study. If friends are able to know when one is intentionally embarrassing the other, does this knowledge reduce the negative effects of intentional embarrassment? Does the ability to "mind read" one's partner affect the consequences of this type of aversive communication? Does it affect the embarrassor's success? These are questions to be addressed in the future.

Whether embarrassors are successful in their quest is dependent on many factors. Bradford and Petronio (in press) note that embarrassors' plans may fail because they do not account for contextual factors or they have insufficient knowledge about possible outcomes, a lack of experience using strategic embarrassment, or a lack of information about the target. Sharkey (1995) argued that intentional embarrassment is based upon the trust built between an embarrassor and a target. That is, for embarrassors to succeed, they must trust that targets are upholding the rules, norms, and so forth of the interaction. Embarrassors must trust *that targets trust* that the would-be embarrassor is also going to uphold the rules, norms, and so forth of the interaction. Embarrassors must also have a working knowledge of what aspects of the target are vulnerable and delicate (i.e., the target's self-identity frame). In addition, embarrassors must trust that their expectations are correct. With this trust in place, embarrassors are able to capitalize on this trust and induce embarrassment in a target.

CONCLUSION

Intentional embarrassment research is still in its infancy. What has been presented thus far is simply a beginning to unraveling the complex nature of intentional embarrassment. With continued research, we may come to realize that the first-order goal of intentional embarrassment is not aversive in and of itself except that it disrupts the flow of interaction. Instead, what should be found is that what is considered aversive embarrassment resides in a relationship. It is based upon individuals' intent and perceptions of intent. Indeed, Fincham (1985) claimed that attributions of intentionality may be one of the more important variables in determining relational outcomes as well as one's behavioral responses. Two parties may agree on one's intent. They may both see the embarrassment as intended to show solidarity or to negatively sanction the target's behaviors. The two parties may disagree as well. An embarrassor may intend to show solidarity using embarrassment, while the target may interpret it as a power move. Or, if the embarrassor intended to establish power, the target may infer the embarrassor's second-order goal was self-satisfaction. The goodness or badness, the positive valence or the negative valence, the rightness or the wrongness of an intentional embarrassment is inextricably tied to what is considered socially appropriate for a particular context which is itself affected by societal, religious, educational, familial, relational, and intrapersonal values, beliefs, and attitudes.

In the end, what is considered an aversive form of interpersonal behavior will be implicitly and explicitly negotiated, within a specified context, between those involved in a relationship. The degree of intent and perception of intent may actually become the most important determinants of outcomes/consequences for each participant, the relationship, and other persons present. There are some relationships in which certain types of intentional embarrassments will be accepted and even expected. For others, embarrassments will be inappropriate. The fear of someone intentionally embarrassing us keeps us from violating rules and norms. But, at the same time, some embarrassments can create novel and enjoyable experiences. In the end, further research that takes into account the influential variables such as intent, perception, culture, self-construal, sex, relationship definition, age, and so on will surely provide a more exacting understanding of this "aversive" form of interpersonal behavior—intentional embarrassment.

REFERENCES

Apsler, R. (1975). Effects of embarrassment on behavior toward others. *Journal of Personality and Social Psychology, 32,* 145–153.

Armstrong, W. D. (1974). The social functions of embarrassment (Doctoral dissertation, The University of Michigan, 1974). *Dissertation Abstracts International, 35,* 2479B.

Berger, C. R. (1988). Planning, affect and social action generation. In R. L. Donohew, H. Sypher, & E. T. Higgins (Eds.), *Communication, social cognition and affect* (pp. 93–116). Hillsdale, NJ: Lawrence Earlbaum.

Berger, C. R. (1990, November). *The many faces of embarrassment: A response*. Paper presented at the meeting of the Speech Communication Association, Chicago, IL.

Berger, C. R. (1995). A plan-based approach to strategic communication. In D. E. Hewes (Ed.), *The cognitive bases of interpersonal communication* (pp. 141–179). Hillsdale, NJ: Lawrence Earlbaum.

Bradford, L. (1993). *A cross-cultural study of strategic embarrassment in adolescent socialization*. Unpublished doctoral dissertation, Arizona State University, Tempe, AZ.

Bradford, L. (1994, February). *Hispanic and non-Hispanic adolescents' use of strategic embarrassment*. Paper presented at the meeting of the Western Speech Communication Association, San Jose, CA.

Bradford, L., & Petronio, S. (in press). Strategic embarrassment: The culprit of emotion. In P. A. Anderson & L. K. Guerrero (Eds.), *Communication and emotion*. New York: Academic Press.

Braithwaite, D. O. (1991, February). *"Getting his feet wet" II: Cultural communication at "coed" wedding and baby showers*. Paper presented at the International Network on Personal Relationships Conference, Bloomington-Normal, IL.

Braithwaite, D. O. (1995). Ritualized embarrassment at "coed" wedding and baby showers. *Communication Reports, 8,* 145–157

Brown, B. R. (1970). Face-saving following experimentally induced embarrassment. *Journal of Experimental Social Psychology, 6,* 255–271.

Brown, B. R., & Garland, H. (1971). The effects of incompetency, audience acquaintanceship, and anticipated evaluative feedback on face-saving behavior. *Journal of Experimental Social Psychology, 7,* 490–502.

Buck, R. W., & Parke, R. D. (1972). Behavioral and physiological responses to the presence of a friendly or neutral person in two types of stressful situations. *Journal of Personality and Social Psychology, 24,* 143–153.

Buck, R. W., Parke, R. D., & Buck, M. (1970). Skin conductance, heart rate, and attention to the environment in two stressful situations. *Psychonomic Science, 18,* 95–96.

Buss, A. (1980). *Self-consciousness and social anxiety*. San Francisco, CA: W. H. Freeman.

Buss, A. H., Iscoe, I., & Buss, E. H. (1979). The development of embarrassment. *The Journal of Psychology, 103,* 227–230.

Cann, A., & Blackwelder, J. G. (1984). Compliance and mood: A field investigation of the impact of embarrassment. *Journal of Psychology, 117,* 221–226.

Chapman, D. E. (1993). *An examination of intentional embarrassment tactics: Perceived appropriateness and effectiveness by self-monitoring social actors*. Unpublished masters thesis, San Diego State University, CA.

Cupach, W. R., & Metts, S. (1990). Remedial processes in embarrassing predicaments. In J. A. Anderson (Ed.), *Communication yearbook* (Vol. 13, pp. 323–352). Beverly Hills, CA: Sage.

Cupach, W. R., & Metts, S. (1994). *Facework*. Thousand Oaks, CA: Sage.

Darwin, C. (1965). *The expression of the emotions in man and animals*. Chicago: The University of Chicago Press. (Original work published 1872)

Dillard, J. P. (1990). A goal-driven model of interpersonal influence. In J. P. Dillard (Ed.), *Seeking compliance: The production of interpersonal influence messages* (pp. 41–56). Scottsdale, AZ: Gorsuch Scarisbrick.

Druian, P. R., & DePaulo, B. M. (1977). Asking a child for help. *Social Behavior and Personality, 5,* 33–39.

Duck, S. (1988). *Relating to others*. Pacific Grove, CA: Brooks/Cole.

Edelmann, R. J. (1982). The effect of embarrassed reactions upon others. *Australian Journal of Psychology, 34,* 359–367.

Edelmann, R. J. (1987). *The psychology of embarrassment*. Chichester, England: John Wiley & Sons.

Edelmann, R. J., & Hampson, S. E. (1979). Changes in non-verbal behaviour during embarrassment. *British Journal of Social and Clinical Psychology, 18,* 385–390.

Edelmann, R. J., & Hampson, S. E. (1981). Embarrassment in dyadic interaction. *Social Behavior and Personality, 9,* 171–177.

Fincham, F. D. (1985). Attributions in close relationships. In J. Harvey & G. Weary (Eds.), *Attribution: Basic issues and applications* (pp. 203–234). New York: Academic Press.

Fink, E. L., & Walker, B. A. (1977). Humorous responses to embarrassment. *Psychological Reports, 40,* 475–485.

Foss, R. D., & Crenshaw, N. C. (1978). Risk of embarrassment and helping. *Social Behavior and Personality, 6,* 243–245.

Garfinkel, H. (1956). Conditions of successful degradation ceremonies. *American Journal of Sociology, 61,* 420–424.

Garland, H., & Brown, B. R. (1972). Face-saving as affected by subjects' sex, audiences' sex and audience expertise. *Sociometry, 35,* 280–289.

Goffman, E. (1953). *Communication conduct in an island community.* Unpublished doctoral dissertation, University of Chicago, IL.

Goffman, E. (1967). *Interaction ritual: Essays on face-to-face behavior.* New York: Pantheon.

Goffman, E. (1973). *The presentation of self in everyday life.* Woodstock, NY: Overlook Press. (Original work published 1959)

Gonzales, M. H., Pederson, J. H., Manning, D. J., & Wetter, D. W. (1990). Pardon my gaffe: Effects of sex, status, and consequence severity on accounts. *Journal of Personality and Social Psychology, 58,* 610–621.

Grasmick, H. G., Bursik, R. J., & Kinsey, K. A. (1991). Shame and embarrassment as deterrents to noncompliance with the law: The case of an antilittering campaign. *Environment and Behavior, 23,* 233–251.

Gross, E. (1984). Embarrassment in public life. *Society, 21,* 48–53.

Gross, E., & Stone, G. P. (1964). Embarrassment and the analysis of role requirements. *American Journal of Sociology, 70,* 1–15.

Harré, R. (1990). Embarrassment: A conceptual analysis. In W. R. Crozier (Ed.), *Shyness and embarrassment: Perspectives from social psychology* (pp. 181–204). Cambridge, England: Cambridge University Press.

Martin, W. B. W. (1987). Students' perceptions of causes and consequences of embarrassment in the school. *Canadian Journal of Education, 12,* 277–293.

McPherson, M. B., & Kearney, P. (1992, February). *Classroom embarrassment: Types, goals, and face saving strategies.* Paper presented at the meeting of the Western States Communication Association , Boise, ID.

Metts, S., & Cupach, W. R. (1989). Situational influence on the use of remedial strategies in embarrassing predicaments. *Communication Monographs, 56,* 151–162.

Miller, R. S. (1987). Empathic embarrassment: Situational and personal determinants of reactions to the embarrassment of another. *Journal of Personality and Social Psychology, 53,* 1061–1069.

Miller, R. S. (1995). On the nature of embarrassability: Shyness, social evaluation, and social skill. *Journal of Personality, 63,* 315–339.

Miller, R. S. (1996).*Embarrassment: Poise and peril in everyday life.* New York: Guilford Press.

Modigliani, A. (1966). *Embarrassment and social influence.* Unpublished doctoral dissertation, University of Michigan, Ann Arbor, MI.

Pawluk, C. J. (1989). Social construction of teasing. *Journal for the Theory of Social Behaviour, 19,* 145–167.

Petronio, S. (1984). Communication strategies to reduce embarrassment differences between men and women. *Western Journal of Speech Communication, 48,* 28–38.

Petronio, S., Olson, C., & Dollar, N. (1988). Relational embarrassment: Impact on relational quality and communication satisfaction. In D. O'Hair & B. R. Patterson (Eds.), *Advances in interpersonal communication research: Proceedings of the annual conference of the Western States Communication Association* (pp. 195–206). Las Cruces, NM: Communication Resources Center.

Petronio, S., Olson, C., & Dollar, N. (1989). Privacy issues in relational embarrassment: Impact on relational quality and communication satisfaction. *Communications Research Reports, 6,* 21–27.

Petronio, S., & Snider, E. (1990, November). *Planned strategic embarrassment.* Paper presented at the Seventy-Sixth Annual Conference of the Speech Communication Association, Chicago, IL.

Petronio, S., & Snider, E. (1992, February). *Planning strategic embarrassment: Testing a theory.* Paper presented at the Sixty-Third Western States Communication Association Conference, Boise, ID.

Sattler, J. M. (1965). A theoretical, developmental, and clinical investigation of embarrassment. *Genetic Psychology Monographs, 71,* 19–59.

Seidner, L. B., Stipek, D. J., & Feshbach, N. D. (1988). A developmental analysis of elementary school-aged children's concept of pride and embarrassment. *Child Development, 59,* 236–377.

Sharkey, W. F. (1990a). [Intentional embarrassment: Goals, tactics, responses and consequences]. Unpublished raw data.

Sharkey, W. F. (1990b). *Intentional embarrassment: Goals, tactics, responses and consequences.* Unpublished doctoral dissertation, The Ohio State University, Columbus, OH.

Sharkey, W. F. (1991). Intentional embarrassment: Goals, tactics and consequences. In W. R. Cupach & S. Metts (Eds.), *Advances in interpersonal communication research 1991: Proceedings of the annual conference of the Western States Communication Association* (pp. 105–128). Normal, IL: Personal Relationships Research Group.

Sharkey, W. F. (1992). Use and responses to intentional embarrassment. *Communication Studies, 43,* 257–275.

Sharkey, W. F. (1993). Who embarrasses whom?: Relational and sex differences in the use of intentional embarrassment. In P. Kalbfleisch (Ed.), *Interpersonal communication: Evolving interpersonal relationships* (pp. 147–168). Hillsdale, NJ: Erlbaum.

Sharkey, W. F. (1995, February). *Intentional embarrassment: The issue of "Trust."* Paper presented at the Sixty-Fifth Annual Conference of the Western States Communication Association, Portland, OR.

Sharkey, W. F., Diggs, R., & Kim, M. S. (1993, May). *Why did you deliberately embarrass me? The effects of attribution.* Paper presented at the Forty-Third Annual Conference of the International Communication Association, Washington, DC.

Sharkey, W. F., Kulp, C., Carpenter, B. M., Lee, C., & Rodillias, U. (1996, February). *Embarrassment: The effects of embarrassor and embarrassee perception.* Paper presented at the Sixty-Sixth Annual Conference of the Western States Communication Association, Pasadena, CA.

Sharkey, W. F., & Singelis, T. M. (1995). Embarrassability and self-construal: A theoretical integration. *Personality and Individual Differences, 19,* 919–926.

Sharkey, W. F., & Stafford, L. (1990). Responses to embarrassment. *Human Communication Research, 17,* 315–342.

Sharkey, W. F., Tamashiro, P., Igawa, C., & Muranaka, D. (1996). [Various cultures' use of intentional embarrassment]. Unpublished raw data.

Sharkey, W. F., & Waldron, V. R. (1990, November). *The intentional embarrassment of subordinates in the work place.* Paper presented at the Seventy-Sixth Annual Conference of the Speech Communication Association, Chicago, IL.

Singelis, T. M., & Sharkey, W. F. (1995). Culture, self-construal, and embarrassability. *Journal of Cross-Cultural Psychology, 26,* 622–644.

Snider, E. (1992). *Strategic embarrassment and face saving strategies.* Unpublished master's thesis, Arizona State University, Tempe, AZ.

Tracy, K. (1990). The many faces of facework. In H. Giles & W. P. Robinson (Eds.), *Handbook of language and social psychology* (pp. 209–226). Beverly Hills, CA: Sage.

Weinberg, M. S. (1968). Embarrassment: Its variable and invariable aspects. *Social Forces, 46,* 382–388.

Wolchover, D. (1988). Attacking confessions with past police embarrassments. *Criminal Law Review, September,* 573–583.

CHAPTER 5

COMPLAINING
WHAT'S ALL THE FUSS ABOUT?

ROBIN M. KOWALSKI AND JANET R. ERICKSON

> Whenever you are tempted to tell your troubles to other people, remember that half your listeners aren't really interested and the rest are glad that you're finally getting what's coming to you.
>
> BAUGHMAN, 1959

Most of us can readily recall an incident in the not too distant past in which an acquaintance droned on and on about every misfortune that had befallen him or her that day. This person seemed to expect us to react supportively and empathically and to feel privileged that he or she had selected us as a listener. However, each time that we offered advice for how to deal with the problem, we were readily dismissed with "Yes, but...." As the listener in this scenario, we are quick to label this person a complainer and often make every effort to avoid subsequent interactions with him or her.

Given that we all complain at least occasionally, however, how can we be so quick to judge another's expressions of dissatisfaction? For that

---

ROBIN M. KOWALSKI AND JANET R. ERICKSON • Department of Psychology, Western Carolina University, Cullowhee, North Carolina 28723. kowalski@wcuvax1.wcu.edu

Aversive Interpersonal Behaviors, edited by Kowalski
Plenum Press, New York, 1997

matter, given our own frequency of complaining, why is complaining even included in a book on aversive interpersonal behaviors? Indeed, Shuy (1988) claimed that "complaining is humankind's first function, manifested by crying at birth" (p. 147).

When most people think of aversive interpersonal behaviors, they conjure up images of actions that people perform only rarely, when, perhaps, they feel that there is no other means available to them to handle a problem. For example, in an informal poll of the behaviors my students considered aversive, answers typically revolved around types of abuse, i.e., emotional, physical, and sexual abuse. However, many of the behaviors that fall under the rubric of aversive interpersonal behaviors are aversive simply because of the frequency with which they occur. Complaining is a good illustration of this. Everyone complains at least occasionally, voicing dissatisfaction with aspects of themselves, other people, or the environment. "I'm so tired." "I have too much work to do." "If these people are going to walk so slowly why don't they move over to the side instead of walking right down the middle of the aisle?"

Like many other behaviors, complaints used in moderation can be beneficial, a point that will be addressed later in this chapter. Indeed, people who never complain may be perceived as secretive, mysterious, and dishonest. Taken to the extreme, however, incessant whining can be very aversive and detrimental to relationships. For some individuals, the sound of another's whining voice is enough to send chills down the spine.

In this chapter, we will define complaining and then present a theoretical model of complaining followed by an examination of the reasons why people complain. We will then discuss conditions that make complaining aversive. Specific attention will be devoted to perhaps the most aversive of complainers: the help-rejecting complainer.

DEFINITIONAL ISSUES

An examination of common definitions of complaining suggests that complaining is a behavioral expression of an unfavorable attitude toward an object, person, or event. For example, *Webster's Third International Dictionary* defines complaining as "expressing discontent, dissatisfaction, protest, resentment, or regret." Similarly, in many of the consumer approaches to complaining, people express dissatisfaction when their expectations regarding a product or service have been disconfirmed (Fornell & Westbrook, 1979).

Were people to complain only when they were truly dissatisfied, this chapter would probably not be included within a book on aversive interpersonal behaviors. With minor exceptions, few people are so chronically dissatisfied that their complaining would become bothersome to other people. However, people do not limit their complaints to those occasions in which they are truly dissatisfied. In fact, people often complain not when they are subjectively dissatisfied but when they perceive that complaining will be instrumental to the attainment of intrapsychic or interpersonal goals. For example, people may complain about their health not because they actually feel sick but because the "sick role" allows them to achieve secondary gains such as sympathy from others or the avoidance of aversive events (Leary & Miller, 1986; Skelton & Pennebaker, 1982; Smith, Snyder, & Perkins, 1983; Synder & Smith, 1982). What child hasn't complained of poor health to avoid a test at school?

The fact that dissatisfaction is sufficient but not necessary for complaining suggests that people have separate thresholds for experiencing dissatisfaction (dissatisfaction threshold) and expressing dissatisfaction (complaining threshold). Even though someone may not currently be dissatisfied (i.e., events do not exceed the dissatisfaction threshold), his or her motivation to complain for other interpersonal reasons may prompt complaining behavior (i.e., the complaining threshold has been reached). For example, if a person is perfectly satisfied with his or her job (the dissatisfaction threshold is high) but perceives that expressing dissatisfaction will nonetheless allow him or her to achieve some desired outcome, such as increased pay or an increased travel allowance (the complaining threshold is low), he or she will voice dissatisfaction. If, however, this same individual perceives that any benefits of complaining will be offset by undesired social consequences (i.e., appearing greedy by one's colleagues), he or she will presumably inhibit complaints or expressions of dissatisfaction. Alternatively, if this same individual is genuinely dissatisfied with the job (the dissatisfaction threshold is low), he or she may or may not complain (i.e., the complaining threshold is low or high, respectively) depending on the situational constraints bearing on his or her behavior. In light of the existence of these two thresholds, complaining has been defined as "an expression of dissatisfaction, whether subjectively experienced or not, for the purpose of venting emotions or achieving intrapsychic goals, interpersonal goals, or both" (Kowalski, 1996, p. 180).

A THEORY OF COMPLAINING

The fact that people sometimes complain when they are dissatisfied and other times complain even when they are not subjectively dissatisfied suggests that the processes underlying complaining are two-fold, with one process influencing the subjective experience of dissatisfaction and the other affecting complaining in the absence of dissatisfaction (Kowalski,

1996). Whether or not complaining arises from genuine feelings of dissatisfaction, a state of self-focus underlies every complaint episode. Self-focus triggers an evaluative process in which people compare current events with their standards for those events. When actual events do not measure up to the individual's standards for those events, dissatisfaction and negative affect result. Because negative affect is, by definition, unpleasant, people are motivated to reduce the discrepancy (Carver & Scheier, 1981; Ingram & Smith, 1984; Pyszczynski, Hamilton, Greenberg, & Becker, 1991). However, before complaining, people who subjectively feel dissatisfied must determine the perceived utility of complaining (i.e., the degree to which complaining will promote the achievement of desired intrapsychic or interpersonal goals such as reducing the discrepancy between current and ideal states, altering others' impressions, or obtaining social comparison information).

Thus, a perceived discrepancy between expectations and reality will result in complaining behavior as a means of reducing the discrepancy as long as the perceived utility of complaining is high. If the perceived utility is low, then individuals will inhibit their expressions of dissatisfaction—the complaining threshold rises—resulting in a further intensification of negative affect, thereby maintaining a state of self-regulatory perseveration (Pyszczynski, Greenberg, Hamilton, & Nix, 1991) or rumination about the cause of the dissatisfaction.

As already noted, however, people frequently complain when they are not subjectively dissatisfied. In cases in which the dissatisfaction threshold is high and the complaining threshold is low, complaining varies entirely as a function of its perceived utility. If an individual is perfectly satisfied with a relationship but perceives that voicing dissatisfaction to his or her spouse will result in increased attention, flowers, etc., he or she will likely complain.

However, simply being self-focused may produce negative thoughts and feelings (Gibbons, 1990; Ingram, Cruet, Johnson, & Wisnicki, 1988; Sedikides, 1992; Smith & Greenberg, 1981), at least among individuals whose self-conception valences (Sedikides, 1992) are predominantly negative. Thus, even in the absence of a discrepancy between current and ideal states, self-focus may lower a person's dissatisfaction threshold if his or her internal state is already negative.

FUNCTIONS OF COMPLAINING

As noted in the definition of complaining, complaints may be expressed to achieve interpersonal goals (such as altering another person's behavior or changing an aversive situation), intrapsychic goals (such as changing the complainer's internal state), or both. For example, by expressing dissatisfaction with the behavior of another person (an interpersonal function), the complainer may change his or her own internal state (an intrapsychic function). In examining the utility of complaining in achieving intrapsychic and/or interpersonal goals, four specific functions of complaining have been proposed: catharsis, self-presentation, social comparison, and calls for accounts (Kowalski, 1996). At the general level, the first function represents an intrapsychic goal and the other three functions reflect interpersonal considerations.

CATHARSIS

Complaining is a way for people to vent their frustrations and dissatisfactions (Alicke et al., 1992). In this sense, complaining provides an emotional release. For example, today while the first author was working on this chapter, the hot water heater in her home "flooded" a room. The plumber then spent over *five* hours installing a new hot water heater. As if that wasn't bad enough, the hot water heater valve that accompanied the *new* hot water heater didn't work. Then, after spending over $200 on the hot water heater itself, she wrote a check for $165 to the plumber. Although I'm sure she should feel grateful that the bill wasn't higher given the amount of time it took, she was less than thrilled. And, although she is aware that expressing these complaints will not change the events that transpired today or that will occur in the future, she nevertheless feels better after writing this paragraph.

Thus, the benefits of cathartic complaining stem from its capacity to make a person feel better. In a study designed to examine the extent to which affective changes actually accompanied cathartic complaining, Kowalski, Cantrell, and Van Hout (1996, Experiment 1) randomly assigned low and high propensity complainers to one of three experimental conditions. After everyone was given the opportunity to think about a person with whom they were dissatisfied, a third were instructed to write about what they had done the previous day, a third wrote about their dissatisfaction as if they were addressing the researcher, and a third wrote a letter to the source of their dissatisfaction. After completing the writing exercise, low propensity complainers felt better when they wrote about their dissatisfaction (to either the person or a third party) relative to when they wrote about the events of yesterday. No significant differences were observed among high propensity complainers as a function of experimental condition.

The link between complaining and improved affect is more readily understood by examining the consequences experienced by people who inhibit or suppress expressions of dissatisfaction. When people inhibit complaining, they frequently ruminate about the causes of their dissatisfaction, often blowing them out of proportion. In this respect, not complaining may be more interpersonally damaging than complaining. Rather than expressing frustrations and minor irritations as they arise, people who silence their complaints until they become unmanageable risk serious damage to their relationships.

People who show this tendency to suppress emotional distress are said to have the type-D personality type. The "chronic suppression of negative emotions" demonstrated by people with type-D personality has been implicated in an increased incidence of coronary heart disease compared to non-type-D personality individuals (Denollet, 1991; Denollet et al., 1996). The tendency to inhibit complaining has also been linked to depression (Folkman & Lazarus, 1986).

Not disclosing emotional distress presents a problematic scenario. Failure to disclose emotional distress heightens negative affect, thereby lowering the dissatisfaction threshold even farther, subsequently increasing the need to complain (Stiles, 1987; Stiles, Schuster, & Harrigan, 1992). By complaining, the individual should experience reduced feelings of dysphoria (see Pennebaker, 1990). However, if inhibitory processes are still operating or the social costs of complaining are too high, the person will experience even further dissatisfaction.

Self-Presentation

Self-presentation (also known as impression management; Leary, 1995; Leary & Kowalski, 1990) refers to the process by which people attempt to regulate the impressions that others form of them. Much of what people do or don't do is based upon their concerns with what others will think about those actions. In the same way, many of the instances in which people choose to complain or to inhibit their complaints stem from self-presentational concerns (Kowalski, 1996).

Self-presentational complaints can take any of a number of different forms, depending on the desired impression. People may complain to convey to others that they have high standards (i.e., things simply do not measure up to their expectations). People may complain about other people as a means of making themselves look superior (Jones & Pittman, 1982). People may also complain to excuse untoward behavior or as a self-handicap in an effort to save face (Kowalski, 1996; Weiner, 1992). For example, people may complain about being sick in order to distance themselves from poor performance on the job or they may use physical health complaints before performing a job-related task so that they will have an excuse should the outcome not be favorable. Finally, people may complain to avoid evaluative situations or undesired activities altogether

(Kolb, 1982; Snyder & Smith, 1982). For example, by expressing physical health complaints, an individual may be able to avoid work or responsibilities at home (Parsons, 1951).

However, concerns with the impressions that others are forming may also lead people to inhibit their complaints. People who complain too much are ostracized and labeled as whiners and gripers. Because of the negative connotations surrounding complaining, people may worry about the negative image implications of expressing dissatisfaction. Or, if they decide to complain, some individuals may choose to be selective in choosing their audience. Complaining to a marathon runner about your fatigue following a 2-mile jog is unlikely to elicit a sympathetic response to the same degree that expressing the same complaint to someone who never exercises would. Indeed, complaining may be regarded as aversive when people are indiscriminant in selecting a listener and seem oblivious to the impressions they are creating through their constant whining and griping.

Social Comparison

In some instances, people complain to obtain information about the thoughts and feelings of others. For example, one employee may complain about the difficulty of a particular job assignment to elicit an assessment of the assignment from another employee. In this way, people can test the validity of and support for their own ideas, a process referred to as social comparison.

Complaints voiced to obtain social comparison information vary as a function of the complainer's initial state of dissatisfaction and the perceived utility of complaining. The lower the person's dissatisfaction threshold, the higher his or her likelihood of complaining to seek social comparison information should be (Wills, 1983). For example, the more difficult the employee found the job assignment to be, the more inclined he or she should be to obtain social comparison information. Second, to the extent that the employee perceives that complaining about the assignment will be useful in acquiring social comparison information, he or she should be more likely to complain.

Call for Accounts and Remediation

Complaints may also be voiced to call others to account for their behavior (Alberts, 1988) or to redress grievances (Fornell & Westbrook, 1979). When our behavior is called into question by another, we typically offer some type of explanation or account for the behavior (Alberts, 1988).

For example, if your partner inquires about your lateness, you typically offer an explanation to account for your whereabouts.

Complaints issued as a call for accounts stem from a perceived discrepancy between a person's expectations for another's behavior and the other's actual behavior (Fincham, 1992; Scott & Lyman, 1968). The likelihood of complaining depends upon the size of the perceived discrepancy between expectations and outcomes. With small discrepancies, people tend to assimilate the discrepancy into their original attitude toward, for example, the other person or the product or manufacturer (Gilly & Gelb, 1982). Alternatively, with larger discrepancies, the discrepancy is magnified resulting in a contrast effect (Gilly & Gelb, 1982).

Used as calls for accounts, complaints may be viewed as manipulative tools by which the complainer can attempt to get others to engage in desired behaviors (behavioral instigation; Buss, 1992; Buss, Gomes, Higgins, & Lauterbach, 1987) or not to perform undesired behaviors (behavioral termination). For example, by chronically complaining about a person always being late, the complainer is actively attempting to induce the other individual to arrive earlier. The problem with complaining as a means of manipulating or changing another's behavior is that it typically sets off a defensive reaction in the target of the complaint. Few of us like to have our behavior called into question and, naturally, react negatively when we are challenged.

THE AVERSIVENESS OF COMPLAINING

Given that we all complain and spend a considerable part of our time listening to others complain, complaining in and of itself could not be entirely aversive. Certain features must distinguish aversive complaining from the occasional rumbles of dissatisfaction with which we are all familiar. Although certainly not an exhaustive list, and perhaps reflecting our own "pet peeves" with complaining, we believe that there are seven variables that influence the aversiveness of complaining. All but one of these elements involve aspects of the complaint or complainant. The last element focuses on aspects of the listener that influence the degree to which complaints are perceived to be aversive.

Incessant Complaining

When voiced in moderation, complaints are seldom aversive. People who infrequently voice dissatisfaction about another person, their job, or some other situational stimulus are seldom viewed negatively. Indeed, some complaining may be welcomed as a means of finding out people's feelings toward certain individuals or issues. In this way, complaining may serve as a check on the current state of a relationship, for example. Such complaining only becomes aversive when people seem not to know when to turn off the complaints and when they seem desensitized to the repercussions of their complaining for those called upon to listen.

People who complain incessantly are rarely perceived to be expressing genuine sentiments of dissatisfaction because their feelings of dissatisfaction seem to be so indiscriminant. Generally speaking, these people have ulterior motives for their incessant complaining other than cathartic release or advice-seeking. In this sense, they resemble a monopolist. According to Yalom (1985), the monopolist is "a person who feels compelled to chatter on incessantly....Interestingly, the monopolist uses compulsive speech for self-concealment" (p. 378). Like the monopolist, the chronic complainer tends to be uncomfortable with conversational lags and is likely to turn others' complaints around to reflect his or her own concerns. Unfortunately, through this behavior they are alienating others and, therefore, to use Yalom's terms, committing social suicide.

One strategy for dealing with the incessant ramblings of others is to suggest to them that they find some other avenue to vent their frustrations. For people complaining about computer problems, you could suggest that they contact *InfoWorld's* Gripe Line (Foster, April 3, 1995). Similarly, some newspapers have columns devoted solely to people's complaints. *The Atlanta Constitution*, for instance, has a column entitled "The Vent" that contains people's complaints.

Aversive Complaint Content

People who are perceived to have a legitimate gripe will seldom be criticized for complaining, almost regardless of how much they complain about the person, object, or event. For example, people who are visibly in pain and complaining about the degree to which they hurt will rarely be met with negative reactions. However, complaints about events of little consequence or issues that are perceived by others as having little merit are more frequently the object of derision. In other words, complaining is perceived to be aversive when the complaint has certain features.

Authentic versus Inauthentic Complaints

Authentic complaints stem from the complainer's genuine feelings of dissatisfaction. For example, people who complain to the management when the dry cleaners burn a hole in their suit are perceived to have an authentic complaint. Inauthentic complaints, on the other hand, stem not from true feelings of dissatisfaction but rather from the desire to achieve desired rewards or to avoid undesired punishments (Caron, Whitbourne, & Halgin, 1992). Although inauthentic complaints are not inherently aversive, listeners may be less tolerant of inauthentic expressions of dissatisfaction.

Regardless of the complaint's true authenticity, the important factor in social encounters is complaint recipients' perceptions of a complaint's authenticity. If listeners perceive that a complaint stems from underlying dissatisfaction, they should be more receptive to maintaining an interpersonal exchange with the complainer. If, however, they perceive that the complainer has an ulterior motive, then they should be less tolerant of the complainer's rantings. Indeed, as suggested by Shuy (1988), "felicitous complaints must [among other things] be sincere [and] show evidence that the complaint event complained about is true" (p. 149).

Because of the frequency with which they complain, habitual complainers' expressions of dissatisfaction are often viewed as inauthentic. Recollections of encounters with habitual complainers suggest that they rarely complain for intrapsychic reasons (i.e., to relieve genuine feelings of frustration or dissatisfaction). Because most of their complaints are oriented toward interpersonal goals, such as altering the perceptions or behaviors of others, they are more likely to be perceived as manipulative compared to infrequent complainers. Complainers who are perceived to be using their complaints to manipulate the reactions of others are, not surprisingly, evaluated negatively.

Verifiable versus Nonverifiable Complaints

Complaints can be verifiable or nonverifiable, depending on the degree to which the claims constituting the complaint can be supported by objective evidence. Complaints that are verifiable are those that can be substantiated by objective evidence. Nonverifiable complaints, on the other hand, are those complaints involving claims that reflect purely subjective, personal opinions. Although it is usually more difficult to refute complaints for which there is no objective evidence (i.e., nonverifiable complaints) than claims for which verification can be obtained (i.e., verifiable complaints), people tend to be more tolerant of others' complaints when the source of their dissatisfaction is clear.

Direct and Indirect Complaints

We have all had people complain to us about their frustrations with another individual. Our typical, usually unstated, response to such complaints is "Why are you telling me this? Why don't you tell the person who made you mad?" Of course, the response would be something to the effect of not wanting to confront or upset the other individual. The problem is that indirect complaints have the potential to be more interpersonally damaging than direct complaints. Direct complaints stated in a nonthreatening, nonjudgmental manner are actually quite effective in changing another person's behavior. They provide valuable feedback to people about their behavior (Krishnan & Valle, 1979) which they can then use to undertake behavioral or, in some cases, characterological change. However, by voicing indirect complaints, the complainant not only expresses his or her own dissatisfaction with the object of the complaint but sensitizes others to that dissatisfaction as well. Hearing another's dissatisfaction with a particular person or event may make us aware of our own feelings of dissatisfaction with that person or event. The end result may be a self-fulfilling prophecy where the listener to the original complaint behaves toward the target in a manner that elicits the behavior being complained about by the complainant.

Complaint Instrumentality

A third variable influencing the aversiveness of complaining is the perceived instrumentality of the complaint. With perhaps the exception of people who fabricate stories to achieve free services or coupons, most consumer complaints, for example, are expressed with the purpose of implementing change (i.e., instrumental complaints). However, as already noted, people frequently complain not because they expect changes to be made but, rather, because complaining simply makes them feel better (i.e., expressive complaints; Stilwell & Salamon, 1990). Thus, noninstrumental complaints may serve a cathartic function.

The instrumental versus expressive nature of a complaint affects our perception of the complaint and the individual complaining. People who repeatedly express dissatisfaction but do nothing to alter the dissatisfying situation are considered to be "all talk and no action." On the other hand, if we hear people complain but view them as attempting to bring about an end to the aversive situation, we are more tolerant of their complaints.

This is not to imply that expressive complaining is never beneficial. Few people will react negatively to the occasional expressive complaint. The issue becomes problematic only when that is the only type of complaint expressed, even by infrequent complainers.

Instrumental complaints, however, may be perceived as aversive if the individual gives the initial impression of attempting to alleviate a dissatisfying situation yet ultimately rejects all efforts at problem-solving. Although most people never expect others to accept their advice unquestioningly, continued rejection of problem-solving attempts has much the same impact that criticism does.

INTENTIONALITY

The aversiveness of a complaint episode is also affected by the intent perceived to be underlying the complaint. Were most people to be confronted with their complaining behavior, they would probably abashedly state that they were unaware that they were complaining. This type of mindless complaining represents the vast majority of the complaints that people express on a daily basis, and highlights the prevalence of complaining in our everyday lives. Because we are all guilty of mindless complaining, few of us will cast aspersions on people who engage in mindless complaining, unless the person complaining appears to be a truly disgruntled, unhappy person, who knows no limits to his or her own complaining.

Some complaints, however, are not voiced mindlessly but, rather, reflect strategic attempts to call others' behavior into question (i.e., to call others to account for their behavior). Few people like to have their behavior called into question so this type of complaining is far more likely to trigger a defensive reaction than mindless complaining. In addition, in spite of our tolerance of the mindless gripes of others, we are far less conciliatory when the complaints are preplanned and manipulative.

Interestingly, the intentional, aversive type of complaining is, in the long run, the most adaptive, at least in terms of relationship functioning. Typically, when people call others' behavior into question, they are attempting to change the person's behavior with the ultimate goal of improving the quality of the relationship. Mindless complaining, on the other hand, by its very nature, has little interpersonal value although it may have intrapsychic value to the complainer.

MOOD CONTAGION

Were other people's complaints independent of our own mood states, we probably would have few, if any, negative reactions to them. In fact, however, hearing others' complaints can set up a contagion of complaining that includes a spreading of the affect accompanying the complaint. What emerges is a domino effect of both complaining and affect. In one of the Winnie the Pooh stories, Christopher Robin states that the residents of the Hundred Acre Wood appear to be suffering from a "bad case of the Galloping Grumps" (Birney, 1992). In response to Piglet's question regarding whether the galloping grumps are catching, Christopher Robin says "Very catching...Grumpiness and grouchiness gallop quickly from one person to another." Three reasons may account for the mood contagion associated with complaining.

First, hearing another person's complaints may make a listener more aware of his or her own negative feelings toward an object, person, or event. The negative affect that develops will, then, trigger the listener's own desire to complain (Stiles, 1987).

Second, hearing another person discuss troublesome or problematic situations may create a cognitive burden in the listener that he or she feels can only be alleviated by complaining to someone else. The phenomenon resembles that confronting individuals who have been told a secret. The urge to confess the secret often becomes overwhelming.

Third, others' complaints frequently remind people of events in their own history, setting the stage for one-upmanship. For example, one individual might complain of a traffic accident he or she recently experienced. The listener, reminded or his or her own experiences with traffic accidents, may proceed to tell his or her own story, perhaps in an attempt to outdo the original story.

Interactional Dilemmas

Complaining is also interpersonally aversive because it creates interactional dilemmas. Like other interpersonal behaviors, complaints involve a mutual pattern of influence between the complainer and his or her audience. The complainer's expressions of dissatisfaction influence the listener whose response to the complaint subsequently affects the complainer's behavior and affect. "The reciprocal nature of complaint episodes suggests that interactions are complementary, meaning that people who express their dissatisfactions with a person's behavior, for example, in a nonthreatening, nondestructive manner may be met with a constructive, supportive reception. However, to the extent that the affect and content of the complaint are derogatory and negative, the target of the complaint responds with hostility" (Kowalski, 1996, p. 190).

Where this principle of complementarity becomes problematic is that, over the course of repeated interactions with chronic complainers, people gradually lose their sensitivity and supportiveness in responding. Specifically, people lose their ability to accommodate or withhold responding to destructive comments with destructive responses (Rusbult, Verette, Whitney, Slovik, & Lipkus, 1991). Typically, people respond to others' occasional expressions of dissatisfaction with either supportive or problem-solving responses (Erickson & Kowalski, 1996). Because those are the most frequently desired responses (Kowalski et al., 1996, Experiment 2), generating these responses to others' complaints maintains smooth interpersonal interactions.

Second, people who complain frequently but repeatedly fail to adopt the advice that is given them also fail to engage in complementarity. While having little effect on the chronic complainer's behavior, listeners are forced into a situation where they are uncertain of how to respond. Without getting hostile or defensive and without countercomplaining, how does one respond when continually being rebuffed?

Listener Characteristics

Just as beauty is in the eye of the beholder, so apparently is the aversiveness of complaining. Some people display a remarkable ability to listen to others' incessant grumblings that boggles the mind. For example, in a recent survey of hospital complaint representatives, over 90% indicated that they were very satisfied with their jobs (Kowalski & Brendle, 1996). What is it that allows some people patiently and willingly to listen to others complain on a regular basis?

One variable that facilitates an individual's ability to engage in active listening with a chronic complainer is emotional detachment. People involved in professions such as patient representation, clinical psychology, or counseling are able to remain satisfied with their positions because they adopt a detached affective stance when interacting with their patients. In this way, they can effectively listen to their clients without experiencing adverse psychological side effects.

Although we have not empirically tested this idea, men and women would also be expected to differ in their perceptions of the aversiveness of chronic complainers. Two factors may account for this hypothesized gender difference. First, because of women's greater relational orientation relative to men, they may be more inclined to maintain aversive interpersonal interactions with chronic complainers. Specifically, although they may perceive the interaction to be aversive, they may be unwilling to terminate the exchange out of concern for the feelings of the other individual.

Second, women and men may differ in their perceptions of what constitutes complaining. What men label complaining, women may perceive as simply emotional self-disclosure. Such differential perceptions of what constitutes complaining would be expected to influence the responses that they give to the individual who is self-disclosing.

Although a number of dispositional variables that influence perceptions of the aversiveness of complaining could be proposed (i.e., empathy, locus of control, etc.) that would be beyond the purpose of the present chapter. One additional variable, however, deserves mention. People's perception of the aversiveness of complaining should be influenced by their own propensity to complain. On one hand, chronic complainers may feel that listening to other people complain is aversive simply because it takes up time when they could be complaining. On the other hand, infrequent complainers may perceive that habitual complainers should simply deal with their problems instead of whining about them.

HELP-REJECTING COMPLAINERS

One group of complainers is the epitome of everything that makes complaining aversive. In 1952, Jerome Frank coined the term *help-rejecting complainer* to describe certain individuals who were difficult to treat, particularly in psychotherapy. The help-rejecting complainer is notorious for complaining as a means of seeking help and advice and then rejecting any and all help that is offered (Yalom, 1985). Although not referring to them as help-rejecting complainers, Berne (1964) referred to the same genre of individuals as those who play the "Why don't you...yes but" game. As Berne described the game, an individual brings to others' attention a problem he or she is having. In an effort to help the individual, others offer solutions that typically take the form of "Why don't you...". To each of these advice statements, the individual responds with "Yes, but...". According to Berne, individuals who play the "Why don't you...yes but" game have as their goal to "demonstrate that no one can give them an acceptable suggestion" (p. 119).

Whether perceived as help-rejecting complainers or people who play a therapeutic game, these individuals have a tendency to exaggerate their problems to the point that they may appear insurmountable, feel their problems deserve more attention than others', adopt a position of hopelessness toward their own problem, and are passive in attempts to alleviate their dissatisfaction. Two reasons may account for the apparent passivity of the help-rejecting complainer. First, others are unlikely to offer solutions that have not occurred to the complainer. Second, even when novel suggestions are presented to the complainer, he or she will still reject them (Berne, 1964). "The purpose of the game is not to get suggestions, but to reject them" (Berne, 1964, p. 118). When concerns arise that perhaps the game is going too far, the help-rejecting complainer may verbally consent to follow through on a particular suggestion, when in fact he or she has no intention of doing so (Frank et al., 1952).

Although the help-rejecting complainer has been studied primarily in clinical settings, generally, and group psychotherapy settings, specifically, similar behavioral patterns can be observed among some individuals with whom we interact on a daily basis. Like the chronic complainer, the help-rejecting complainer seldom complains to achieve intrapsychic functions (Berger & Rosenbaum, 1967). Rather, the help-rejecting complainer appears constantly to seek the attention and support of others. Where these individuals differ from others whom one might characterize as excessively dependent is in their rejection of the assistance offered to them. It is perhaps this quality of the help-rejecting complainer more than the incessant complaining that is most aversive. Not only do others tire of the complaining itself, but they become frustrated and hopeless themselves in their efforts to help the individual (Frank et al., 1952). In this way, the help-rejecting complainer creates in others the very feelings he or she is currently experiencing.

People interacting with help-rejecting complainers find themselves in a Catch-22. The emotional reactions that they exhibit in response to their frustration with the help-rejecting complainer may actually be more informative to others about them than about the complainer. For example, if the listener eventually responds to the help-rejecting complainer with anger, others may be afraid to ever complain to the listener. On the other hand, to not respond with some indication of frustration or annoyance is to perpetuate the help-rejecting complainers' behavior (Frank et al., 1952).

Berne (1964) suggested some methods that can be used to deal effectively with help-rejecting complainers. He suggested that one reason that people become frustrated when dealing with people like help-rejecting complainers is because the listeners are playing their own game of "I'm only trying to help you." People playing this game will immediately react defensively when dealing with help-rejecting complainers. Berne suggests that a more effective strategy is to acknowledge that the complainer's problem has been heard and then ask what the complainer plans to do about the problem himself or herself. In this way, the help-rejecting complainer or any complainer for that matter is forced into the position of generating solutions to his or her own problem. Alternatively, in circumstances in which it is clear to the listener that the complaint has no instrumental value and that no solution is possible, the most strategic response is simply to acknowledge that the problem was heard.

TESTING YOUR OWN SAVVY AS A COMPLAINER

To discover the aversive associations that people had with chronic complaining, we used an act nomination procedure (Buss & Craik, 1984). In the first stage of this procedure, 139 male and female participants were instructed to think of people whom they perceived to be chronic complainers. With these people in mind, the participants were then asked to write down "acts or behaviors that these people perform that reflect or exemplify their chronic complaining."

On average, participants in this study generated 10 behaviors each. After eliminating redundancies and acts with shared meanings, 237 acts or behaviors were retained from the first step. Ninety-seven men and women were then asked to imagine someone they knew whom they perceived to be a chronic complainer. With this person in mind, the participants were asked to "rate how likely it is that each act or disposition describes a chronic complainer." A list of some of the items that received the highest ratings can be found in Table 1. Examination of some of the descriptors of chronic complainers leaves little doubt regarding the aversive nature of chronic complaining. Examining how characteristic each of these descriptors is of you may provide you with an index of the degree to which others may perceive your complaining as aversive.

TABLE 1 Descriptors of Chronic Complainers

Bring other people down
Are never satisfied with efforts made to deal with their complaints
Feel that they are always worse off than someone else
Interrupt discussions to make personal comments
Expect others to cater to them
Think that anything negative is someone else's fault
Want your opinion to be what they want to hear
Get upset when they don't get their way
Are pessimistic
Try to justify their complaining
Are argumentative
Move from one person to another to find someone who will listen to them complain
Nag constantly
Get along with people who do exactly what they want them to do
Have high expectations and complain when those expectations are not met
Hate to admit they are wrong
Are moody
No advice will work with them
Criticize other people
All of their conversations include a complaint
Complain to make themselves feel better
Use complaining to get attention
Complain about things that don't really matter
Try to get other people's sympathy
Are impossible to please
Are stubborn
Complain about other people behind their backs
Complain about things that are not relevant to them
Look for things to complain about
Are always wishing for things to be different
Try to outdo the complaints of others
Whine
Complain about things over which they have no control

SUMMARY

Like most other interpersonal behaviors, complaining can be used to achieve any of a number of desired goals. People may complain to make themselves feel better, to control the impressions that others form of them, to obtain social comparison information from others, or to call others to account for their behavior. Whether or not complaining is the behavior invoked to achieve any or all of these goals, however, depends on both the individual's dissatisfaction threshold and his or her complaining threshold. Thus, an individual who is very dissatisfied with a person or event may or may not complain depending on the social implications of complaining.

In spite of the frequency with which people complain, too much or too little complaining may be aversive. People who never complain may suffer just as many aversive intrapsychic and interpersonal consequences as those who complain too much because they are perceived to be secretive and mysterious. Thus, moderation is probably the best policy to adopt with complaining. In addition, not all complaints are alike. Complaints that are incessant, that contain aversive complaint content, that are expressive and manipulative, that create negative affect in the listener and that produce interactional dilemmas are perceived to be the most aversive. Epitomizing most, if not all, of these characteristics is the help-rejecting complainer or the individual playing Berne's game of "Why don't you...yes, but." These individuals not only annoy others with their incessant whining, but fail to take any advice that is offered to them.

REFERENCES

Alberts, J. K. (1988). An analysis of couples' conversational complaints. *Communication Monographs, 55,* 184–197.

Alicke, M. D., Braun, J. C., Glor, J. E., Klotz, M. L., Magee, J., Sederholm, H., & Siegel, R. (1992). Complaining behavior in social interaction. *Personality and Social Psychology Bulletin, 18,* 286–295.

Baughman, M. D. (1959). *Teacher's treasury of stories for every occasion.* Englewood Cliffs, NJ: Prentice-Hall.

Berger, M., & Rosenbaum, M. (1967). Notes on help-rejecting complainers. *International Journal of Group Psychotherapy, 17,* 357–370.

Berne, E. (1964). *Games people play.* New York: Ballantine Books.

Birney, B. (1992). *Oh, bother! Somebody's grumpy.* Racine, WI: Western Publishing Company.

Buss, D. M. (1992). Manipulation in close relationships: Five personality factors in interactional context. *Journal of Personality, 60,* 477–499.

Buss, D. M., & Craik, K. H. (1994). Acts, dispositions, and personality. In B. A. Maher & W. B. Maher (Eds.), *Progress in experimental personality research* (pp. 241–301). New York: Academic Press.

Buss, D. M., Gomes, M., Higgins, D. S., & Lauterbach, K. (1987). Tactics of manipulation. *Journal of Personality and Social Psychology, 52,* 1219–1229.

Caron, M. D., Whitbourne, S. K., & Halgin, R. P. (1992). Fraudulent excuse-making among college students. *Teaching of Psychology, 19,* 90–93.

Carver, C. S., & Scheier, M. F. (1981). *Attention and self-regulation.* New York: Springer-Verlag.

Denollet, J. (1991). Negative affectivity and repressive coping: Pervasive influence on self-reported mood, health, and coronary-prone behavior. *Psychosomatic Medicine, 53,* 538–556.

Denollet, J., Sys, S. U., Stroobant, N., Rombouts, H., Gillebert, T. C., & Brutsaert, D. L. (1996). Personality as independent predictor of long-term morality in patients with coronary heart disease. *Lancet, 347,* 417–421.

Erickson, J., & Kowalski, R. M. (1996). *Responses generated in complaint episodes.* Unpublished manuscript, Western Carolina University.

Fincham, F. D. (1992). The account episode in close relationships. In M. L. McLaughlin, M. J. Cody, & S. J. Read (Eds.), *Explaining one's self to others: Reason-giving in a social context* (pp. 167–191). Hillsdale, NJ: Erlbaum.

Folkman S., & Lazarus, R. S. (1986). Stress process and depressive symptomatology. *Journal of Abnormal Psychology, 95,* 107–113.

Fornell, C., & Westbrook, R. A. (1979). An exploratory study of assertiveness, aggressiveness, and consumer complaining behavior. In W. L. Wilkie (Ed.), *Advances in consumer research* (Vol. 6, pp. 105–110). Ann Arbor, MI: Association for Consumer Research.

Foster, E. (1995, April 3). The gripe line is on your side, but we can't promise results for everyone. *InfoWorld,* 48.

Frank, J. D., Ascher, E., Margolin, J. B., Nash, H., Stone, A. R., Varon, E. J. (1952). Behavioral patterns in early meetings of therapeutic groups. *American Journal of Psychiatry, 108,* 771–778.

Gibbons, F. X. (1990). Self-attention and behavior: A review and theoretical update. In M. P. Zanna (Ed.), *Advances in Experimental Social Psychology, 23,* 249–303.

Gilly, M. C., & Gelb, B. D. (1982). Post-purchase consumer processes and the complaining consumer. *Journal of Consumer Research, 9,* 323–328.

Ingram, R. E., Cruet, D., Johnson, B. R., & Wisnicki, K. S. (1988). Self-focused attention, gender, gender role, and vulnerability to negative affect. *Journal of Personality and Social Psychology, 55,* 967–978.

Ingram, R. E., & Smith, T. W. (1984). Depression and internal versus external focus of attention. *Cognitive Therapy and Research, 8,* 139–152.

Jones, E. E., & Pittman, T. S. (1982). Toward a general theory of strategic self-presentation. In J. Suls (Ed.), *Psychological perspectives on the self* (Vol. 1, pp. 231–262). Hillsdale, NJ: Erlbaum.

Kolb, L. C. (1982). Attachment and pain complaints. *Psychosomatics, 23,* 413–425.

Kowalski, R. M. (1996). Complaints and complaining: Functions, antecedents, and consequences. *Psychological Bulletin, 119,* 179–196.

Kowalski, R. M., & Brendle, M. (1996, May). *Profiles of a patient representative.* Paper presented at the meeting of the Carolinas Society for Patient Representation and Consumer Affairs, Charlotte, NC.

Kowalski, R. M., Cantrell, C. C., & Van Hout, M. (1996). *Interpersonal and affective consequences of complaints and complaint responses.* Unpublished manuscript, Western Carolina University.

Krishnan, S., & Valle, V. A. (1979). Dissatisfaction attributions and consumer complaint behavior. In W. L. Wilkie (Ed.), *Advances in consumer research* (Vol. 6, pp. 445–449). Ann Arbor, MI: Association for Consumer Research.

Leary, M. R. (1995). *Self-presentation: Impression management and interpersonal behavior*. Dubuque, IA: Brown & Benchmark.

Leary, M. R., & Kowalski, R. M. (1990). Impression management: A literature review and two-component model. *Psychological Bulletin, 107,* 34–47.

Leary, M. R., & Miller, R. S. (1986). *Social psychology and dysfunctional behavior*. New York: Springer-Verlag.

Parsons, T. (1951). *The social system*. Glencoe, IL: Free Press.

Pennebaker, J. W. (1990). *Opening up*. New York: Avon.

Pyszczynski, T., Greenberg, J., Hamilton, J., & Nix, G. (1991). On the relationship between self-focused attention and psychological disorder: A critical reappraisal. *Psychological Bulletin, 110,* 538–543.

Pyszczynski, T., Hamilton, J. C., Greenberg, J., & Becker, S. E. (1991). Self-awareness and psychological dysfunction. In C. R. Snyder & D. R. Forsyth (Eds.), *Handbook of social and clinical psychology* (pp. 138–157). New York: Pergamon Press.

Rusbult, C. E., Verette, J., Whitney, G. A., Slovik, L. F., & Lipkus, I. (1991). Accomodation processes in close relationships: Theory and preliminary empirical evidence. *Journal of Personality and Social Psychology, 60,* 53–78.

Scott, M. B., & Lyman, S. M. (1968). Accounts. *American Sociological Review, 33,* 46–62.

Sedikides, C. (1992). Attentional effects on mood are moderated by chronic self-conception valences. *Personality and Social Psychology Bulletin, 18,* 580–584.

Shuy, R. W. (1988). Discourse level language functions: Complaining. In J. Staton, R. W. Shuy, J. K. Peyton, & L. Reed (Eds.), *Dialogue journal communication: Classroom, linguistic, social, and cognitive views* (pp. 143–161). Norwood, NJ: Ablex Publishing Corporation.

Skelton, J. A., & Pennebaker, J. W. (1982). The psychology of physical symptoms and sensations. In G. S. Sanders & J. Suls (Eds.), *Social psychology of health and illness* (pp. 99–128). Hillsdale, NJ: Erlbaum.

Smith, T. W., & Greenberg, J. (1981). Depression and self-focused attention. *Motivation and Emotion, 5,* 323–331.

Smith, T. W., Snyder, C. R., & Perkins, S. C. (1983). The self-serving functions of hypochondriacal complaints: Physical symptoms as self-handicapping strategies. *Journal of Personality and Social Psychology, 44,* 787–797.

Snyder, C. R., & Smith, T. W. (1982). Symptoms as self-handicapping strategies: The virtues of old wine in a new bottle. In G. Weary & H. L. Mirels (Eds.), *Integrations of clinical and social psychology* (pp. 104–127). New York: Oxford University Press.

Stiles, W. B. (1987). "I have to talk to somebody": A fever model of disclosure. In V. J. Derlega & J. H. Berg (Eds.), *Self-disclosure: Theory, research, and therapy* (pp. 257–282). New York: Plenum Press.

Stiles, W. B., Schuster, P. L., & Harrigan, J. A. (1992). Disclosure and anxiety: A test of the fever model. *Journal of Personality and Social Psychology, 63,* 980–988.

Stilwell, N. C., & Salamon, M. J. (1990). Complaining behavior in long-term care: A multifactorial conceptualization. *Clinical Gerontologist, 9,* 77–90.

Weiner, B. (1992). Excuses in everyday interaction. In M. L. McLaughlin, M. J. Cody, & S. J. Read (Eds.), *Explaining one's self to others: Reason-giving in a social context* (pp. 131–146). Hillsdale, NJ: Erlbaum.

Wills, T. A. (1983). Social comparison in coping and help-seeking. In B. M. DePaulo, A. Nadler, & J. D. Fisher (Eds.), *New directions in helping: Help-seeking* (Vol. 2, pp. 109–141). New York: Academic Press.

Yalom, I. D. (1985). *The theory and practice of group psychotherapy*. New York: Basic Books.

CHAPTER 6

BLOWHARDS, SNOBS, AND NARCISSISTS

INTERPERSONAL REACTIONS TO EXCESSIVE EGOTISM

MARK R. LEARY, RICHARD BEDNARSKI, DUDLEY HAMMON, AND TIMOTHY DUNCAN

Few interactions are as annoying, exasperating, and unpleasant as those with people whom we perceive are behaving egotistically. The words commonly used to describe egotistical individuals are extremely disparaging; we call them arrogant, haughty, big-headed, vain, conceited, stuck-up, or pretentious, and brand them blowhards, show-offs, snobs, narcissists, pompous asses, or worse. Of the 300 adjectives on the Adjective Check List, those that connote egotism—arrogant, boastful, conceited, egotistical, snobbish, and the like—rank among those rated most unfavorably (Gough & Heilbrun, 1983). Simply put, we don't like egotistical people. Our interest in this chapter is on the interpersonal aspects of egotism—why egotistical behavior evokes such strong negative reactions in other people, the consequences of egotism for both the egotistic individual and others who are present, and why, given the negative reactions of others, people often act egotistically.

MARK R. LEARY, RICHARD BEDNARSKI, DUDLEY HAMMON, AND TIMOTHY DUNCAN • Department of Psychology, Wake Forest University, Winston-Salem, North Carolina 27109. leary@wfu.edu

Aversive Interpersonal Behaviors, edited by Kowalski
Plenum Press, New York, 1997

FEATURES OF EGOTISTICAL BEHAVIOR

As we use the term, *egotism* is characterized by an exaggerated estimate of one's intellect, ability, importance, appearance, wit, or other valued personal characteristics. Egotistical behavior is behavior that conveys to others that the individual holds an exaggerated perception of himself or herself.

THE CONCEPT OF EGOTISM

We propose that there are two distinct, though overlapping, types of egotistical behavior. *Absolute egotism* is characterized by the belief that one possesses more positive attributes than one actually does. If a woman fancies herself an outstanding athlete despite considerable evidence that she is only average, she would display absolute egotism. *Relative egotism* is characterized by the belief that one possesses more positive attributes than some other individual or individuals when such is not the case. If the woman thinks she is a better athlete than her roommate when, in fact, the roommate is just as athletically skilled, we would characterize her as showing relative egotism.

Absolute and relative egotism often occur together; people who have an exaggerated sense of their own characteristics often believe they are better than other people as well. However, the two types of egotism may occur separately. On one hand, people may think they are better than they truly are and, at the same time, recognize that they are not as good as most other people (absolute egotism). On the other hand, people may perceive themselves accurately (that is, they are not egotistical in an absolute sense), yet still believe they are better than other people because they underestimate others' characteristics (so they demonstrate relative egotism). Although interactions with people who display either type of egotism are unpleasant, people whose behavior conveys *both* absolute and relative egotism are particularly aversive.

For clarity, we should distinguish egotism from four related concepts with which it is sometimes confused. First, egotism should not be confused with *egocentrism*, which reflects excessive preoccupation with oneself. When people respond egocentrically, they perceive the world primarily from their own perspective and do not take others' perspectives or interests into account. Although egotistical individuals are often egocentric (partly because they overestimate their own importance in events), overvaluing oneself is not equivalent to having a narrow, self-centered perspective. In fact, egocentrism is often decidedly nonegotistical, as in the case of paranoia or depression in which the person's thoughts are egocentric but not egotistical.

Nor is egotism the same as *egoism*. Egoistic behavior refers to actions that are motivated primarily by self-interest. Again, when responding egotistically, people are often motivated by self-interest, partly because their lofty self-views give them a sense of being entitled to certain resources or treatment by others. However, egoists may selfishly pursue their own interests without having an overblown sense of self.

Egotism should also be distinguished from mere *bragging*. A successful person may brag about his or her attributes or accomplishments without being egotistical. As long as the claims do not overstate reality, egotism is not involved, although others may regard him or her as arrogant or braggartly.

Finally, a distinction must be drawn between egotism and *narcissism*. Narcissism is best conceptualized as a syndrome of reactions that involves not only heightened egotism, but also a sense of entitlement, a lack of empathy, and an exploitative approach toward other people. According to the *Diagnostic and Statistical Manual of Mental Disorders, Fourth Edition* (*DSM-IV*, American Psychiatric Association, 1994), the criteria for narcissistic personality disorder include: (a) a grandiose sense of self-importance (i.e., excessive egotism), (b) preoccupation with fantasies involving one's success, power, or brilliance, (c) the belief that one is a "special" person who can be understood and appreciated only by other special people, (d) an excessive need for admiration by others, (e) a sense of entitlement, (f) a tendency to exploit other people, (g) low empathy, (h) envy of other people, often accompanied by the belief that others are envious of him or her, and (h) arrogant or haughty behavior or attitudes.

In our view, the central component of narcissism is that of excessive absolute and relative egotism. Most of the other features appear to be consequences of the belief that one is better than most other people. A person who honestly believes that he or she is important and special might quite naturally think about success, power, and brillance. These would be regarded as "fantasies" only by other people; the narcissist would see them as goals, plans, or daydreams. Excessive egotism would be accompanied by the sense of being special, by the belief that one should be admired, and by the assumption that one is entitled to special treatment. Although narcissism always involves egotism, not all instances of egotism are necessarily narcissistic. Even so, as we will see, research on narcissism can shed a great deal of light on the social psychological aspects of egotism.

Inferring Egotism from Behavior

Egotism may be conceptualized both objectively and subjectively. On one hand, it sometimes is not difficult to demonstrate objectively that a person's self-image is biased in a positive direction. If a person claims to possess a superior intellect and otherwise appears to believe that he or she is more intelligent than evidence suggests, yet the person struggles with standard high school courses, scores poorly on standardized tests, and is unable to solve even moderately difficult intellectual problems, the discrepancy between the person's self-image and the objective evidence would suggest that the individual is egotistical.

However, more often, people do not have access to objective indices that unequivocally indicate that an individual's self-beliefs are exaggerated. Even so, people may conclude that another person is being egotistical if he or she appears to hold self-beliefs that are more positive than observers' subjective impressions of him or her. In such instances, egotism is best regarded as an inference or attribution of the observer rather than as a characteristic of an individual per se.

Because no previous research has examined the cues that people use to infer that others are egotistical, we conducted an informal, unsystematic survey of university students in search of clues regarding how people infer that another person is "stuck-up." Our respondents indicated that the most direct way to detect egotism was through people's verbal claims regarding their abilities or accomplishments, or about their standing relative to others. However, because excessive self-aggrandizement is discouraged, if not censured (Schlenker & Leary, 1982), most people refrain from making blatantly egotistical claims. Even when others do not explicitly enhance themselves, however, people may infer that they hold highly positive views of themselves when they talk about themselves a great deal, and particularly when they do so in a self-important fashion, with excessive emphasis and dramatic flair. In fact, narcissistic individuals do use first-person personal singular pronouns more frequently than people who are low in narcissism, and they tend to talk more about personally relevant topics (Raskin & Shaw, 1988).

Observers also infer that other people are "stuck on themselves" through nonverbal channels. Particular ways of talking, gazing, standing, or moving can convey an impression of egotism. For example, common wisdom maintains that people who think very highly of themselves strut when they walk, with their head held high, their shoulders back, and their chest thrust slightly forward. They are assumed to be overly concerned with their appearance and clothing, and frequently preen themselves publicly (straightening their clothes, removing lint, checking their hair). People also make attributions of egotism when others seem disinterested in or unimpressed by others' contributions to conversations, and particularly when they downplay or denigrate others' experiences or accomplishments. Egotists are also assumed to interact with others in an overly controlled, reserved, or distant fashion. They do not pay others an appropriate amount of visual attention, and maintain an inappropriately large interpersonal distance. In fact, extreme egotists sometimes do not acknowledge other people at all. They may pass acquaintances on the street without appearing to see them. Through their apparent disinterest in other people, egotists convey that others are less important than themselves.

Undoubtedly, these inferences are sometimes incorrect; we have all concluded that another individual was "stuck-up" only to discover later that we had erred in our initial impression. (Often, shyness seems to be interpreted as conceit, for example.) Even so, the average person seems to think he or she can detect egotists; whether this is true is an interesting question for research.[1]

EGOTISM AS AN ASPECT OF HUMAN NATURE

Virtually everyone is egotistical from time to time. Behavioral researchers have documented that human beings have a penchant for thinking and behaving egotistically. Most people tend to see themselves as better than the average person, which is obviously a logical and statistical impossibility (Alicke, 1985; Brown, 1986). They also tend to overestimate their responsibility for favorable outcomes and underestimate their responsibility for unfavorable events (Bradley, 1978). For example, students are likely to claim responsibility for scoring well on tests, but tend to deny that their failures are their fault (Forsyth, 1986; Whitley & Frieze, 1985). Likewise, therapists attribute client improvement to their own clinical skills but blame the client when therapy goes poorly (Roberts & McCready, 1987). Similarly, people working together in groups show a strong tendency to believe that they were more influential in the group's performance than other group members when their group succeeds but less responsible than most of the other members if the group fails (Forsyth & Schlenker, 1977; Schlenker & Miller, 1977; Schlenker, Miller, Leary, & McCown, 1979). People in unhappy marriages tend to blame their marital problems mostly on their partners, but those in happy marriages take personal credit (Bradbury & Fincham, 1990). And, people generally rate themelves more positively than other people do; for example, American workers rate their job performance higher than their supervisors rate the workers (Farh,

[1] Many respondents had difficulty identifying more than a couple of vague cues that led them to infer that someone was egotistical, but they nonetheless maintained that they could "just tell" someone was stuck-up. From listening to their suggestions regarding how egotists may be detected, we got the sense that some people convey an "aura of egotism" that is difficult to precisely identify or define even though observers may independently agree that, in fact, the person thinks too highly of himself or herself.

Dobbins, & Cheng, 1991). (For reviews of the literature on self-serving illusions, see Blaine & Crocker, 1993; Taylor & Brown, 1988.)

The pervasive tendency for people to behave egotistically led Greenwald (1980) to characterize the human ego as inherently "totalitarian." Just as a totalitarian regime controls information to lead its citizens to perceive the government in a particular desired fashion, the ego fabricates and revises information in a way that preserves the individual's desired image of himself or herself.

This tendency toward egotism is not only apparently normal and natural, but presumably also functional because it is sometimes adaptive to overestimate one's ability or importance. Egotism may help people escape the paralyzing effects of self-doubt, motivate them to pursue difficult and imposing goals, and reduce the shame of personal failure (Greenwald, 1980). It may also promote certain aspects of mental health by enhancing personal contentment, increasing one's ability to help others, and enhancing the capacity for creative, productive work (Taylor & Brown, 1988, 1994; see, however, Colvin & Block, 1994). Moreover, some evolutionary psychologists have suggested that egotistic tendencies evolved because they conferred benefits for survival and reproduction. For example, early human beings were more successful in impressing others (thereby increasing their social status, access to resources, and reproductive success) if they *believed* the inflated self-images they conveyed to others. Trivers (1976) suggested that evolutionary pressures may have selected for a degree of self-deception, that would allow people to convey highly postive impressions of themselves to others without giving themselves away by appearing deceitful or guilty. Whatever its source, a tendency toward at least mild egotism appears to be an undeniable aspect of human nature.

Although we grant the benefits of occasional egotism, like most adaptations, excessive egotism can be personally and interpersonally maladaptive. For the individual, egotistical biases can lead to nonjudicious behavioral choices. People who overestimate their ability will likely bite off more than they can chew, persist on tasks that are beyond their objective ability, and take excessive risks (Colvin & Block, 1994). Furthermore, convinced that they are more knowledgeable and capable than others, egotistical individuals may ignore sage advice from other people. And, perceiving themselves as virtually infallible, extreme egotists may not learn from their own mistakes. Sullivan (1953) marveled at "the failure of learning which has left their capacity for fantastic, self-centered delusions so utterly unaffected by a life-long series of educative events" (p. 80). Thus, despite its occasional benefits, egotism has serious liabilities for the egotistic individual. Although such intrapsychic consequences are of considerable importance, we confine ourselves in this chapter to the interpersonal aspects of egotism.

INTERPERSONAL CONSEQUENCES OF EGOTISTICAL BEHAVIOR

If people judiciously kept their egotistical beliefs to themselves, hiding any hint that they viewed themselves positively, egotistical actions would have few interpersonal consequences, and there would be little need to consider egotistical behaviors as a class of aversive interpersonal behavior. But, people often convey, intentionally or not, impressions that observers regard as exaggerated, inflated, or even delusional.

Most people find interactions with egotistical individuals aversive, and those who behave in ways that others view as egotistical are disliked and avoided. In Anderson's (1968) study of the "likableness" of 555 trait adjectives, terms that connoted egotism were among the most disliked. For example, the traits conceited, snobbish, bragging, egotistical, and boastful each ranked among the 15% most disliked personal attributes. Experimental research also confirms that people disparage those who behave in egotistical ways. In three studies that examined people's reactions to those whose claims understated or overstated their real level of performance, Schlenker and Leary (1982) showed that people who egotistically claimed to have performed better on a task than they actually did were evaluated significantly less favorably than those who accurately represented themselves.

In small group settings, people who behave egotistically are disliked. Forsyth, Berger, and Mitchell (1981) assessed group members' reactions to other members who made egotistical attributions for the group's performance. Members who took excessive responsibility for the group's success were evaluated unfavorably, as were those who disclaimed responsibility for group failure. Given that other members dislike and resent those who respond egotistically, group cohesion may be weakened when people make egotistical attributions (Leary & Forsyth, 1987). In a study of people's reactions to bonafide narcissists (Carroll, Corning, Morgan, & Stevens, 1991), participants rated narcissistic women significantly less positively than both psychologically healthy and dependent women, and indicated less interest in interacting with them (see also Carroll, Hoenigmann-Stovall, King, Wienhold, & Whitehead, in press).

People in various cultures may differ in how they react to displays of egotism. Farh et al. (1991) suggested that, "while exaggerated self-perceptions may be accomodated and even reinforced in individualistic cultures, inflated self-perceptions are inconsistent with collectivistic cultures that encourage interpersonal harmony, interdependence, solidarity, and group cohesion" (p. 131). Thus, we would not only expect to find less egotism in collectivist than in individualistic cultures, but less tolerance for expressions of egotism as well.

In a study that compared workers' self-ratings of their performance with the ratings that their supervisors gave them, Farh et al. (1991) found that, whereas American workers typically rated themselves more highly than their supervisors did, workers in the Republic of China (Taiwan) rated their job performance less favorably than their supervisors. Importantly, this difference was due to differences in the workers' self-ratings rather than to the supervisors' ratings (which were similar in the two cultures). Along the same lines, Smith (1990) found that Asian-American women scored lower on a measure of narcissism than Caucasian and Hispanic Americans. Although some of this difference may be attributable to items that are only indirectly related to narcissism (such as "I am assertive"), the groups clearly differed on items that are at the heart of egotism. For example, 72% of the Caucasian Americans endorsed the item "I think I am a special person," whereas only 21% of the Asian Americans did so.

What is unclear is whether these cross-cultural differences reflect true differences in egotism or whether only the *expression* of egotism differs. That is, it is possible that the true incidence of egotism is comparable across cultures, but people in certain cultures are more reluctant to express inflated self-views. Alternatively, perhaps socialization leads people in some cultures to develop less egotistical beliefs about themselves. Either way, presumably people from cultures in which egotistical responding is infrequent would have a more negative reaction to those who act egotistically than people from cultures in which egotism is more common.

People not only evaluate egotists unfavorably but sometimes challenge their egotistical behavior. These challenges range from subtle and implicit to direct and even violent. Mild, somewhat subtle challenges include snide and sarcastic retorts ("Okay, Mr. Know-it-all") and semi-humorous or good-natured disparagement ("I sure wish I could be as perfect as you"). Challenges may also include explicit denials that the person is as good as he or she says. Observers may offer evidence that corrects or contradicts the person's egotistical claims, or poke holes in his or her egotism in other ways. Adler and Adler (1989) discussed how college athletic coaches criticize and mock their star players in team meetings to keep their egos in check.

In extreme cases, challenges may take a violent turn, particularly if, in behaving egotistically, the offending individual casts aspersions on other interactants. For example, one primary cause of violence between juvenile gangs is one gang's belief that another gang sees itself as superior.

Insults from one gang to another easily escalate into overt violence (Jankowski, 1991). Baumeister, Smart, and Boden (1996) have suggested that violence may occur when a person with high but fragile self-esteem is confronted with a threat to his or her ego. To the extent that egotism can threaten the self-esteem of others who are present (by indicating that one is superior to other people), we suspect that egotism sometimes provokes aggressive responses.

WHY IS EGOTISM AVERSIVE?

In our view, the interesting question is *why* interactions with egotistical people are so aversive and evoke negative reactions from other people. The answer to this question is not as obvious as it may first appear: if some self-absorbed, big-headed egotist thinks he or she is better than he or she is (or even better than other people), why should anyone else mind? Why do we find it so difficult to tolerate conceited people? Below we suggest six factors that may contribute to the nearly universal dislike of egotistical people.

SELF-ESTEEM THREAT

First, as noted earlier, egotistical behavior often threatens the self-esteem of other interactants. When one individual conveys that he or she is superior to other people, the others are, by implication, deemed inferior. In essence, then, egotism can function much like a veiled insult, disparaging other people in a subtle, oblique fashion.

Threats to self-esteem are, of course, typically unpleasant. At best, people must perform the cognitive work necessary to dismiss the egotist's unflattering comparisons as the delusions of a narcissist; at worse, they may suffer a loss of self-esteem if they begin to question their own relative competence, appearance, skill, or whatever. However, not all egotistical behavior is ego-threatening. If a person is egotistical on a dimension that others view as irrelevant to their own identity, they should not experience much of a threat to their self-esteem nor find the braggart's claims particularly objectionable (although they may be tiresome nonetheless). However, if a person is egotistical on a dimension that others regard as relevant to themselves, they will experience the other's egotism more negatively (Tesser, 1988).

According to the sociometer theory of self-esteem (Leary & Downs, 1995; Leary, Tambor, Terdal, & Downs, 1995), self-esteem is a subjective monitor of interpersonal inclusion and, thus, self-esteem is threatened by events that undermine the person's sense of acceptance or belonging. The sociometer perspective raises the possibility that egotism sometimes causes self-esteem to decrease because it threatens the individual's sense of social acceptance. This could occur via two routes.

First, by touting their superiority, egotists (particularly relative egotists) essentially claim that they are more socially desirable and, thus, more interpersonally acceptable than other people. To the extent that people are sometimes in implicit competition for others' attention, admiration, and acceptance, one person's egotism can imply a threat to others' social inclusion. Second, people with more positive personal qualities typically have more interpersonal options than those with less positive qualities. People who are attractive, competent, and of high status, for example, find it easier to leave one social interaction or relationship for a more desirable one. Indeed, the detachment and disinterest of egotistical people connote less than complete acceptance of other people. Implying that one is superior connotes that others may not have much to offer the egotistical person, who may seek greener interpersonal pastures. In light of this, people may feel that their relationships with egotistical people are more tenuous than their relationships with those who are more down-to-earth, and, thus, experience lowered self-esteem when interacting with them.

Misrepresentation

Social norms dictate that people must be who and what they claim to be. As Goffman (1959) observed, "an individual who implicitly or explicitly signifies that he has certain social characteristics ought in fact to be what he claims he is" (p. 13). Smooth and effective social interaction requires that people can trust others to represent themselves accurately. Although we tolerate a certain amount of fudging, people who frequently or extensively misrepresent themselves break this social contract, disrupt social encounters, and consequently provoke the ire of other interactants. Because the sanctions associated with misrepresentation are severe, people generally try to present themselves to others in ways that are consistent with what others already know or are likely to learn about them (Baumeister & Jones, 1978; Schlenker, 1975).

In the eyes of observers, egotism is essentially misrepresentation. The individual who implicitly or explicitly purports to be more knowledgeable, capable, or whatever than he or she really is makes claims that are not supported by the evidence. This creates difficulties for other interactants. They must decide whether to respond to the egotistical individual as they actually perceive him or her or as the individual claims to be. Either tactic creates a certain degree of interpersonal stress. Other interactants must either risk the possibility of a confrontation if they deny the egotist's claims or struggle through a farce if they pretend to accept them.

ENTITLEMENT AND EXPLOITATION

At various times and places, people who are unusually successful at professional, financial, intellectual, athletic, or military pursuits have been treated as special. Given the egotistical person's self-perceived superiority, he or she is likely to expect a certain degree of deference, tribute, and influence, and possibly a disproportionate share of resources.

Furthermore, narcissism and arrogance correlate moderately with dominance (Emmons, 1984; Raskin, Novacek, & Hogan, 1991b). Bennett (1988) found that narcissism was associated with a heightened need to influence others. People who think they are superior tend to believe not only that they are more capable of making decisions that affect others but also that they have the right to do so. In extreme cases, people who believe they are superior may believe they have the right to exploit other individuals, feeling they are entitled, by virtue of their superiority, to draw upon their time, energy, or goodwill. Observers who do not share the egotist's inflated self-image are understandably more likely to regard these attempts to extract additional respect, deference, or resources as megalomania rather than as legitimate claims commensurate with the individual's contributions or status.

Some of the worst cases of exploitation in history can be traced to one group's belief that it was superior to another, and, thus, had a right to treat the supposedly inferior group as it desired. The subjugation of slaves, the domination of Native Americans, apartheid in South Africa, and the Holocaust all involved the egotistical belief that, due to their superiority, some people had a right to exploit others.

DEFENSIVENESS

Egotists do not take criticism well. This is not an entirely unreasonable response from a person who is, in fact, superior to most other people; most of us have more difficulty accepting negative feedback from those we regard as inferior to us on the dimension in question than those whom we regard as superior. (We resent "the pot calling the kettle black.") Given how difficult it is for average individuals to accept criticism they know is valid, consider how difficult it must be for individuals who believe themselves to be superior. Thus, it is rarely fruitful to provide unfavorable feedback to egotistical individuals. Employers, teachers, coworkers, family, and friends often feel they must walk on eggshells when they approach an egotistical person with a criticism or reprimand.

Furthermore, egotists often require a great deal of overt adulation. Their ego must be stroked regularly. For example, people who score high on the superiority factor of the Narcisstic Personality Inventory (this factor is essentially an index of egotism) were rated as expecting "everyone to admire him or her" (Emmons, 1984). If others are not appropriately acclaiming and deferential, the egotist may interpret the absence of positive feedback as actual disparagement.

When they do not receive the respect they believe they deserve (whether that involves lack of positive attention or explicitly negative evaluations), egotists are prone to respond with hostility. They are highly defensive to indications that they are not as successful, intelligent, skilled, or attractive as they believe themselves to be. Self-perceived superiority and narcissism correlate moderately with tendencies toward hostility and aggression (Emmons, 1984; Raskin et al., 1991b; Rhodewalt & Morf, 1995). In extreme cases, egotists sometimes display "narcissistic rage" in the face of criticisms or insults. They may even contemplate ways to seek revenge upon those they perceive have disparaged them. As noted previously, Baumeister et al. (1996) reviewed evidence that suggests that some people with high self-esteem may become violent when their ego is threatened.

The hyperdefensiveness of egotistical people is paradoxical. On one hand, a sense of superiority correlates with social imperturbability, low public self-consciousness, and low social anxiety (Emmons, 1984; Raskin & Novacek, 1989), suggesting that people who feel superior do not concern themselves with others' evaluations as much as people who feel less superior. On the other hand, egotistical people sometimes overreact to criticism, insults, and slights. We return below to the question of why someone who was convinced of his or her superiority might be hypersensitive to others' reactions.

Illegitimate Self-Esteem

People who succeed are justifiably entitled to feel proud of their accomplishments. However, by the same token, people are not entitled to enjoy successes that they have not legitimately earned. Yet the egotist enjoys the emotional benefits of success without having performed in an exemplary fashion. The person who feels superior may experience high self-esteem, a sense of pride, and the attendant emotions without having earned them legitimately. Although we know of no evidence on this issue, we propose that people dislike those who reap the emotional benefits of success without earning them.

Boredom

Finally, people simply find egotistical individuals tedious. As Dale Carnegie observed, people are far more interested in their own concerns than in the affairs of others. Although we are quite willing to share the floor in interpersonal encounters, we typically find conversations that focus exclusively on another person less interesting and involving than those that focus on us as well. In a factor analytic study of the antecedents of interpersonal boredom, participants rated behaviors that conveyed self-preoccupation as "moderately" boring (Leary, Rogers, Canfield, & Coe, 1986). Thus, whatever other negative responses egotistical people elicit, boredom may be among them.

SUMMARY

We have identified six reasons that egotism evokes negative responses in other people. Egotistical people may threaten others' self-esteem, be viewed as misrepresenting themselves, have a sense of entitlement (if not actually exploit other people), respond defensively when they do not receive the deference they think they deserve, be perceived as reaping an undeserved sense of self-satisfaction, and bore other people. Negative reactions to egotistical behavior are multiply determined, which may explain why egotism is so aversive.

PERSPECTIVES ON EGOTISM

Most people realize that egotistical behavior is regarded negatively. For example, when undergraduate students rated 56 adjectives in terms of how accepted or rejected they would feel if someone used each adjective to describe them, the three adjectives that connoted aspects of egotism (arrogant, snobbish, and selfish) were rated as highly rejecting; in contrast, the adjective "modest" was associated with acceptance. Similarly, when other respondents were asked how they would describe themselves to get another person to dislike them, they included adjectives that connoted conceit.

Given that most people regard egotists unfavorably and do not wish to be regarded as egotistical themselves, it is perhaps surprising that anyone should ever boast or brag at all. The fact that egotistical behavior is quite common raises the provocative question of why people so often act in egotistical ways. Why would people risk the censure and derogation associated with egotism? Note that the question here is not why people sometimes perceive themselves better than they are or better than other people. A great deal has been written about the possible cognitive, motivational, and evolutionary causes of self-serving biases (see Blaine & Crocker, 1993; Greenwald, 1980; Taylor & Brown, 1988). Rather, our interest is in why people would convey their inflated self-views to others. Three primary hypotheses will be considered that we call the veridical, defensive, and strategic perspectives.

VERIDICAL EGOTISM

The most straightforward explanation is that egotistical people believe their inflated self-views and, thus, don't stop to consider that others may not share their self-perceptions or regard them as arrogant. As Calvin (of the cartoon, *Calvin and Hobbes*) observed after a playmate accused him of being a conceited blowhard, "When you're great, people often mistake candor for bragging." But why do some people come to see themselves more positively than they really are?

Some people become egotistical through excessive glorification by others. For example, children whose parents treat them as particularly special may grow up with an inflated self-concept. Similarly, people who have distinguished themselves through their accomplishments—such as entertainment celebrities, sports heroes, political and military leaders—may have difficulty keeping their egos in check as they receive constant adulation from the public. They may even be aware of the fact that they are becoming big-headed, and even try to fight it, yet eventually succumb to the adoration (Adler & Adler, 1989). From a symbolic interactionist perspective, the development of a "gloried self" under such circumstances is understandable. To the extent that people's self-concepts are affected by how they believe others perceive them (Felson, 1993; Shraugher & Schoneman, 1979), the person who is adored by others would be expected to develop a very positive view of self.

The puzzling thing is that most people realize that, even when the acclaim is deserved, others regard those who trumpet their own accomplishments as braggarts. Thus, it would seem that even people who were truly great would exercise restraint in advertising their abilities and virtues, particularly given that, in many cases, others are already aware of them (Baumeister & Jones, 1978). Yet, ironically, people who advertise their accomplishments appear not to realize that their sense of self-importance has a negative effect on other people's reactions to them or that others see them as egotistical and arrogant.

Part of the reason may lie in the fact that people typically do not challenge egotistical people on their behavior. This may be particularly true for individuals who are truly superior and acclaimed in a particular area; even superstars' best friends may hesitate to tell them that they have become haughty. And, even if the egotist perceives that others are responding unfavorably, he or she may attribute others' reactions to envy rather than justified annoyance. Furthermore, some egotistical people may lack the interpersonal skills necessary to convey desired impressions without stepping over the line into conceit. Studies suggest that particularly narcissistic people may be deficient in empathy and role-taking skills and, thus, may have difficulty perceiving the negative effect they have on others (Watson & Morris, 1991).

Veridical egotism may also become aversive when glorified people turn their egotism against their devotees. The supporters and fans of political leaders, religious figures, sports luminaries, and other celebrities may idolize their heroes, yet be distressed when it becomes obvious that the celebrity thinks too highly of himself or herself. Realizing that the superstar has placed himself or herself above the fans may turn hero worship to resentment and disillusionment. In contrast, notables who retain the "common touch" despite their stardom are often particularly admired. The irony, of course, is that the egotistical celebrity often develops an overblown ego because of the excessive adulation of the same fans who subsequently resent the celebrity's arrogance.

Defensive Egotism

Many people have been skeptical that highly egotistic or narcissistic people truly believe their inflated self-views. The assumption seems to be that egotistical behavior emerges from a fragile sense of self and that the apparently high self-esteem of egotistical people is, in fact, a compensation or defense against a negative or fragile self-concept. According to this view, people who behave egotistically do not really have an inflated ego. Rather, they are behaving egotistically to convince themselves (and, perhaps, others) that they are more competent and self-assured than they really feel (Harder, 1984). Likewise, many theoretical views of narcissism have assumed that narcissists are characterized by low self-esteem, if not self-loathing (e.g., Kohut, 1971).

Little direct evidence supports this hypothesis, however. On the contrary, a wealth of data supports the notion that egotistical, narcissistic behavior is more common among people who truly perceive themselves positively. Not only do highly egotistical/narcissistic people have high self-esteem (Emmons, 1984; Raskin, Novacek, & Hogan, 1991a), but they make blatantly egotistical attributions for events in their lives, claiming personal responsibility for their successes (Hartouni, 1992; Ladd & Welsh, 1996; Rhodewalt & Morf, 1995).

However, proponents of the defensive perspective claim that what appears to be high self-esteem is, in reality, *defensive* self-esteem. In support of this, highly egotistical people often do not appear to have the confidence and poise one expects out of people who truly think they are great. In fact, some evidence suggests that, rather than having the positive affective effects often associated with high self-esteem (Taylor & Brown, 1988), narcissists are typically anxious and distressed (Kohut, 1977; Watson & Morris, 1991). As Emmons (1984) noted, this is a paradox; why do some people who hold grandiose views of themselves appear insecure and defensive?

We accidentally stumbled upon a partial resolution of the "narcissistic paradox" (Emmons, 1984) in a study designed to examine how narcissistic people deal with unflattering feedback from others (Bednarski & Leary, 1995). Participants who had completed a measure of narcissism described themselves to another person, then received feedback from this individual. The intriguing finding relevant to the narcissistic paradox was that, among participants who scored low in narcissism, feelings of state self-esteem were strongly negatively correlated with subjective anxiety ($r = -.68$, $p < .001$). In contrast, among high narcissists, self-esteem and anxiety were *uncorrelated*, ($r = .02$, ns.). We replicated this finding in a second study that used a different paradigm; in the second study, self-esteem and anxiety correlated –.70 ($p < .001$) for low narcissists but only –.28 for high narcisists (*ns.*) (Bednarski & Leary, 1996).

One interpretation of these data is that highly egotistical people do, in fact, possess high self-esteem, but their positive self-regard does not buffer them against anxiety and uncertainty as it does for most people. Put differently, highly egotistical people *think* more highly of themselves but, for some reason, they don't *feel* better about themselves. Why chronically egotistical people do not experience the same affective benefits of high self-esteem as other people is not clear, but this may help to explain the egotist's endless search for affirmation and security.

Strategic Egotism

A third alternative explanation of egotistical behavior is that people may intentionally behave in egotistical ways when they believe that doing so has interpersonal benefits for them. Self-enhancement can have positive consequences. When other people have no reason to doubt the egotist's claims, they may, in fact, be suitably impressed (Schlenker & Leary, 1982). As Francis Bacon recommended, "Praise yourself daringly, something always sticks." Thus, egotism can be viewed as a variety of self-presentational tactic that is designed to impress or intimidate other people.

The interpersonal benefits of judicious self-aggrandizement are obvious. Overall, people who are perceived as competent, powerful, attractive, and confident attain greater social and material rewards than people who are regarded less positively (Schlenker, 1980). Thus, it is not at all surprising that many people wish to be perceived in these desired ways and occasionally manage their impressions to convey such images (Leary,

1995). Presumably, a great deal of egotistical behavior is intended to serve these self-presentational functions.

But why would tactics designed to convey certain impressions often be so aversive to other people? We see three possible reasons. First, often the egotist's goal is not to be liked, but to be respected or even feared. In Jones and Pittman's (1982) taxonomy, egotists' self-presentational goal is typically *self-promotion* (being perceived as competent) or *intimidation* (being seen as threatening) rather than ingratiation (being seen as likeable). If one does not care about being liked or about being regarded as a desirable interactant, whether one's behaviors are aversive to others may of little concern. Along these lines, one study suggested that narcissistic individuals strongly wish to be admired but are indifferent about social approval per se (Raskin & Novacek, 1991; Raskin et al., 1991a, 1991b).

Second, many instances of blatant, aversive egotism may reflect self-presentational miscalculations. The person may have intended to present highly favorable self-presentations to enhance his or her image in others' eyes but misjudged how his or her behavior would be perceived by others. The person who desires to be admired walks a fine line between conveying an image that will result in accolades and being disparaged as egotistical.

The third reason involves a breakdown in audience segregation. We often do not mind people being egotistical toward other individuals and, in fact, may want those with whom we are linked in some way to think highly of themselves. For example, we want our own political candidates, athletic coaches, and company presidents to convey the impression that they (and, by implication, our political party, team, or company) are the best. In fact, under certain circumstances, a political, military, or group leader's egotism may be beneficial in maintaining the confidence and cohesiveness of the group. This is one instance in which egotistical behavior may not be regarded as aversive and, in fact, may be encouraged and reinforced by other people.

However, we do not like it when *other people's* candidates, coaches, company presidents, or group leaders are equally egotistical. The difficulty is that, unless the egotistical person can keep the in-group and out-group audiences segregated, the egotistical self-presentations admired by one's adherents will evoke negative reactions among members of the out-group.

CONCLUSIONS

We have examined several factors that underlie people's antipathy toward egotists and the aversiveness of our interactions with them, as well as reasons that people continue to behave egotistically despite the interpersonal consequences. The veridical, defensive, and strategic explanations of egotism (and narcissism) may each have merit; there is no reason to assume that all egotistical behavior occurs for the same reason. In different instances, egotism may arise from a deep (but erroneous) belief in one's own superiority, a desparate attempt to ward off feelings of inferiority, or an intentional (though sometimes misguided) attempt to make particular impressions.

We find it ironic that, in a culture that regards having high self-esteem as a virtue, people who think too highly of themselves are so greatly disliked. American culture offers a mixed message regarding egotism and modesty. We encourage people to be the best they can be and to think well of themselves, yet when they let others know that they do, in fact, think highly of themselves, we often disparage and avoid them. And, we rarely instruct children regarding how to walk the fine line between appropriate self-esteem and excessive self-aggrandizement. Behavioral researchers have been of little help in this respect; indeed, they disagree among themselves regarding the extent to which egotistical biases and high self-esteem are beneficial (Baumeister et al., 1996; Colvin & Block, 1994; Taylor & Brown, 1988, 1994). Growing evidence suggests that viewing oneself positively is a mixed blessing and suggests that the consequences of egotism—both for egotistical individuals and those with whom they interact—deserve further attention.

REFERENCES

Adler, P. A., & Adler, P. (1989). The gloried self: The aggrandizement and constriction of self. *Social Psychology Quarterly, 52,* 299–310.

Alicke, M. (1985). Global self-evaluation as determined by the desirability and controllability of trait adjectives. *Journal of Personality and Social Psychology, 49,* 1621–1630.

American Psychiatric Association (1994). *Diagnostic and statistical manual of mental disorders* (4th ed.). Washington, D.C.: Author.

Anderson, N. H. (1968). Likableness ratings of 555 personality-trait words. *Journal of Personality and Social Psychology, 9,* 272–279.

Baumeister, R. F., & Jones, E. E. (1978). When self-presentation is constrained by the target's knowledge: Consistency and compensation. *Journal of Personality and Social Psychology, 36,* 608–618.

Baumeister, R. F., Smart, L., & Boden, J. M. (1996). Relation of threatened egotism to violence and aggression: The dark side of high self-esteem. *Psychological Review, 103,* 5–33.

Bednarski, R. F., & Leary, M. R. (1995, November). *Narcissistic reactions to interpersonal evaluations.* Paper presented at the meeting of the Society of Southeastern Social Psychologists, Del Ray Beach, FL.

Bednarski, R. F., & Leary, M. R. (1996, March). *The paradox of narcissism: When high self-esteem fails.* Paper presented at the meeting of the Southeastern Psychological Association, Norfolk, VA.

Bennett, J. B. (1988). Power and influence as distinct personality traits: Development and validation of a psychometric measure. *Journal of Research in Personality, 22,* 361–394.

Blaine, B., & Crocker, J. (1993). Self-esteem and self-serving biases in reactions to positive and negative events. In R. F. Baumeister (Ed.), *Self-esteem: The puzzle of low self-regard* (pp. 55–85). New York: Plenum Press.

Bradbury, T. N., & Fincham, F. D. (1990). Attributions and behavior in marital interaction. *Journal of Personality and Social Psychology, 63,* 613–628.

Bradley, G. W. (1978). Self-serving biases in the attribution process: A reexamination of the fact or fiction question. *Journal of Personality and Social Psychology, 36,* 56–71.

Brown, J. D. (1986). Evaluations of self and others: Self-enhancement biases in social judgments. *Social Cognition, 4,* 353–376.

Carroll, L., Corning, A. F., Morgan, R. R., & Stevens, D. M. (1991). Perceived acceptance, psychological functioning, and sex role orientation of narcissistic persons. *Journal of Social Behavior and Personality, 6,* 943–954.

Carroll, L., Hoenigmann-Stovall, N., King, A., Wienhold, J., & Whitehead, G. I. (in press). Interpersonal consequences of narcissistic and borderline personality disorders: A comparative investigation. *Journal of Social and Clinical Psychology.*

Colvin, C. R., & Block, J. (1994). Do positive illusions foster mental health? An examination of the Taylor and Brown formulation. *Psychological Bulletin, 116,* 3–20.

Emmons, R. A. (1984). Factor analysis and construct validity of the Narcissistic Personality Inventory. *Journal of Personality Assessment, 48,* 291–300.

Farh, J., Dobbins, G. H., & Cheng, B. (1991). Cultural relativity in action: A comparison of self-ratings made by Chinese and U.S. Workers. *Personnel Psychology, 44,* 129–145.

Felson, R. B. (1993). The (somewhat) social self: How others affect self-appraisals. In J. Suls (Ed.), *Psychological perspectives on the self* (Vol. 4; pp. 1–26). Hillsdale, NJ: Erlbaum.

Forsyth, D. R. (1986). An attributional analysis of students' reactions to success and failure. In R. Feldman (Ed.), *The social psychology of education* (pp. 17–38). New York: Cambridge University Press.

Forsyth, D. R., Berger, R., & Mitchell, T. (1981). The effects of self-serving vs. other-serving claims of responsibility on attraction in groups. *Social Psychology Quarterly, 44,* 59–64.

Forsyth, D. R., & Schlenker, B. R. (1977). Attributing the causes of group performance: Effects of performance quality, task importance, and future testing. *Journal of Personality, 45,* 220–236.

Goffman, E. (1959). *The presentation of self in everyday life.* Garden City, NY: Doubleday.

Gough, H. G., & Heilbrun, Jr., A. B. (1983). *The adjective check list manual.* Palo Alto, CA: Consulting Psychologists Press.

Greenwald, A. G. (1980). The totalitarian ego: Fabrication and revision of personal history. *American Psychologist, 35,* 603–618.

Harder, D. W. (1984). Character style of the defensively high self-esteem man. *Journal of Clinical Psychology, 40,* 26–35.

Hartouni, Z. S. (1992). Effects of narcissistic personality organization on causal attributions. *Psychological Reports, 71,* 1339–1346.

Jankowski, M. S. (1991). *Islands in the street: Gangs and American urban society.* Berkeley, CA: University of California Press.

Jones, E. E., & Pittman, T. (1982). Toward a general theory of strategic self-presentation. In J. Suls (Ed.), *Psychological perspectives on the self* (Vol. 1, pp. 231–262). Hillsdale, NJ: Erlbaum.

Kohut, H. (1971). *The analysis of the self.* New York: International Universities Press.

Kohut, H. (1977). *The restoration of the self.* New York: International Universities Press.

Ladd, E. R., & Welsh, M. C. (1996, March). *Narcissism and causal attribution.* Paper presented at the meeting of the Southeastern Psychological Association, Norfolk, VA.

Leary, M. R. (1995). *Self-presentation: Impression management and interpersonal behavior*. Boulder, CO: Westview Press.

Leary, M. R., & Downs, D. L. (1995). Interpersonal functions of the self-esteem motive: The self-esteem system as a sociometer. In M. H. Kernis (Ed.), *Efficacy, agency, and self-esteem* (pp. 123–144). New York: Plenum.

Leary, M. R., & Forsyth, D. R. (1987). Attributions of responsibility for collective endeavors. In C. Hendrick (Ed.), *Group processes* (pp. 167–188). Newbury Park, CA: Sage.

Leary, M. R., Rogers, P. A., Canfield, R. W., & Coe, C. (1986). Boredom in interpersonal encounters: Antecedents and social implications. *Journal of Personality and Social Psychology, 51,* 968–975.

Leary, M. R., Tambor, E. S., Terdal, S. K., & Downs, D. (1995). Self-esteem as an interpersonal monitor: The sociometer hypothesis. *Journal of Personality and Social Psychology, 68,* 518–530.

Raskin, R., & Novacek, J. (1989). An MMPI description of the narcissistic personality. *Journal of Personality Assessment, 53,* 66–80.

Raskin, R., & Novacek, J. (1991). Narcissism and the use of fantasy. *Journal of Clinical Psychology, 47,* 490–499.

Raskin, R., Novacek, J., & Hogan, R. (1991a). Narcissism, self-esteem, and defensive self-enhancement. *Journal of Personality, 59,* 19–38.

Raskin, R., Novacek, J., & Hogan, R. (1991b). Narcissistic self-esteem management. *Journal of Personality and Social Psychology, 60,* 911–918.

Raskin, R., & Shaw, R. (1988). Narcissism and the use of personal pronouns. *Journal of Personality, 56,* 393–404.

Rhodewalt, F., & Morf, C. C. (1995). Self and interpersonal correlates of the Narcissistic Personality Inventory: A review and new findings. *Journal of Research in Personality, 29,* 1–23.

Roberts, J. E., & McCready, V. (1987). Different clinical perspectives of good and poor therapy sessions. *Journal of Speech and Hearing research, 30,* 335–342.

Schlenker, B. R. (1975). Self-presentation: Managing the impression of consistency when reality interferes with self-enhancement. *Journal of Personality and Social Psychology, 32,* 1030–1037.

Schlenker, B. R. (1980). *Impression management: The self-concept, social identity, and interpersonal relations*. Monterey, CA: Brooks/Cole.

Schlenker, B. R., & Leary, M. R. (1982). Audiences' reactions to self-enhancing, self-denigrating, and accurate self-presentations. *Journal of Experimental Social Psychology, 18,* 89–104.

Schlenker, B. R., & Miller, R. S. (1977). Egocentrism in groups: Self-serving biases or logical information processing? *Journal of Personality and Social Psychology, 35,* 755–764.

Schlenker, B. R., Miller, R. S,, Leary, M. R., & McCown, N. E. (1979). Group performance and interpersonal evaluation as determinants of egotistical attributions in groups. *Journal of Personality, 47,* 575–594.

Shrauger, J. S., & Schoeneman, T. J. (1979). Symbolic interactionist view of selrf-concept: Through the looking glass darkly. *Psychological Bulletin, 86,* 549–573.

Smith, B. M. (1990). The measurement of narcissism in Asian, Caucasian, and Hispanic American Women. *Psychological Reports, 67,* 779–785.

Sullivan, H. S. (1953). *Conceptions of modern psychiatry*. New York: Norton.

Taylor, S. E., & Brown, J. D. (1988). Illusion and well-being: A social psychological perspective on mental health. *Psychological Bulletin, 103,* 193–210.

Taylor, S. E., & Brown, J. D. (1994). Positive illusions and well-being revisited: Separating fact from fiction. *Psychological Bulletin, 116,* 21–27.

Tesser, A. (1988). Toward a self-evaluation maintenance model of social behavior. In L. Berkowitz (Ed.), *Advances in experimental social psychology, 21*, 181–227.

Trivers, R. (1976). Foreward. In R. Dawkins, *The selfish gene*. New York: Oxford University Press.

Watson, P. J., & Morris, R. J. (1991). Narcissism, empathy, and social desirability. *Personality and Individual Differences, 12*, 575–579.

Whitley, B. E., & Frieze, I. H. (1985). Children's causal attributions for success and failure in achievement settings: A meta-analysis. *Journal of Educational Psychology, 77*, 608–616.

CHAPTER 7

SOCIAL OSTRACISM

KIPLING D. WILLIAMS

You hesitate to stab me with a word, and know not silence is the sharper sword.

—Anonymous

INTRODUCTION

If we asked people to generate a list of aversive interpersonal behaviors, we might expect them to include various examples of verbal and physical abuse. After all, insults and punches are observable, measurable behaviors that we find aversive. This chapter, however, focuses on what many may overlook when constructing such a list, perhaps because it is not considered to be a behavior at all, but rather a "nonbehavior." I refer to the pervasive and universal phenomenon of *ostracism*—the general process of exclusion and rejection. As we shall see, ostracism is not only an aversive interpersonal behavior, but also a response to aversive interpersonal behaviors. I review briefly experimental, observational, and case studies from anthropology, sociology, animal behavior, and psychology that pertain to ostracism. I then present a taxonomy and model of ostracism that I hope to be inclusive enough to cover its various forms, as well as specific

---

KIPLING D. WILLIAMS • School of Psychology, University of New South Wales, Sydney, NSW 2052 Australia. kip.williams@unsw.edu.au; http://www.psy.unsw.edu.au/~kipw

Aversive Interpersonal Behaviors, edited by Kowalski
Plenum Press, New York, 1997

enough to generate testable hypotheses. The general framework of the model is depicted in Figure 1. Next, I present a new experimental ostracism paradigm that we have employed in our laboratory to test a few hypotheses derived from this model. I also summarize ongoing qualitative interviews with long-term users and victims of the "silent treatment," a form of ostracism commonly used in close dyadic relationships. Finally, directions for future research are discussed.

One way to evaluate the merits of studying any particular social phenomenon is to gauge its frequency and its impact in real life. How often does it happen? How long has it been happening? How many individuals and groups does it affect? What kind of effects does it have? In short, does it happen often enough and are its effects strong enough to warrant scientific scrutiny? I believe that on these two criteria, ostracism is arguably one of the most important social phenomena we could choose to study.

Ubiquity of Ostracism

We have many names for ostracism: we call it being ignored, avoided, excluded, rejected, shunned, exiled, banished, cut off, frozen out, given the "cold shoulder" or "silent treatment," feeling invisible, or, for the British, being "sent off to Coventry." Regardless of what we call ostracism, its use on individuals and groups by individuals and groups can be documented from the time of early Greek civilization (Zippelius, 1986) to present-day societies. It is practiced by governments, cultures, religions, military institutions, tribes, small groups, and even individuals, as a response to individuals or groups who deviate, either in the way they look or act, from acceptable expectations. It occurs in organizations, in the workplace, and in the home. Sometimes, the decision to ostracize is formal and explicit. The South African government, for instance, exiled outspoken anti-Apartheid newspaper editor Donald Woods within his own country, preventing him from speaking to those within and without his country. Other times, ostracism occurs spontaneously without laws, explicit rules, or public proclamation. Benjamin O. Davis, Jr. was the first black cadet at West Point in the 20th century. For four years, his fellow cadets "silenced" him, never talking to him except in the line of duty. Davis believed (no doubt, accurately) that he was silenced because he was black (Davis, 1991). According to Gruter and Masters (1986b), ostracism has been "observed in virtually all known human societies" (p. 150). We recently conducted a survey of a representative sample of over 2,000 men and women in the United States. When asked about their experiences with the "silent treatment," over 75% admitted that it had been used on them by a loved one; and almost 70% say that they used it themselves on a loved one (Williams,

Sherman-Williams, & Faulkner, 1996). Indeed, humans are not alone in their widespread use of ostracism: many species of animals have been found to employ ostracism on conspecifics as well (Goodall, 1986; Kling, 1986; Lancaster, 1986; McGuire & Raleigh, 1986). Yet, despite its universality, psychologists have devoted little attention to understanding why we use it or examining its consequences.

STRONG IMPACT

It is clear that social and biological scientists agree that ostracism has an enormous impact on its victims. The effects on the perpetrators of ostracism are less clear. Although experimental social psychologists have given little attention to ostracism per se, they implicitly recognize the behavioral and emotional consequences of anticipated social exclusion. In order to avoid exclusion from others, we conform, obey, comply, inhibit our socially undesirable or idiosyncratic behaviors, change our attitudes, work harder, and generally try to present ourselves in a favorable manner (see Baumeister & Leary, 1995). Biologists and physiologists claim ostracism causes general "physiological deregulation": it interferes with our immunological functioning and hypothalamic reactions that are related to aggression and depression. Case studies report stomach ulcers (Gruter, 1986), fear of public gatherings, and loss of tribal leadership (Boehm, 1986) as a result of ostracism. Psychotic behaviors are more likely to occur in prisoners who are subjected to solitary confinement (as reported in McGuire & Raleigh, 1986). On the positive side, ostracism is believed to be an effective means to control counternormative behaviors, punish deviance, and increase in-group cohesion (Alexander, 1986; Barner-Barry, 1986; Basso, 1972; Boehm, 1986; Mahdi, 1986). One of the most widely recommended and successful forms of disciplining children by teachers and parents is to remove a child from social attention by issuing a "time-out" (Brooks, Perry, & Hingerty, 1992), and some therapists are now advocating using time-outs within families to ward off family violence (Veenstra & Scott, 1993).

REVIEW OF EXISTING LITERATURE

There are numerous articles written in a variety of disciplines about ostracism. In fact, a special issue of *Ethology and Sociobiology*, edited by Gruter and Masters (1986a), was devoted exclusively to social and biological analyses of ostracism. In that volume, ethologists, physiologists, medical researchers, sociologists, anthropologists, political scientists, legal experts, and zoologists (apparently, no psychologists) presented an impressive array of treatises documenting the existence, importance, and complexities of ostracism. Although the working definition of ostracism in that special issue was exclusion and rejection from others, definitions from one article to another ranged from derisive comments to the termination of life (Boehm, 1986)! Clearly, rejection is an important component (but not the only component) of ostracism. But, at least for my purposes, all forms of rejection are not examples of ostracism. For instance, rejection includes other psychologically distinct concepts, such as verbal and physical abuse, and these forms of aversive behavior can be studied in their own right. Likewise, whereas execution may be viewed as both an extreme form of rejection and exclusion, attempting to assess the psychological impact of ostracism on a dead person presents difficulties.

One clear message of the Gruter and Masters' special issue is that the term "ostracism" has many definitions, some of which I will not include in this chapter. I will restrict my review of the literature primarily to instances in which individuals or groups are socially or physically excluded (but are not physically assaulted or killed) from interacting with others. Interestingly, except for a few animal studies examining social isolation from mothers or peers, no examples of ostracism experiments were included in the special issue. Outside this volume, there are only a handful of social psychological experiments that have been published in which ostracism is experimentally manipulated. I will review briefly the research from the special issue and the scattering of articles found elsewhere.

In Ethology and Biology

The ethological orientation to ostracism is that it serves an adaptive function: to weed out undesirables from the group, resulting in increased reproductive competitiveness in the remaining members (see also, Goodall, 1986; Lancaster, 1986; de Waal, 1986), as well as to promote cohesiveness among the remaining members of the group. Kling (1986) suggests that tendencies toward social isolation in three nonhuman primates lead to their being ostracized. This is an interesting notion because it places the blame on the victim. He further suggests that these tendencies could be related to specific structures of the brain. McGuire and Raleigh (1986; Raleigh & McGuire, 1986) propose that, eventually, physiological research will assist in identifying persons who may be genetically predisposed to engage in ostracism and those persons who are physiologically vulnerable to being ostracized. McGuire and Raleigh's research on monkeys shows that short-term isolation from mothers or peers causes changes in the limbic system, increasing the whole blood seratonin levels which are associated with aggression and suicide.

It is worth noting that these animal studies tend to group together, both conceptually and behaviorally, animals who are ostracized and animals who are violent or aggressive. As such, the assumption is that those who are ostracized deserve to be ostracized. Once ostracized, further deterioration in physiology and behavior occur, including altered immune functioning, and decrements in problem-solving capabilities.

In Anthropology and Sociology

Several accounts of ostracism in humans show striking resemblances to the observations and assumptions behind its use in nonhuman primates. Mahdi (1986) analyzed the ostracism of members of the Pathan Hill tribes in Afghanistan. Ostracism is the form of punishment that is observed by these tribespeople, but is liberally defined as ranging from insult to exile to execution. As with the primates, the purpose of ostracism was to deter deviant behavior that threatened the group, to punish the offending member, and to unify the remaining members. Even Alexander's (1986) analysis of humor as ostracism suggests that humor serves to exclude outgroup members (the target of the jokes) and promote ingroup cohesiveness. In some cases, this literally occurs, as with certain Greenland Eskimos who resolve their quarrels through joke telling contests, with the one getting the least laughs going into exile.

Gruter (1986) discussed the practice of Meidung among the Amish. Meidung is a commandment from the church established in 1632 in Article 17 of the Dortrecht Confession of Faith, which establishes shunning as the means of disciplining group members. In one example of Meidung, an Amish man (Yoder) violated church doctrine by purchasing a car so that he could transport his polio-stricken one-year-old daughter to frequent doctor's appointments. The community's Amish Bishop and two preachers punished Yoder by invoking a declaration of Meidung. Neighbors, close friends, and even family members could not speak to him or eat with him, for fear of being shunned themselves. Meidung continues until the offending member agrees to comply with the elders' wishes (or, in this specific and apparently unusual case, until a court-order demanded payment to the plaintiff and a cessation of the Meidung. Payment was made, but informal Meidung continued).

Barner-Barry (1986) analyzed an instance of an informal, spontaneous emergence of ostracism. In the process of conducting a participant-observation study of 33 children on a playground, she noted a specific boy who was bullying other children around. The bullied children avoided playing with him, probably to protect themselves, and other children modeled this avoidance. Soon, he was ostracized by all the children and was verbally rejected when he tried to join others in play. Within a few days his bullying behaviors diminished.

In Psychology

There are many areas of research in psychology that study phenomena that are related to ostracism, although few actually focus on the causes, consequences, or psychological experience of ostracism itself. Developmental psychologists have documented the use of shunning and exclusion behaviors in children, used among other techniques as a form of peer-rejection (Asher & Coie, 1990; Asher & Parker, 1989; Dodge, Pettit, McClaskey, & Brown, 1986). Cairns and her colleagues found that over one-third of the same-gender conflicts among seventh grade girls involved the manipulation of group acceptance through ostracism, alienation, or character defamation (Cairns & Cairns, 1991). In a longitudinal study of fourth graders (through to the tenth grade), they found an increase in social aggression and ostracism in female-female conflicts (Cairns, Cairns, Neckerman, & Ferguson, 1989). These themes were rarely reported in boys, who were more likely to use physical styles of aggression.

Likewise, the efficacy of using time-outs in the schools and in special education programs has received considerable attention. Despite the fact that there is no thorough narrative or meta-analytic review of the time-out literature, individual studies (case studies, quasi-experiments, and a few experiments) have examined a large variety of time-out techniques (cf. Heron, 1987). Although time-outs vary from physical exclusion to social exclusion, and with respect to the feedback and personal control given to the child, these variations are not considered from a theoretical perspective. Clearly, it is assumed that being given a time-out is a punishment, either by administering an aversive stimulus (e.g., inattention) or taking away a rewarding stimulus (e.g., attention). Researchers in this area appear to restrict their interest in time-out only to a practical concern for the technique's short-term effectiveness in controlling undesired behaviors.

With adults, Miceli and Near (1992) have presented an excellent and programmatic analysis of the phenomenon of "whistleblowing," in which employees disclosed illegal, immoral, or illegitimate practices that took place within their organizations. Although Miceli and Near report that whistleblowers frequently mention being shunned by their coworkers and supervisors as a consequence of whistleblowing, the researchers do not refer to this form of coworker punishment as retaliation. Rather, retaliation is operationally defined in terms of denied promotions, involuntary transfers, demotions, and other (more easy to document) forms of punishment.

Research in the use of power tactics to achieve compliance has produced a theoretically useful taxonomy of tactics, their likelihood and frequency of being used by specific groups (i.e., males versus females, low power versus high power individuals, etc.), and their use and effectiveness in organizations and interpersonal relationships (Kipnis, Schmidt, & Wilkinson, 1980). In this taxonomy, they mention the silent treatment and categorize it as "disengagement" or "withdrawal." Falbo (1977) refers to explicit announcements of withdrawing verbal interaction if compliance is not forthcoming as "threats." The silent treatment is operationally defined as withdrawing from the setting or breaking off the interaction (for a review, see Forsyth, 1990). Using the terminology of power researchers, ostracism would be regarded as "indirect" (Falbo & Peplau, 1980—or "weak," Kipnis, 1984) or "direct" if it was a threat (Falbo, 1977), "nonrational," and "unilateral" (Falbo & Peplau, 1980). Falbo and Peplau (1980) found that nonrational, unilateral power tactics are more commonly used by the individual who has less power in the relationship, and this was found in both heterosexual and homosexual relationships. For their heterosexual sample, withdrawal was much more likely to be used by females. Relatively little attention has been given in this literature, however, to the effectiveness or consequences of ostracism, including possible negative side-effects for the individuals involved.

Relevant research in interpersonal attraction and close relationships research can be found as well. Insko and Wilson (1977) instructed triads to engage in a round-robin sequence of consecutive dyadic conversations. During each dyadic conversation, the remaining member was excluded from social interaction, but was still physically present. Because of an ostensible time constraint, the sequence was truncated after two rounds, resulting in one member having interacted once with each of the other two, whereas the other two had not interacted with each other. Because the exclusion was clearly not punitive, nor even under the control of the participants, it might be regarded as minimal and unlikely to have much impact. Nevertheless, compared with ratings of the members with whom they interacted, participants rated the group member who did not interact with them (and vice versa) as less likable and less interpersonally attractive on a variety of dimensions. Participants also surmised that that individual would not like them, either.

Rusbult, Verette, Whitney, Slovik, and Lipkus (1991) employ a response typology in their model of accommodation (inhibiting destructive reactions and engaging constructive reactions to bad behavior by one's partner). This typology, similar to Hirschman's (1970) typology for responses to declining organizations and governments, refers to two orthogonal dimensions (destructive-constructive and active-passive) producing a matrix with four resulting classes of responses: "exit"—separating, moving out of the relationship (but also actively destroying the relationship with verbal or physical abuse), "voice"—actively and constructively attempting to improve conditions, "loyalty"—passively staying in the relationship and hoping for improvement, and "neglect"—ignoring the partner or spending less time together (but also including destructive criticisms and treatment). According to this typology, ostracism could be classified primarily as "neglect" (but not incorporating the destructive criticisms and treatment beyond being ignored). It could only apply to "exit" with respect to physical separation, but would not include verbal and physical abuse. Rusbult, Johnson, and Morrow (1986) found that the primary marker for good functioning couples was avoiding destructive acts (exit or neglect) rather than maximizing constructive responses. This research did not extract the solely exclusionary forms of ostracism for the analyses, so questions regarding its frequency of use in functioning versus nonfunctioning couples, or its impact on the couple, were not addressed.

Buss, Gomes, Higgins, and Lauterbach (1987) asked couples to answer the question, "When you want to get your partner to do something (or to stop doing something), what do you do?" Factor analysis revealed six factors, one of which was the silent treatment. The silent treatment was found to be fifth in frequency of use, not more likely to be used by males or females, more often used to terminate behaviors than to elicit them, and positively correlated with measures of neuroticism.

Two areas where one might expect to see recognition of and attention to the use of the silent treatment are clinical and counseling psychology. Given our survey results (Williams et al., 1996) indicating nearly three-quarters of the people using the silent treatment on their loved ones (and having it used on them), it would be expected that the use of the silent treatment in families and marriage would have been documented, examined, and discussed, perhaps even warranting its own special therapy, yet little or no mention has been given to the silent treatment in these fields. Self-help books offer much advice to couples as to what to say and what not to say when they are arguing, but, surprisingly, nothing is said about saying nothing. One exception to the silent treatment being overlooked is in the research on communication interaction patterns in marriages (particularly "at-risk" marriages) by John Gottman and his colleagues (Gottman, 1979, 1980; Gottman & Krokoff, 1992). Gottman categorizes silence as withdrawal, notes its importance in triggering violence, and sees it as symptomatic in deteriorating relationships. It is interesting that withdrawal included both physical and social withdrawal, and distinctions between the two are not considered.

The few studies in social psychology that have explicitly examined ostracism, shunning, or being ignored indicate a general conclusion that being excluded or ignored results in negative psychological consequences. Geller, Goodstein, Silver, and Sternberg (1974) found that females ignored by two female confederates during a conversation reported feeling more alone, withdrawn, shy, dull, frustrated, anxious, nervous, and bored compared to included participants. They found also that ignored females were less likely than included females to reward the confederates later. Craighead, Kimball, and Rehak (1979) found that participants who imagined the act of being ignored (also in conversations) generated significantly fewer positive self-referent statements than participants who imagined successful attempts at social interaction. Specifically, ostracized individuals imagined that they would experience more sadness, frustration, anger, disengagement, passivity, puzzlement, rejection, loneliness, and feelings of unworthiness than included individuals.

Some evidence suggests that excluded individuals, particularly those low in self-esteem (Dittes, 1959) or high in public self-consciousness (Fenigstein, 1979), are less likely to want to work with the rejecting group in the future (Pepitone & Wilpizeski, 1960). Other evidence suggests that the desire for group membership does not decrease when the rejecting group is viewed as highly attractive (Jackson & Saltzstein, 1957). Snoek (1962) had groups reject individuals by not talking to them, either because ostensibly they were not worthy of group membership (personal) or because the group was too large (impersonal). He found that, when people were rejected for impersonal reasons, their desire to affiliate with the group decreased. But when they were rejected for personal reasons, people maintained their desire to belong. Snoek concluded that personally rejected individuals possessed a "need for social reassurance" that could be fulfilled only by remaining in the group. These results suggest that the causal attributions for the ostracism play an important role in determining the impact it has on the individual. Snoek provided participants with an attribution; in other situations, however, ostracized individuals may have to generate their own attributions, and these may mediate the emotional, cognitive, and behavioral impact of ostracism.

In summary, research from a number of disciplines has documented the frequent and ubiquitous use of social ostracism. A systematic, theory-based program of research into the causes and consequences of ostracism is clearly needed. Because definitions of ostracism are far ranging, even within the general domain of exclusion from interaction, it is worth noting important dimensions on which they vary, especially when it is plausible that these different forms or types of ostracism may be used for different purposes, interpreted differently by victims, and, consequently, have different effects. What follows is a taxonomic structure of dimensions along which forms of ostracism vary.

A TAXONOMIC STRUCTURE OF OSTRACISM

Ostracism is a broadly used term referring generally to the exclusion of an individual or group from other individuals or groups. There are, however, several types of ostracism. Boehm's (1986) analysis of ostracism in tribal Montenegro led him to articulate 20 levels of ostracism. They ranged from "slight coolness in tone of voice, denial of eye contact, obvious reticence to speak to someone" through to "physical avoidance, exclusion from social or ritual activities, denial of all social intercourse, temporary and permanent expulsion from groups, and finally, execution" (p. 308). Other levels included gossiping behind one's back, laying on curses, making witchcraft accusations, and using sorcery. In the taxonomic structure presented here, as shown in Figure 1, I suggest four dimensions of ostracism that describe many of its complex variations. These dimensions are intended to assist the understanding of these variations, although they are not necessarily exhaustive nor mutually exclusive. The development of this taxonomic structure represents work in progress, and, as such, reflects variations that I believe ought to be psychologically consequential. With more research, some distinctions may be unnecessary, and will, in future versions, be removed; likewise, it is also possible that future research will indicate that additional or finer distinctions be made.

All of these dimensions allude to, directly or indirectly, a particular feature of ostracism: it is inherently ambiguous. I believe it is chosen by so many people as the initial (or even habitual) response to hurt feelings, anger, or fear precisely because it is ambiguous — it is not clear to the victim *if* it is occurring or *why* it is occurring. There is always the possibility that ostracism is not occurring, but resides only in the mind of the victim. Realizing this possibility undoubtedly causes them to pause, speculate, doubt, worry, and anguish. In other types of punishments (verbal and physical abuse), the aversive behaviors are clearly occurring, and, even though aversive, are unlikely to produce the additional anxiety associated with ostracism's ambiguity.

VISIBILITY OF THE VICTIM/USER

Some forms of ostracism involve exclusion of the victim to the extent of being removed from the sight of others, whereas other forms involve exclusion while still being visible. The two essentially dichotomous levels of this dimension are *physical* versus *social* ostracism. Physical ostracism describes the invisibility inherent in physical separation, which includes expulsion, banishment, exile, solitary confinement, "time-out" in a separate room, or, at an interpersonal level, spending less time with an individ-

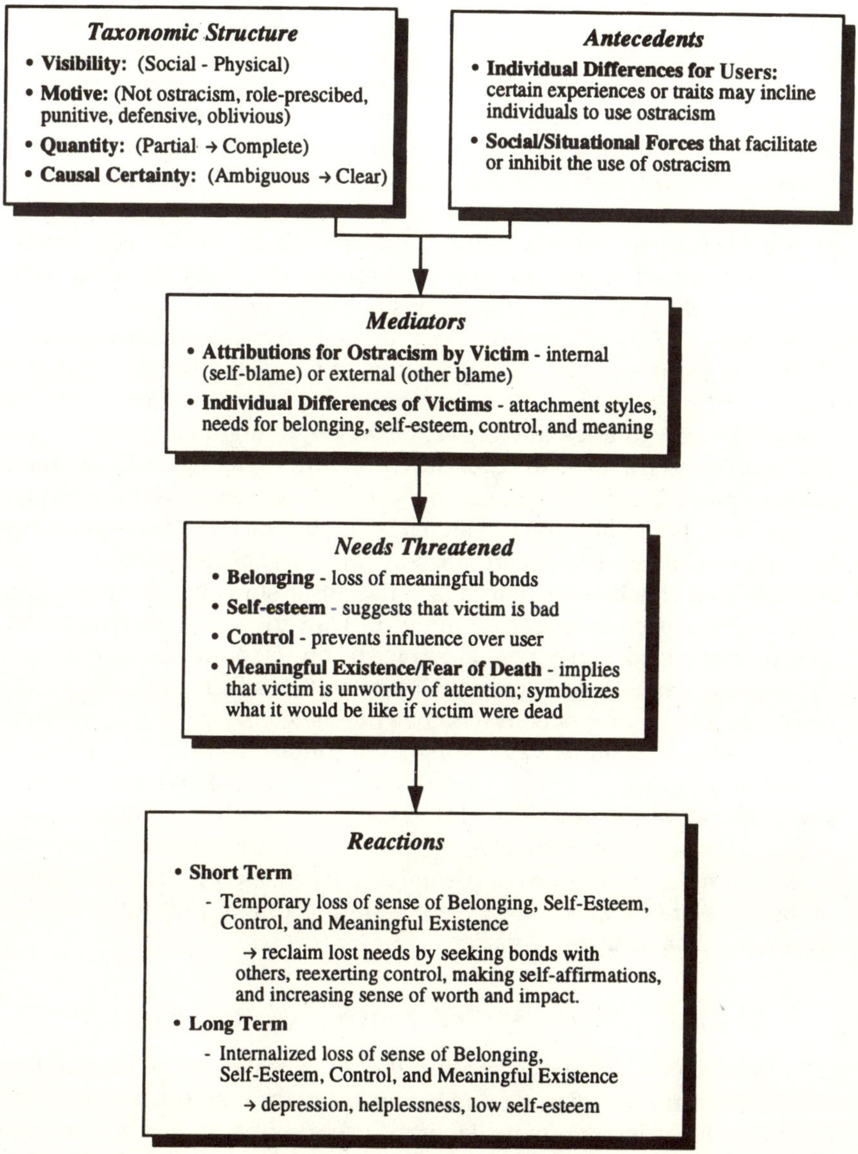

FIGURE 1. Model of ostracism.

ual or leaving his or her presence. Relatively speaking, physical ostracism is less ambiguous, although even physical ostracism can occur without notice or warning. Imagine, for example, people who, because of anger or hurt feelings, choose not to visit or spend time with their friends without giving notice. Conversely, social ostracism describes instances in which ostracized individuals remain visible to others; they are being ignored while still in the physical presence of the others. Phrases such as "silent treatment," "cold shoulder," and "freezing out" refer to social ostracism. Ironically, even though victims are visible during social ostracism, it is with this type of ostracism that people may actually *feel* invisible; victims of physical ostracism who are, in fact, not seen probably do not feel invisible.

From the user's perspective, choosing to physically ostracize someone might reflect several factors. In his analysis of exit, voice, and loyalty, Hirschman (1970) proposed that exit (akin to physical ostracism) is more likely to occur if loyalty (i.e., commitment to the relationship) is absent, or voice (active discussion and working out of problems to arrive at solutions) is perceived to be ineffective. However, it might also be employed as a short-term response to "cool down" before engaging in discussion in order to prevent escalating conflict. From both the user's and the victim's perspective, physical ostracism signals disapproval and an unwillingness to engage in bilateral conflict resolution. But, it might also permit thoughtful reflection of behaviors that caused the ostracism in the first place. This type of introspection might be more difficult to engage in while being socially ostracized. During social ostracism, one is continuously reminded about being ignored. As Boehm (1986) states, "To inflict such exclusionary treatment on a living person who has nowhere else to go is an ultimate punishment — in some ways worse than solitary confinement or death, since the person is reminded continually of the active and total rejection that is taking place" (pp. 313–314). Instead of allowing the individual to reflect upon whatever instigated the conflict, social ostracism might result in increasing anger or hurt, persistent attempts to recapture the attention of the ostracizer (e.g., apology, or escalating verbal or physical abuse), or retaliating by also using ostracism.

The Perceived/Intended Motive for the Ostracism

A second distinction involves the intended or perceived motives behind the ostracism. Based upon the review of the literature and response protocols of participants in my laboratory work, five categories of motives are considered: the behavior is *not ostracism, role prescribed, punitive, defensive,* or *oblivious*. The first two types are instances that help create the overall ambiguity of ostracism. In many instances, what may be perceived as ostracism may *not* be *ostracism*. While we anguish over why our friend or spouse or coworker did not look at us or speak to us this morning, we also consider the possibility that it was not intentional, that their minds were on other issues, and that we are blowing things out of perspective. *Role prescribed* ostracism is another excusing condition, one in which intentions to hurt or express superiority are not intended or perceived. Such would be the case in instances for which temporary roles dictate that a person playing one role does not acknowledge or speak to someone playing the other role, such as the inattention we give wait staff at restaurants. (It is possible that this sort of inattention is not perceived to be appropriate and is, instead, a manifestation of power. Once again we see the possibility of ambiguity. If this is the perception, then it would be regarded by the target as indicative of the user's self-perception of superiority, even though this might not be intended by the user. I will refer to this as oblivious ostracism and will discuss it shortly.)

Punitive ostracism refers to acts of ignoring that are perceived to be or are intended to be deliberate and aversive. Exile, banishment, shunning, and the silent treatment are examples of this. Ironically, as the "object of inattention," the target of punitive social ostracism may become highly self-aware, a psychological state often experienced by people who are the object of attention. This form of ostracism is the most widely discussed and is the assumed purpose in many accounts that I have reviewed already. The assumed purpose of punitive ostracism is either temporarily or permanently to exclude an offending individual. If temporary, the punishment is intended to modify the behavior of the offending party to be once again appropriate. It is also a means to resolidify the remaining members of the group, apparently by reminding them of what behaviors define the group and by giving them an outgroup member with whom to compare themselves.

Defensive ostracism is preemptive in nature, and may be used in anticipation of negative, threatening feedback from another, or even to expected ostracism by others; it is meant more as ego-protection or as a means to suspend vanishing control over the situation, rather than as an offensive weapon. Baumeister and Leary (1995) suggest that when people do not believe that they will be regarded in ways that will lead to acceptance, they might avoid absolute rejection by disaffiliating. By doing this, they "reduce the risk of saying or doing something that others might regard negatively...giving others few reasons to reject..." (p. 520). In Basso's (1972) examination of a Western Apache tribe, he noted several prescribed occasions in which community and family members ostracized individuals. These included not talking to recently widowed women or to adolescents who recently returned from "white man's world." The interesting pattern was that, in all such occasions, it was anticipated by those who employed the silent treatment that they would be derogated by the targeted individual. Widows were feared to be possessed and returning adolescents were feared to hold condemning attitudes of their tribe and family. So, to preempt the derogation, they chose to ostracize first and wait for the victim to come to them and speak (in a civil manner).

Oblivious ostracism refers to those occasions when the ostracizer has no intention to be punitive, in fact, the target of oblivious ostracism is not worth being punished. Punishment implies that the user cares enough about the victims to invest the time and energy to punish them. But oblivious ostracism occurs when the users' attitudes or beliefs are, or are perceived to be, that the victim is unworthy of their attention. It is simply not worth the time or energy of the user to recognize the existence of the target, or so it may be interpreted by the victim. Examples of oblivious ostracism include how people regard individuals who occupy lower social classes (such as seen between different members of caste systems, races, or religions). In Ralph Ellison's (1952) *Invisible Man*, the unnamed protagonist claims, "I am invisible, understand, simply because people refuse to see me" (p. 3). Rather than being the object of inattention, the obliviously ostracized person feels invisible or unworthy of attention. Ellison's invisible man goes on to say, "...you often doubt if you really exist" (p. 3).

The Quantity of Ostracism Perceived or Intended

A third distinction refers to the quantity of ostracism, a continuum running from *partial* to *complete* ostracism. Partial ostracism could be short, barely sufficient replies to queries, or could include a minimum concession to social norms (e.g., saying "excuse me" when passing by, or "pass the salt" at the dinner table). Similarly, in Boehm's (1986) hierarchy of ostracism, the lowest degrees of ostracism include coolness in tone of voice and denial of eye contact. Complete ostracism would be the total absence of verbal address, eye contact, and attention to verbalizations of the victim. (It could be argued that the most complete form of ostracism would be physical ostracism, because then there would be the additional absence of any form of social stimulation. However, I prefer not to confound the two dimensions, because I anticipate qualitatively different reactions to complete social ostracism compared with complete physical ostracism.) From the user's perspective, the choice to employ partial ostracism may reflect the desire to avoid escalation of conflict or retaliation, or it may be an opportunistic exploitation of ostracism's ambiguity. One can maintain deniability ("I wasn't ignoring you, I said 'excuse me!' "), thereby not being held accountable for its use. Choosing complete ostracism would probably reflect intense anger, lack of concern for immediate consequences, and no desire to disguise these feelings. From the victim's perspective, partial ostracism creates greater attributional ambiguity as to whether he or she is really being ostracized, and makes it difficult to render clear interpretations and appropriate reactions. Whereas complete ostracism may be perceived by the victim as more extreme, it is also easier to detect, evaluate as punishment, and retaliate.

THE DEGREE OF CAUSAL CERTAINTY

Finally, another dimension pertains to the perceived reasons for ostracism. These can vary from causally ambiguous to causally certain. Ostracism that is high in *causal ambiguity* occurs when the target is completely baffled as to why it is happening to him or her. In Franz Kafka's sketch entitled, *Gemeinschaft*, he writes of five men excluding a sixth for no reason (inapparent even to themselves) other than he is not one of the five (reprinted in Rehbinder, 1986). Although purposely absurd, there are similar occasions when we find ourselves ostracized by friends, coworkers, or family, but we do not know why.

Ostracism that is high in *causal certainty* occurs when an explicit declaration is made that ostracism will occur for a specific reason. For the Amish, everyone is aware that the punishment for disobeying the elders is Meidung (shunning), so, for them, ostracism has high causal certainty. The dimension of causal certainty is important because it can influence the impact of the ostracism and the means with which we cope with it. Undoubtedly, the sixth man must have devoted considerable thought as to why the others were excluding him, just as we all would when confronted with unexplained silent treatment. I propose that ostracism that is highly ambiguous, although not explicitly punitive, may actually threaten someone's self-concept more, because its victims may be highly motivated to manufacture myriad self-deprecating internal attributions to account for the ostracism (e.g., "It's because I was late for dinner," "The last time I saw him I must have insulted him," "They don't like me because I'm different from them"). It may even trigger doubts of one's existence (e.g., "Am I here?") if one attributes the cause to oblivious, rather than punitive, reasons.

A NEED-THREAT MODEL OF OSTRACISM

I propose that social ostracism can prevent individuals from fulfilling four fundamental needs (Williams, 1993), as shown in Figure 1. I will refer to these as needs, rather than desires or wants, because there is substantial evidence that when any of them are lacking, people "exhibit pathological consequences beyond mere temporary distress" (Baumeister & Leary, 1995, p. 498). These needs are not exclusively threatened by ostracism; in fact, they represent a synthesis of fundamental motivational needs assumed to underlie most human social behavior (see, for example, Smith & Mackie, 1995). I believe, however, that these needs are peculiarly and immediately triggered by even short-term exposure to ostracism. I am also not arguing that these needs are necessarily mutually exclusive; indeed, the authors who champion each need often indicate that the other needs are subordinate to, and serve in the maintenance of, their particular need (cf. Greenberg et al., 1992). I will leave to others the task of debating which of these needs envelopes the others. It is sufficient for my purposes merely to recognize the importance of these needs, particularly as they relate to ostracism.

First, ostracism deprives people of a sense of *belongingness* to others (e.g., Baumeister & Leary, 1995; Baumeister & Tice, 1990), a need that is argued to be not only emotionally desirable, but evolutionarily adaptive (Buss, 1990). Baumeister and Leary (1995) argue that the need to belong, defined as the desire for frequent, positive, and stable interactions with others, is a fundamental human motivation that guides cognitive processing and leads to positive affect. Studies show that the absence of affiliation and intimacy with others produces a host of negative psychological consequences, including depression, anxiety, stress, and physical and mental illness. Theories of social identity (Brewer, 1991, 1993; Hogg & Abrams, 1988; Tajfel & Turner, 1986) and group level social comparison (Goethals & Darley, 1987) also postulate that feelings of belongingness strengthened by ingroup distinctiveness are central to the maintenance of self-esteem and a positive self-concept. Being ostracized may be one of the clearest methods of attacking a sense of belonging. People can be criticized or chastised for any number of behaviors, and can feel bad about themselves with respect to those behaviors, but may still feel attached to the individual or group who is punishing them. The humanistic approach to reproval tries to indicate to the individual, "I love (or like) you, but I don't like your behavior." This message implies continued belonging and connectedness despite disapproval. Yet, when the silent treatment or some other form of ostracism is meted out, then the explicit or symbolic message is that the offending person risks losing the attachment to the other individual or group. Whereas Baumeister and Leary (1995) argue that all forms of disapproval may trigger fears of rejection, ostracism would seem to be the clearest and most direct method of evoking such a fear.

Second, people are ostracized often because someone dislikes who they are or what they have done. For either reason, it poses a threat to its victims' *self-esteem*, the belief that they are good and worthy people. Many theorists argue that the need for maintaining high self-esteem is pervasive and adaptive (e.g., Greenwald, 1980; Steele, 1988; Tesser, 1988) and is central to many theories as a primary determinant of self-efficacy and mental health (e.g., Bandura, 1995; Barnett & Gotlib, 1988; Leary, Tambor, Terdal, & Downs, 1995). As has been discussed, ostracism is most commonly regarded as a response to deviant or inappropriate behavior, or, in some instances, to one or more physical characteristics of the individual that sets him or her apart from the rest (i.e., physical handicap, different color, carrier of a disease, etc.). As such, it carries with it the message that something about the individual is bad or unwanted. This message directly threatens an individual's sense of being good and worthy to others and can lead to an internalized belief in one's undesirable nature and shortcomings. In the short run, research has found that individuals are rather resilient to attacks on their self-esteem, and they either use defense mechanisms, or redeem themselves in the specific domain of attack, or even affirm their goodness in other domains (Steele, 1988). In the long run, however, continued diminution of their self-esteem can lead to negative expectations and self-fulfilling prophecies resulting in a downward spiral toward lower self-esteem and undesirable behaviors.

Third, ostracism also robs individuals of a sense of *control* over their understanding of their social environment and interactions with others (Bruneau, 1973; see also Skinner, 1996), and over desired outcomes (i.e., low self-efficacy), all of which control theorists argue are necessary to one's psychological well-being and self-efficacy (e.g., Bandura, 1995; Seligman, 1975; Taylor & Brown, 1988; Taylor et al., 1992). Unlike most other forms of aversive behavior, ostracism involves a unilateral stance by one person (or group) over another. There is no give and take. In a verbal argument, regardless of the intensity and insulting nature of the verbal barbs, it is still the case that each person is responsive to the other. I call you a name and you call me one back. Despite its negativity, it continues to provide a sense of control. What one person says affects (has control over) what the other person says. The same thing can be said for physical aggression. Although unpleasant and potentially dangerous, there is still the opportunity for a responsive exchange. A person who is physically threatened can escape, or cover himself or herself, in an attempt to avoid future attack, or can attack back, all involving control. But someone who is ostracized is deprived of the bilateral nature of conflict. No matter what is said or done, the other person appears unaffected, as though the victim of ostracism did not exist. The story of the tar baby in the Uncle Remus (Harris, 1948) classic comes to mind. To catch Brer Rabbit, Brer Fox dresses up a baby made of tar along a path that Brer Rabbit travels. Being the gregarious fellow that Brer Rabbit is, he attempts to engage the tar baby in a conversation. For reasons obvious to the reader (but not to Brer Rabbit), the tar baby does not respond. The outcome of this frustrating nonexchange is that Brer Rabbit resorts to physical aggression to try to achieve some response from the tar baby. Kicking and punching the tar baby, Brer Rabbit becomes stuck, allowing Brer Fox to capture him. I have two reasons for bringing up this story: one is to illustrate the frustration that the silent treatment causes...a frustration resulting from losing any feeling of social control; the second is the frightening message that the silent treatment may encourage escalating aggression, possibly in the form of physical violence.

Fourth, because ostracism involves a withdrawal of attention or recognition by others, individuals exposed to it may be reminded of their fragile and temporary existence, and its lack of meaning and worth. They may even be reminded of their own death. Theory and research indicates we have a need to maintain our beliefs in a *meaningful existence* (e.g., Cooley, 1902; James, 1890; Mead 1934) and to avoid thoughts of our own death (Solomon, Greenberg, & Pyszczynski, 1991). In fact, it could be argued that ostracism symbolizes (or is a metaphor for) death. While being ostracized, it could occur to us that this is what it would be like if we were dead, the sort of realization Dickens instilled in Scrooge in *The Christmas Carol* (1880). In terror management theory, Greenberg, Pyszczynski, and Solomon (1986; Solomon et al., 1991) argue that a fundamental human anxiety that drives social behavior is our fear of our own mortality and meaningless existence. The terror management position claims that "...people need self-esteem because it is the central psychological mechanism for protecting individuals from the anxiety that awareness of their vulnerability and mortality would otherwise create" (Greenberg et al., 1992, p. 913). Interestingly, other authors allude either metaphorically or literally to the similarity between ostracism and death. William James (1890) likened the phenomenological horror of being socially ostracized to feeling as though "every person we met cut us dead" (p.294). Mahdi (1986) argues that the most severe form of ostracism is the "termination of life" (p. 295). Service (1975) writes that the usual punishment by any society is some amount of disapproval or withdrawal, the most extreme being ostracism, which he describes as, "...in primitive society a fate practically equivalent to death" (p. 54). In writing about the ostracism used by primates, Lancaster (1986) states, "...the 'cold shoulder' is only a step along the way to execution" (p. 216). In Gruter's (1986) account of Amish Meidung, she writes, "Meidung [in this rural community] means slow death" (p. 274). Finally, Boehm (1986) considers the connection between death by execution and social ostracism: "The act of execution is not much more than the strongest manifestation of the 'silent treatment' itself when this [treatment] persists for a long time. Either involves what amounts to the social death of the individual" (pp. 313–314). Based on these accounts of ostracism, it does not seem such an enormous leap to suggest that ostracism (perhaps particularly social ostracism) threatens both a sense of meaningful existence, and a glimpse of what things would be like if one were dead. Both of these reactions ought to bring us closer to the terror that Greenberg, Solomon, and Pyszczynski believe we fight so diligently to buffer.

REACTIONS TO THREATENED NEEDS

There are two overriding hypotheses that derive from this model. One considers reactions to isolated or short-term incidences of ostracism; the other considers reactions to long-term exposure to ostracism. Depending upon which need or needs have been threatened or activated by the ostracism, the individual will, in the short-run, react in such a way to regain or strengthen that need. This homeostatic notion of a direct causal link between need deprivation and need fulfillment has been suggested or demonstrated for studies on belonging (Baumeister & Leary, 1995), control (e.g., Friedland, Keinan, & Regev, 1992; Pittman & D'Agostino, 1989; Pittman & Pittman, 1980; Wortman & Brehm, 1975), self-esteem (Steele, 1988), and meaningful existence (Greenberg et al., 1990). If, however, an individual endures long-term ostracism, attempts to regain these needs may give way to despair and helplessness. This is consistent with research and theory on long-term loss of control (Peterson, Maier, & Seligman, 1993; Seligman, 1975) and rejection (Leary, 1990).

As mentioned earlier, the needs are not necessarily mutually exclusive. An increased sense of belongingness may raise self-esteem (Baumeister & Leary, 1995); increased self-esteem might provide one with a greater feeling of control and efficacy (Bandura, 1995) or buffer the fear of meaningless existence and death (Greenberg et al., 1986). However, depending upon the type of ostracism that is used or perceived, threats to one of these needs may be more salient, causing corrective action to focus on ameliorating that particular threat.

Types of ostracism that emerge from the taxonomic structure above may threaten different needs, and, as a consequence, have a different impact on the thoughts, feelings, and behaviors of its victims. For instance, punitive ostracism may cause a person to seek self-affirmation, or, if it threatens feelings of connectedness or a sense of belonging, it may cause a desire to seek out others with whom to associate and belong. This can also augment self-esteem (Leary et al., 1995). I would venture to speculate that oblivious ostracism might be the worst type of ostracism in that it is likely to threaten all four needs: one would simultaneously feel a loss of belonging, control, self-esteem, and meaningful existence. Each type might also provide its users different strategic value. Partial ostracism may provide its user with a "safe sanctuary" from accountability (e.g., "You must be paranoid, I wasn't ignoring you"), whereas complete ostracism may be a more clear and demonstrative statement of punishment and exclusion.

AN EXPERIMENTAL PARADIGM TO STUDY EFFECTS OF SHORT-TERM SOCIAL OSTRACISM

My aim was to capture the psychological drama of being socially ostracized in a laboratory setting. I was hoping to create a procedure that was fairly simple and uncomplicated by extraneous context, but that caused individuals to notice and feel, in a relatively short period of time, that they were being ostracized. The eventual procedure stemmed from an event that actually happened to me several years ago when I was relaxing in a park with my dog. A Frisbee rolled by me, and I picked it up and saw two men who had obviously been playing with it. I threw it back to them, and they began to include me in their Frisbee exchange. They were strangers to me, but I felt as though I belonged to their group. After a minute or so, I noticed that they had not thrown me the Frisbee on the last several tosses. Almost immediately, I felt ostracized. I wondered what I had done to cause it. I thought I was throwing the Frisbee pretty well, but I figured I had done something wrong. They still did not throw me the Frisbee, so I sheepishly withdrew from them and went back to my dog (who, I was happy to see, was willing to accept me). This episode led to a laboratory analogue of social ostracism.

BALL-TOSSING

I have developed a "minimal ostracism" paradigm in which individuals are either included or ostracized in a ball-throwing session between two other participants (who are actually accomplices of the experimenter). One participant and two confederates arrive for an experiment. The participant and confederates enter a room that contains three chairs arranged in a triangular formation, approximately five feet apart from one another. The confederates occupy the two chairs placed against the walls, leaving the participant to sit in the remaining chair, allowing us a clear view to observe and videotape the participant through an observation mirror. Next to one confederate is a small crate filled with toys, a ball, and books. Above the crate hangs a sign reading "Child Play Behavior." Similar signs reading "Child Observation" were hung in the hallway next to the laboratory, all to create the illusion that the same laboratory was used for conducting another study (for which the toys and observation mirror were necessary).

All participants are asked to give their written consent for the research, and to allow us to videotape them. The experimenter then administers a "Pre-Experimental Questionnaire," which assesses such background information as class rank, age, and major. The purpose of the questionnaire is to prevent participants from initiating conversation with the confederates. The experimenter then announces that, for various reasons depending upon the specific experiment, the participants are to wait quietly because it is important for the upcoming task that no one talks. The experimenter then leaves the room for five minutes and observes the participant and confederates through the one-way mirror. During this period, some of the participants experience social inclusion and some experience social ostracism.

When the participant completed the questionnaire, one confederate began rummaging through the crate, ostensibly to pass the time. After looking through a book and examining a few toys, the confederate "noticed" a racquetball and began bouncing the racquetball, first by himself/herself, then to the other group members (i.e., the other confederate and participant). The confederates include the participant, both by bouncing him or her the ball and by smiling and making eye contact.

The procedure for ostracized participants is exactly the same as in the inclusion condition, except that, after approximately one minute passes, the confederates begin bouncing and tossing the ball only to each other. They neither look nor smile at the participant for the remaining four minutes. When the confederates hear the experimenter walking toward the room, they quickly toss the ball back into the crate.

Measures of nonverbal behavior, attributions, self-reported mood, subsequent choices or behaviors in various social contexts, and autobiographical accounts of past experiences of ostracism comprise the dependent variables.

Afterwards, great care is taken to re-establish the individual's feelings of acceptance and self-worth. Debriefing lasts for up to 20 minutes. They are reintroduced to the accomplices and debriefed regarding the necessity of deception and the purposes of the research program. Often, great relief is expressed by participants when they find out that the other two participants were instructed to ostracize them. Also frequently, participants disclose similar incidents that have happened to them in the past, with friends, family members or significant others. In many cases, debriefing appears to take on the feeling of catharsis for the participants and it seems as though they appreciate being able to discuss these experiences and feelings.

This paradigm is indeed engaging. Responses vary, but typically follow a pattern of looking at the other two, smiling, looking around, frowning, withdrawing, and sometimes initiating some other activity (e.g., looking in one's wallet). During this time, they were no doubt thinking about what was happening and why it was occurring. The confederates, although willing and able to carry out their research assignments, nevertheless indicated that it was difficult to engage in social ostracism. And from our own perspectives, it was uncomfortable to watch the ostracism take place. When participants were asked to recall episodes of the silent treatment from their past, they wrote more words and were more personally disclosing than what we have become accustomed to in other post-experimental questionnaires. Several participants used curse words to describe episodes in their lives when others had ostracized them. A male admitted beating up his girlfriend in response to her silent treatment, and one female admitted to "poking" her boyfriend continually until he yelled back at her. Almost all reported that they had been given the silent treatment at some point in their lives and that it was memorable and unpleasant. Yet, almost all also reported that they used the silent treatment on friends, loved ones, or relatives as an effective means of punishing or dealing with those people. Usually, they claimed it was the only means that would work in their particular circumstances. These reports strengthen my belief that social ostracism is a widespread and powerful tactic of social influence.

Conversation, Imaging Paradigms

Although the ball-tossing paradigm appears to work quite well, we also recognize that it is useful to employ several paradigms when studying a phenomenon, and that some paradigms may have certain advantages over others, depending upon the specific issues being examined. For this reason, we have also used a conversational paradigm, in which three individuals (again, one participant and two confederates) are discussing various topics for five minutes. For those participants randomly assigned to be ostracized, after the first minute, confederates are instructed to look only at each other, not make any eye contact with the participant, and respond only to each other. This requires them to interrupt and "speak over" the participant if the participant chooses to speak. We have also begun using three actual participants, giving ostracism instructions to two of them prior to the group setting, although the efficacy of this technique is still under investigation.

Finally, on some occasions, we have employed imagery techniques, asking individuals to imagine that they are being ostracized (given the silent treatment), and then asking them to respond to various questions. Although not as engaging, this procedure can be useful in assessing what people think they would do under such circumstances.

Research Findings

We have conducted several experiments in our laboratories some are still in progress and some are in the planning stages. As will be noticed, the data are less than definitive at this point. Some studies show mild support for the hypotheses, and others show qualified support. I will review briefly these studies, and the results when available, as they pertain to the need-threat model.

Two studies examined the control deprivation hypothesis, with mixed success. Williams (1993) tested whether ostracism by two individuals (whom the male participant perceived as either friends or strangers to each other) caused the participant to assert higher levels of social control over a third "participant" who had not been involved in the ostracizing interaction. From an attributional perspective, we might expect that being ostracized by two people who are friends to each other would be less threatening than being ostracized by two people who are strangers to each other. We could perhaps dismiss the ostracism by friends as due to their friendship rather than a personal shortcoming in ourselves. On the other hand, Buss (1990) theorized that exclusion ought not be that threatening unless it is by a perceptibly desirable group. If this is true, then a group of friends would look more attractive than an aggregate of strangers. After the ostracism manipulation in the ball-tossing paradigm, the participant was asked to participate in a study on "mind reading." He was told that studies on hemispheric laterality suggest that individuals perceived different types of nonverbal messages from others depending upon which side of the person's face they focused on. The participant was told that he could, therefore, request of the new participant unlimited "head turns" in an effort to guess what that person was viewing on a card. Exerting social control was measured by the number of head turns the victim requested of the third accomplice. Tendencies for increased social control occurred only when participants were ostracized by two individuals who were perceived to be friends with each other. Perhaps, for males, being ostracized by a desirable intact group poses a greater threat to loss of control, causing them to reassert social control when the opportunity presents itself.

Amy Kaylor (1993) attempted to test the control deprivation hypothesis of social ostracism another way in her honors thesis. Kaylor relied on research by Pittman and his colleagues that indicated that individuals who were deprived of control would engage in deeper cognitive processing as a means to regain control. In one study, control-deprived individuals were more likely to engage in attributional thinking (Pittman & Pittman, 1980), and, in another, Pittman and D'Agostino (1989) found that control-deprived participants attempt to regain control by outperforming baseline standards on a non-ego-threatening cognitive task. Kaylor reasoned that, if being ostracized deprived individuals of a sense of control, then they ought to be more likely to engage in cognitive processing, particularly in non-ego-threatening tasks, than included participants. Using study time as an indicator of cognitive effort, her results were consistent with the predictions, although not statistically significant.

Williams and Sommer (in press) examined aspects of the belongingness hypothesis. The ball-tossing paradigm was used to investigate the effects of social ostracism on individuals' subsequent contributions to a group task. Much research has found a reduction of individual effort when one's contributions are pooled with others on collective tasks (for a review, see Karau & Williams, 1993). Although group cohesiveness lessens the likelihood of social loafing, the other side of the coin has not received attention: What happens when people work with others in noncohesive groups, specifically, those in which the individual has been socially ostracized? For these people, it was predicted that, in order to regain their sense of belonging to the group, ostracized individuals would socially compensate (Williams & Karau, 1991), working harder collectively than coactively. Participants were asked to generate as many uses as they could for an object, either coactively (in which their contributions were individually tabulated) or collectively (in which their contributions were combined with the others') with two others who had earlier either ostracized or included them in a ball-tossing exchange. Ostracized females did socially compensate, whereas non-ostracized females showed neither loafing nor compensation. Yet, both ostracized and non-ostracized males socially loafed. This was interpreted to support other research on sex differences in groups. Females tend to be more concerned with establishing and maintaining group harmony. Thus, when ostracized, they apparently try to reestablish their sense of belonging to the group by working extra hard, even when their contributions to the group task are unidentifiable. Males, however, tend to be more task oriented and agentic in group settings. Ostracized males apparently felt less attraction to the group and less responsible for making group contributions. Attributional measures supported this interpretation in that females tended to attribute the ostracism to their own personal shortcomings, whereas males attributed the ostracism to shortcomings of the other two group members.

Similarly, Predmore and Williams (1983) found that socially ostracized males, when asked whom they would like to work with on an upcoming task, were more likely to want to work with a different group of people, rather than work with the same group who ostracized them, or work alone. In this study, however, participants were instructed to engage in the ball-tossing task so that they could "warm-up" for a subsequent task requiring good hand-eye coordination. When the two confederates stopped throwing the ball to the participant, it is unclear whether the effect was because of ostracism, or was because they thought they were improperly prepared for the upcoming task.

Ko (1994) used the ball-tossing paradigm with high school males invited to participate in research at the University of Toledo. After being either included or socially ostracized, they were asked to take part in a study on perceptions of sporting events at their high school. Asked to recall the outcomes of specific football games from their high school's schedule that fall, ostracized students tended (but not significantly) to use the pronoun "we" more often (44%) than included students (31%), regardless of the team's defeat or victory. This was taken as mild support for the belongingness hypothesis, in that attempts to attach oneself to a group were somewhat greater after ostracism.

Bogle (1994; Sommer, Bogle, Grahe, & Williams, 1995) analyzed the nonverbal reactions of participants from studies just mentioned and found several interesting effects. Ostracized males and females disengaged more from social interaction than their included counterparts, looking away and smiling less often. Furthermore, ostracized females disengaged more than ostracized males. Males were more likely to exhibit object manipulation during the ostracism, interpreted as a face-saving strategy. They would often stand up, look around the room or out a window, take out a comb, or open and examine a book or their wallet. In effect, the message seemed to indicate that they, rather than the other two, had chosen to stop throwing the ball, because they had better things to do.

With respect to the self-esteem hypothesis, Samolis (1994) found that participants who imagined being ignored (in a conversational context at a party) generated significantly fewer positive self-referent statements than did participants who imagined successful attempts at social interaction. And, as mentioned above, Williams and Sommer (in press) found that ostracized females made more negative attributions to self than included females, or males in either condition.

As can be seen, we have conducted a variety of studies that have yielded promising, if not definitive, conclusions for the hypotheses regarding threats against feelings of control, belonging, self-esteem, and meaningful existence. Certainly, more research needs to be conducted before any firm conclusions can be reached.

INTERVIEW METHODOLOGIES TO STUDY EFFECTS OF LONG-TERM OSTRACISM

The theoretical predictions for reactions to ostracism are essentially reversed when we consider individuals who have experienced long-term exposure to ostracism. As has been shown in research on learned helplessness (Seligman, 1975), chronic exposure to events over which people perceive no control no longer causes reactance, but instead leads to resignation and feelings of depression and worthlessness (Wortman & Brehm, 1975). For obvious reasons, it would be neither practical nor ethical to subject participants in the laboratory to long-term ostracism. Experimental work on this question is severely constrained. Perhaps the only way to examine questions on long-term effects will be to use qualitative approaches with populations who have had such experiences. The disadvantages of such research methods involve the inability to determine cause and effect. One may just as easily conclude that individuals who have suffered long-term ostracism are affected as they are because of the ostracism, or that, because they behave as they do, they caused people to ostracize them. As discussed in the beginning of this chapter, ethologists' orientation to studying ostracism begins with the premise that ostracized individuals (people or animals) are anti-social and deviant, and the group chooses to ostracize them in order to punish the offending individuals, and to recapture group cohesiveness. On the other hand, the experimental research suggests that normal individuals who are ostracized experience negative effects, and it is likely that enduring these negative effects over a long period of time will undoubtedly result in pathological consequences. In any case, it will be informative to interview long-term victims (and users) of ostracism to at least provide some information about chronic effects. The model suggests that reactions to long-term social ostracism, however, would include persistent feelings of isolation, disengagement, helplessness, giving up, lowered self-esteem, and the questioning of one's existence (or at least the importance of one's existence).

Sonja Faulkner and I have begun an interview program in which we advertise in a local newspaper for "long time victims and users of the silent treatment." Individuals who answer the advertisement are informed that they will not be paid, nor is any therapy provided. Nevertheless, we have interviewed 32 people over the last year. More women participated in the study than men (69% versus 31%), and most participants ranged in age between 23 and 75 years old (M = 42.2 years). Of the 10 men who were interviewed, four described themselves as victims of the silent treatment, four said that they were users, and two characterized themselves as both users and victims of ostracism. Of the 22 women, 13 claimed to be victims, five said that they were users, and four described themselves as both users and victims of the silent treatment.

Almost all of the victims we interviewed reported that the effects of long-term ostracism have been devastating. Many interviewees used words illustrative of the hypothesized threatened needs. Interviewees reported that chronic or repeated exposure to the silent treatment elicited many negative emotions, such as anger, frustration, sadness, and despair. A 45-year-old woman said, "I was deprived of my childhood because of this. I'm hurt, bitter, and resentful. I don't *belong* anywhere! I'm still trying to find a family. It's so hard to talk about, even now. How would I sum up the silent treatment? It's the second most awful thing you can do to someone. Murder is first." There were also individuals claiming that the silent treatment caused them psychological distress, such as depression and paranoia. "Lee" was silenced for over 40 years by her now-deceased husband. She doesn't have an explanation for his extreme behavior, but says, "I wish he would've beaten me instead of giving me the silent treatment, because at least it would have been a response. This has ruined my life—I have no chance for happiness now." Many suggested that they would have preferred to have been beaten than to have had the silent treatment (interestingly, this statement was even found in the post-experimental questionnaires from our laboratory studies). "Lea" was ostracized by her mother and grandmother, who silenced her frequently as a child and teenager. Most episodes would last six to eight weeks, and, as she explains, "the bottom line is that it's the meanest thing you can do to someone, especially if you know they can't fight back. I never should have been born."

Others reported that the silent treatment precipitated various behavioral outcomes. For example, a female victim of ostracism by her mother since the age of thirteen said, "I coped with the situation by developing anorexia. I dropped to 80 pounds and almost died four years ago. I saw it as the only way to maintain some sort of *control* over my life." Others mentioned promiscuity and attempted suicides. Most of the victims explained that their experiences with the silent treatment have psychologically scarred them for life. Indeed, many reported that their lives were not meaningful, that they would never be completely happy, and some questioned whether they should have been born.

Several interviewees described themselves as users of the silent treatment, and our goal was to determine why someone would choose ostracism over other communication techniques such as yelling, hitting, or throwing things. Also, we were interested in how users justified their behavior and whether they have changed their minds about its use over the years. It is interesting to note that the reasons for employing the silent treatment in a professional setting may be strategically different than when using it in on a significant other, family member, or friend. Specifically, the silent treatment is (presently) legal, so employees may give each other the silent treatment without facing imminent termination or even disciplinary consequences that would follow verbal or physical abuse. In personal relationships, respondents reasoned that the silent treatment was an appropriate strategy to employ, for it prevented physical or verbal abuse. Some described silencing as a "time-out" or cooling-down period after someone upset them, whereas others explained that their ostracism was clearly punitive ("I'll show him how important I really am, and then he'll be sorry when I won't speak to him"). Others used the silent treatment defensively ("I won't let him hurt me, so I just go into my comfort zone, where I can block people out"), and most described the ostracism as a way to control interactions.

Glandry, 42, explained that he uses the silent treatment in both professional and personal settings. "The impact of the silent treatment is always beneficial in a professional setting. It shows the courage of conviction and creates an awareness as to the sincerity and seriousness of the issue at hand. I'm able to maintain a distance, but still have my presence felt. It creates a degree of autonomy, and it feels good to be in control of a situation. Any other alternative would decrease my level of control. As far as my kids, I would rather 'put them on ice' than give them the corporal punishment, because I'm afraid of child abuse. Now all three appreciate the rules and give me begrudging respect. Had I physically punished them, I fear that they would now hate me." Barbara, 62, was another proponent of the silent treatment. She explained that she uses ostracism to control situations and punish people. "I'm not quick-witted and can't debate, nor do I have snappy, sassy comebacks, so when people want to argue, ostracism is my defense. It's like with the Amish. They are non-violent people and they always use the silent treatment. Well, that's like me — I use the silent treatment whenever there may be a fight or confrontation. The silent treatment accomplishes for me all the things that fighting accomplishes for other people: control, power, and punishment. It gives me pleasure, and I'm in control. I also think it's funny how people grovel. I never feel guilty or ashamed, because it's always justifiable. Hey, I can't hurt you, I can't run you out of town, I can't run you out of business, but I can do this. The Rolling Stones talk about satisfaction. This is how I get mine."

FUTURE DIRECTIONS

At this point, it is far easier to ask questions about ostracism than to provide answers. Although it would be desirable to suggest solutions or alternatives to using ostracism, especially at the interpersonal level, it is too early to do so. Instead, more research needs to be done that demonstrates the impact of ostracism on individuals: Are initial reactions aimed at recovering losses in belonging, control, self-esteem, and meaning needs? When people experience long-term ostracism, do they essentially give up and suffer permanent damage to conceptions of self and beliefs in worth and personal efficacy? Are there important individual differences in how people react to ostracism? From the users' perspective, what situational and personality factors contribute to people choosing to use ostracism on others, rather than more direct, bilateral, and rational means of expressing hostility?

Currently, several studies are in progress or are planned.

1. Social ostracism is hypothesized to threaten an individual's sense of belonging. In the short term, this ought to increase the likelihood that one will do what one can to reassert one's feeling of belonging. Specifically, a person who is ostracized ought to think of himself or herself more readily as a member of other groups than one who is not being ostracized. Thinking of oneself as a member of a group could serve two purposes: (a) to re-establish a feeling of connectedness to someone else, thus making ostracized individuals feel as though they "belong" to some important others, and (b) if ostracized individuals picture ostracism as a group level event, (e. g., "those two people who are ostracizing me really represent the fact that the group to which they belong is rejecting the group to which I belong"), then the personal impact (and self-blame) of the ostracism can be diffused. If individuals are prevented from shifting the explanation for the ostracism to a group level event, then they are less able to deflect the negative impact, and are more likely to make an internal attribution for the ostracism (e.g., "there must be something wrong with me.").

   Using a new "email paradigm" in which the ostracism takes place among members of a laboratory chat group, the primary dependent variables will be verbal aggression (called "flaming" on internet commmunications) and attributions. It should pose more threat to be ostracized than included. Those who are ostracized should: (a) send more messages right after being ostracized (attempt to regain control and belonging), but (b) fewer messages thereafter (subsequent disengagement), than those who are not ostracized. The greater the negative impact of the ostracism (i.e., self-blaming would cause greater threat to one's ego than external or group-level blame), the more likely flaming will be used in electronic mail interactions. Therefore, (c) negative reactions to being ostracized should be greatest for those ostracized by one ingroup and one outgroup member because the individual will be less able to deflect the ostracism to either group level attributions, or to external attributions of the ostracizing individuals; somewhat less when being ostracized by ingroup members because the ostracism can be attributed externally and at a group level *if* one chooses to reject and devalue the group; and should be least threatening when ostracized by outgroup members because it is easiest to attribute externally and at a group level. Numbers of messages and a measure of the degree of verbal aggression (i.e., through blind-coders ratings of "flaming") should reflect a similar pattern.

2. Differences are likely to exist with respect to the magnitude and meaning of being ignored by one person compared to being ignored by a group. According to Latané's (1981) social impact theory, negative impact should increase multiplicatively with increasing sources. Also, status within the group has been shown to affect a member's intragroup behavior. Moreland (1985) and Moreland and Levine (1982; 1988) have shown that relative length of membership within a group is highly predictive of normative behaviors by and toward the individual group members. "Newcomers" are less likely to lead, to take initiative, to speak out, or to do other behaviors that draw attention to themselves. "Oldtimers" (even if they have been in the group for only a short time, just as long as there are newer members) are more likely to set policy, take active roles in discussions, get in arguments, and state feelings and beliefs that may differ from others.

   Ostracism by larger sized groups should result in stronger aversive reactions. Attributions for social ostracism may also change accordingly. It would be easier to discount being ostracized by one person, particularly a stranger, by externalizing the attribution (e.g., "something is wrong with that person who is ignoring me"). It would be more difficult to assuage the impact of being ostracized, however, by a group of people. Not only will an individual being ostracized by a group find it more difficult to believe that all members of that group have something wrong with him or her, but he or she must also contend with the possibility that the others *conspired* to ignore him or her. The effects of being a newcomer versus an oldtimer of a group that ostracizes an individual should also cause different reactions. Newcomers assume that they will be ignored initially (Moreland & Levine, 1988); therefore, if one joins a group after it has already been formed, being ostracized ought to have less negative impact on the individual than if one is an oldtimer in a group.

3. Perhaps certain people are less able to cope than others, or certain people who are ostracized are more likely to feel deprived of one particular need (e.g., affirmation), whereas other people feel deprived of other needs (e.g., belonging, or control). One individual difference that may interact with reactions to social ostracism is attachment style. People differ on the degree to which they make

strong affectional bonds to particular others (Bowlby, 1977).

The effect of one's attachment style as it relates to ongoing relationships may dictate the strength of the threat imposed by ostracism, as well as the need and style with which to cope with it. From preliminary work, it is apparent that parent/child- and adult- relationships are salient to our participants following ostracism. On open-ended questionnaires, many write (in surprisingly hostile language) about their parents' use of ostracism on them when they were children, or their boy/girlfriends' use of it on them in their current relationships. For this reason, we hope to conduct research on the interaction between attachment styles and reactions to social ostracism. Nonverbal responses, mood, and attributions for the ostracism will be measured. Secure individuals should be least bothered by the ostracism, and will search for situational explanations for the interaction when ostracized. Dismissive individuals will show greater evidence of object manipulation and will blame the others for the ostracism. Preoccupied individuals will make more attempts to be included in the group, and will blame themselves for their exclusion. Fearful individuals should blame themselves and others, and should withdraw more quickly.

4. Another experiment will examine whether social ostracism denies fulfillment of needs for belongingness, control, self-esteem, and meaningful existence, with an old, yet rarely used projective technique. Self-reports of reactions to ostracism have been problematic. Participants often deny any effects of ostracism (even though behavioral and nonverbal data would say otherwise). They may not want to admit to being threatened psychologically, or they may have already coped successfully with it (outwardly, with nonverbal reactions; inwardly, by attributing it to external causes). The Thematic Apperception Test (TAT, Murray, 1971) is an involving method that is less prone to problems with impression management than are self-reports. With regard to ostracism, several of Murray's (1938) needs may be subsumed under my model. Therefore, participants' responses to the TAT provide the main dependent measures. The TAT, which consists of a set of picture cards, is a projective test designed to expose needs that may or may not be acknowledged by the test taker at a conscious level. Murray purported that the type and frequency of needs are influenced largely by situational factors. That is, when the environment deprives individuals of fulfillment of a particular need, that need will more likely emerge during administration of the TAT. Furthermore, other personality traits may play a particularly

vital role in predicting how people will react to being ignored.

The second goal of this present study is to advance our understanding of the role of personality in predicting reactions to ostracism. Subjects' individual needs for *affiliation*, *aggression*, *dominance*, *social recognition*, and *exhibition* will be assessed. First, it is predicted that the TAT will elicit a significantly higher number of *belonging* and *control* needs/presses in ostracized subjects compared to included subjects. Personality variables may moderate these differences; following ostracism, needs/press for *belonging* should be strongest for subjects high in chronic needs for affiliation, and needs/press for *control* should be strongest for subjects high in stable needs for aggression and dominance. Needs and presses (i.e., situational forces) related to *self-esteem* and *meaningful existence* also are expected to increase for ostracized subjects. Needs/presses for *self-esteem* should be most prevalent in subjects high in needs for social recognition, and needs/presses for *meaningful existence* should prevail in subjects high in needs for exhibition. For ostracized subjects, generally the themes should reflect a preoccupation with the act of ostracism, or related concepts of general rejection.

5. The laboratory paradigm used thus far has examined aspects of social (as opposed to physical) ostracism — being ignored by people who are present. Furthermore, although left ambiguous, it is probably interpreted as punitive (rather than as not happening at all, defensive, oblivious, or role-prescribed), complete (as opposed to partial), and attributionally ambiguous (what victims did to cause it is unclear). The goal of future research will be to manipulate these dimensions experimentally and to determine how they may (a) threaten different needs in the hypothesized model, (b) produce different attributions, and (c) have different consequences on people's thoughts, emotions, and behaviors.

SUMMARY

Ostracism is a ubiquitous and impactful phenomenon. It exists in the animal kingdom in a variety of species. With humans, it occurs at societal, institutional, and small group levels, including the use of the silent treatment in dyadic relationships. It is set apart from other forms of aversive interpersonal behavior because of its invisibility and its ambiguity, which can be exploited by its users and can confound and psychologically cripple its victims. A taxonomic structure has been offered that illustrates the rich and complex variations that ostracism can take, with specific hypotheses regarding how each type may have different causes and consequences. A model was proposed that ostracism directly threatens four fundamental human needs: to belong, to control, to maintain high self-esteem, and to buffer the terror of conceiving of one's existence as meaningless and temporary. A new experimental paradigm was designed to study social ostracism. In order to explore adequately the phenomenology of being ostracized, the procedure had to be behaviorally and emotionally engaging. Participants were first enticed into spur-of-the-moment free-play by tossing a ball around with two other people while awaiting the return of an experimenter. After about a minute, some of the participants found themselves in an odd situation — suddenly, and for the remainder of the waiting period, they were no longer thrown the ball. Several studies have shown promising, yet inconclusive support for the model. Interviews with long-term users and victims have also been undertaken indicating severe and far-reaching negative consequences for the victims, and strategically acknowledged advantages for the users. Future research is needed to understand more fully the effects that ostracism can have in order to determine if there are alternative methods for resolving conflict available that are more likely to promote, rather than destroy, fundamental human needs.

AUTHOR NOTES

I would like to thank the following people for their assistance in the development of the theory or the conduct of the research: Darlene Ammann, Roy Baumeister, Frank Bernieri, Michelle Bogle, Kelly Cady, Brian Gyorki, Sonja Faulkner, Renee Feldstein, Carol Golias, Jon Grahe, Bud Hite, Rob Hitlan, Michael Hogg, Mike Jones, Amy Kaylor, Norbert Kerr, Dustin Langenderfer, Annette Loch, John Levine, Marick Moldawski, Richard Moreland, Matt Nicholas, Matt O'Connor, Melissa Samolis, April Sherida, Wendy Shore, Kristin Sommer, Bill Taylor, Matt West, and Cindy Williams. I would also like to thank the Department of Psychology at the University of Toledo for its support of my research, the University of Toledo Research Awards and Fellowship Program for an internal grant, and the Department of Psychology at the University of Queensland for their assistance and support while I was on sabbatical.

REFERENCES

Alexander, R. D. (1986). Ostracism and indirect reciprocity: The reproductive significance of humor. *Ethology and Sociobiology, 7*, 253–270.

Asher, S. R., & Coie, J. D. (1990). (Eds.). *Peer rejection in childhood*. New York: Cambridge University Press.

Asher, S. R., & Parker, J. G. (1989). Significance of peer relationship problems in childhood. In B. H. Schneider, G. Attili, J. Nadel, & R. P. Weissberg (Eds.), *Social competence in developmental perspective* (pp. 5–23). Amsterdam: Kluwer Academic Publishing.

Bandura, A. (1995). *Self-efficacy in changing societies*. New York: Cambridge University Press.

Barner-Barry, C. (1986). Rob: Children's tacit use of peer ostracism to control aggressive behavior. *Ethology and Sociobiology, 7,* 281–293.

Barnett, P. A., & Gotlib, I. H. (1988). Dysfunctional attitudes and psychosocial stress: The differential prediction of future psychological symptomatology. *Motivation & Emotion, 12,* 251–270.

Basso, K. H. (1972). "To give up on words": Silence in Western Apache culture. In P. P. Giglioli (Ed.), *Language and social context* (pp. 67–86). Baltimore, MD: Penguin Books, Inc.

Baumeister, R. F., & Leary, M. R. (1995). The need to belong: Desire for interpersonal attachments as a fundamental human motivation. *Psychological Bulletin, 117,* 497–529.

Baumeister, R. F., & Tice, D. M. (1990). Anxiety and social exclusion. *Journal of Social and Clinical Psychology, 9,* 165–195.

Boehm, C. (1986). Capital punishment in tribal Montenegro: Implications for law, biology, and theory of social control. *Ethology and Sociobiology, 7,* 305–320.

Bogle (Bowers), M. (1994). *The effects of social ostracism on nonverbal reactions in males and females*. Unpublished honors thesis, University of Toledo.

Bowlby, J. (1977). The making and breaking of affectional bonds. *British Journal of Psychiatry, 130,* 201–210.

Brewer, M. B. (1991). The social self: On being the same and different at the same time. *Personality and Social Psychology Bulletin, 17,* 475–482.

Brewer, M. B. (1993). The role of distinctiveness in social identity and group behaviour. In M. A. Hogg & D. Abrams (Eds.), *Group motivation* (pp. 1–16). London: Harvester Wheatsheaf.

Brooks, N. C., Perry, V., & Hingerty, S. E. (1992). Modifying behavior through time out from positive reinforcement. *Vocational Evaluation and Work Adjustment Bulletin, 25,* 93–95.

Bruneau, T. J. (1973). Communicative silences: Forms and functions. *The Journal of Communication, 23,* 17–46.

Buss, D. M. (1990). The evolution of anxiety and social exclusion. *Journal of Social and Clinical Psychology, 9,* 196–201.

Buss, D. M., Gomes, M., Higgins, D. S., & Lauterbach, K. (1987). Tactics of manipulation. *Journal of Personality and Social Psychology, 52,* 1219–1229.

Cairns, R. B., & Cairns, B. D. (1991). Social cognition and social networks: A developmental perspective. In D. J. Pepler & K. H. Rubin (Eds.), *The development and treatment of childhood aggression* (pp. 249–278). Hillsdale, NJ: Lawrence Erlbaum Associates, Inc.

Cairns, R. B., Cairns, B. D., Neckerman, H. J., & Ferguson, L. L. (1989). Growth and aggression: I. Childhood to early adolescence. *Developmental Psychology, 25,* 320–330.

Cooley, C. H. (1902). *Human nature and the social order*. New York: Scribner's.

Craighead, W. E., Kimball, W. H., & Rehak, P. J. (1979). Mood changes, physiological responses, and self-statements during social rejection imagery. *Journal of Consulting and Clinical Psychology, 47,* 385–396.

Davis, B. O. (1991). *Benjamin O. Davis, Jr., American: An autobiography*. Washington: Smithsonian Institution Press.

Dickens, C. (1880). *A christmas carol*. Springfield, OH: The Crowell Publishing Company.

Dittes, J. E. (1959). Attractiveness of group as function of self-esteem and acceptance by group. *Journal of Abnormal and Social Psychology, 59,* 77–82.

Dodge, K. A., Pettit, G. S., McClaskey, C. L., & Brown, M. M. (1986). Social competence in children. *Monographs of the Society for Research in Child Development, 51,* 1–85.

Ellison, R. (1952). *Invisible man.* New York: Quality Paperback Book Club.

Falbo, T. (1977). Multidimensional scaling of power strategies. *Journal of Personality and Social Psychology, 35,* 537–547.

Falbo, T., & Peplau, L. A. (1980). Power strategies in intimate relationships. *Journal of Personality and Social Psychology, 38,* 618–628.

Fenigstein, A. (1979). Self-consciousness, self-attention, and social interaction. *Journal of Personality and Social Psychology, 37,* 75–86.

Forsyth, D. R. (1990). *Group dynamics* (2nd Edition). Pacific Grove, CA: Brooks/Cole Publishing Company.

Friedland, N., Keinan, G., & Regev, Y. (1992). Controlling the uncontrollable: Effects of stress on illusory perceptions of controllability. *Journal of Personality and Social Psychology, 63,* 923–931.

Geller, D. M., Goodstein, L., Silver, M., & Sternberg, W. C. (1974). On being ignored: The effects of violation of implicit rules of social interaction. *Sociometry, 37,* 541–556.

Goethals, G. & Darley, J. (1987). Social comparison theory: Self-evaluation and group life. In B. Mullen & G. Goethals (Eds.), *Theories of group behavior* (pp. 21–47). New York: Springer-Verlag.

Goodall, J. (1986). Social rejection, exclusion, and shunning among the Gombe chimpanzees. *Ethology and Sociobiology, 7,* 227–236.

Gottman, J. M. (1979). *Marital interaction: Experimental investigations.* New York: Academic Press.

Gottman, J. (1980). Consistency of nonverbal affect and affect reciprocity in marital interaction. *Journal of Consulting and Clinical Psychology, 48,* 711–717.

Gottman, J. M., & Krokoff, L. J. (1992). Marital interaction and satisfaction: A longitudinal view. *Journal of Consulting and Clinical Psychology, 57,* 47–52.

Greenberg, J., Pyszczynski, T., & Solomon, S. (1986). The causes and consequences of the need for self-esteem: A terror management theory. In R. F. Baumeister (Ed.), *Public self and private self* (pp. 189–212). New York: Springer-Verlag.

Greenberg, J., Pyszczynski, T., Solomon, S., Rosenblatt, A., Veeder, M., Kirkland, S., & Lyon, D. (1990). Evidence for terror management theory II: The effects of mortality salience on reactions to those who threaten or bolster the cultural worldview. *Journal of Personality and Social Psychology, 58,* 308–318.

Greenberg, J., Solomon, S., Pyszczynski, T., Rosenblatt, A., Burling, J., Lyon, D., Simon, L., & Pinel, E. (1992). Why do people need self-esteem? Converging evidence that self-esteem serves an anxiety-buffering function. *Journal of Personality and Social Psychology, 63,* 913–922.

Greenwald, A. G. (1980). The totalitarian ego. Fabrication and revision of personal history. *American Psychologist, 35,* 603–618.

Gruter, M. (1986). Ostracism on trial: The limits of individual rights. *Ethology and Sociobiology, 7,* 271–279.

Gruter, M., & Masters, R. D. (Eds.) (1986a). Ostracism: A social and biological phenomenon. Special Issue of *Ethology and Sociobiology, 7,* 149–395.

Gruter, M., & Masters, R. D. (1986b). Ostracism as a social and biological phenomenon: An introduction. *Ethology and Sociobiology, 7,* 149–158.

Harris, J. C. (1948). *The favorite Uncle Remus.* Boston: Houghton Mifflin Company.

Heron, T. E. (1987). Timeout from positive reinforcement. In J. O. Cooper, T. E. Heron, & W. L. Heward (Eds.), *Applied behavior analysis* (pp. 439–453). Columbus, OH: Merrill Publishing.

Hirschman, A. O. (1970). *Exit, voice, and loyalty: Responses to decline in firms, organization, and states*. Cambridge, MA: Harvard University Press.

Hogg, M. A., & Abrams, D. (1988). *Social identifications: A social psychology of intergroup relations and group processes*. London: Routledge.

Insko, C. A., & Wilson, M. (1977). Interpersonal attraction as a function of social interaction. *Journal of Personality and Social Psychology, 35*, 903–911.

Jackson, J. M. & Saltzstein, H. D. (1957). The effect of person-group relationships on conformity processes. *Journal of Abnormal and Social Psychology, 57*, 17–24.

James, W. (1890). *Principles of psychology, Vol. 1*. New York: Dover Publications.

Karau, S. J., & Williams, K. D. (1993). Social loafing: A meta-analytic review and theoretical integration. *Journal of Personality and Social Psychology, 65*, 681–706.

Kaylor, A. (1993). *The effects of social ostracism and ego-threat on regaining a sense of control in a cognitive task*. Unpublished honors thesis, University of Toledo.

Kipnis, D. (1984). The use of power in organizations and in interpersonal settings. In S. Oskamp (Ed.), *Applied social psychology annual* (Vol. 5, pp. 179–210). Newbury Park, CA: Sage.

Kipnis, D., Schmidt, S. M., & Wilkinson, I. (1980). Intraorganizational influence tactics: Explorations in getting one's way. *Journal of Applied Psychology, 65*, 440–452.

Kling, A. S. (1986). Neurological correlates of social behavior. *Ethology and Sociobiology, 7*, 175–186.

Ko, T. (1994). *Social ostracism and social identity*. Unpublished Masters Thesis, University of Toledo.

Lancaster, J. B. (1986). Primate social behavior and ostracism. *Ethology and Sociobiology, 7*, 215–225.

Latané, B. (1981). The psychology of social impact theory. *American Psychologist, 36*, 343–356.

Leary, M. R. (1990). Responses to social exclusion: Social anxiety, jealousy, loneliness, depression, and low self-esteem. *Journal of Social and Clinical Psychology, 9*, 221–229.

Leary, M. R., Tambor, E. S., Terdal, S. K., & Downs, D. L. (1995). Self-esteem as an interpersonal monitor: The sociometer hypothesis. *Journal of Personality and Social Psychology, 2*, 518–530.

Mahdi, N. Q. (1986). Pukhtunwali: Ostracism and honor among the Pathan Hill Tribes. *Ethology and Sociobiology, 7*, 295–304.

McGuire, M. T., & Raleigh, M. J. (1986). Behavioral and physiological correlates of ostracism. *Ethology and Sociobiology, 7*, 187–200.

Mead, G. H. (1934). *Mind, self, and society*. Chicago: University of Chicago Press.

Miceli, M. P., & Near, J. P. (1992). *Blowing the whistle: The organizational and legal implications for companies and employees*. New York: Lexington Books.

Moreland, R. L. (1985). Social categorization and the assimilation of "new" group members. *Journal of Personality and Social Psychology, 48*, 1173–1190.

Moreland, R. L., & Levine, J. M. (1982). Socialization in small groups: Temporal changes in individual group relations. In L. Berkowitz (Ed.), *Advances in experimental social psychology, 15*, 137–192.

Moreland, R. L., & Levine, J. M. (1988). Group dynamics over time: Development and socialization in small groups. In J. E. McGrath (Ed.), *The social psychology of time* (pp. 151–181). Newbury Park, CA: Sage.

Murray, H. A. (and collaborators). (1938). *Explorations in personality*. New York: Oxford.

Murray, H. A. (1971). *Manual of Thematic Apperception Test*. Cambridge, MA: Harvard University Press.

Pepitone, A., & Wilpizeski, C. (1960). Some consequences of experimental rejection. *Journal of Abnormal and Social Psychology, 60*, 359–364.

Peterson, C., Maier, S. F., & Seligman, M. E. P. (1993). *Learned helplessness: A theory for the age of personal control*. New York: Oxford University Press.

Pittman, T. S., & D'Agostino, P. R. (1989). Motivation and cognition: Control deprivation and the nature of subsequent information processing. *Journal of Experimental Social Psychology, 25,* 465–480.

Pittman, T. S., & Pittman, N. L. (1980). Deprivation of control and the attribution process. *Journal of Personality and Social Psychology, 39,* 377–389.

Predmore, S., & Williams, K. D. (1983, May). *The effects of social ostracism on affiliation*. Paper presented at the meeting of the Midwestern Psychological Association, Chicago.

Raleigh, M. J., & McGuire, M. T. (1986). Animal analogues of ostracism: Biological mechanisms and social consequences. *Ethology and Sociobiology, 7,* 201–214.

Rehbinder, M. (1986). Refusal of social cooperation as a legal problem: On the legal institution of ostracism and boycott. *Ethology and Sociobiology, 7,* 321–327.

Rusbult, C. E., Johnson, D. J., & Morrow, G. D. (1986). Impact of couple patterns of problem solving on distress and nondistress in dating relationships. *Journal of Personality and Social Psychology, 50,* 744–753.

Rusbult, C., Verette, J., Whitney, G., Slovik, L., & Lipkus, I. (1991). Accommodation processes in close relationships: Theory and preliminary empirical evidence. *Journal of Personality and Social Psychology, 60,* 53–78.

Samolis, M. M. (1994). *The effects of ostracism and communication level on self and task-referents, feelings, and action*. Unpublished Honors Thesis, University of Toledo.

Seligman, M. E. P. (1975). *Helplessness: On depression, development, and death*. San Francisco: Freeman & Co.

Service, E. R. (1975). *Origins of the state and civilization*. New York: W. W. Norton & Company.

Skinner, E. A. (1996). A guide to constructs of control. *Journal of Personality and Social Psychology, 71,* 549–570.

Smith, E. R., & Mackie, D. M. (1995). *Social psychology*. New York: Worth Publishers.

Snoek, J. D. (1962). Some effects of rejection upon attraction to a group. *Journal of Abnormal and Social Psychology, 64,* 175–182.

Solomon, S., Greenberg, J., & Pyszczynski, T. (1991). A terror management theory of self-esteem and its role in social behavior. In M. Zanna (Ed.) *Advances in experimental social psychology, 24,* 93–159.

Sommer, K. L., Bogle, M., Grahe, J. E., & Williams, K. D. (July, 1995). *Nonverbal and attributional reactions to social ostracism*. Paper presented at the American Psychological Society conference, New York City, New York.

Steele, C. M. (1988). The psychology of self-affirmation: Sustaining the integrity of the self. In L. Berkowitz (Ed.), *Advances in experimental social psychology, 21,* 261–302.

Tajfel, H., & Turner, J. C. (1986). The social identity theory of intergroup behavior. In S. Worchel & W. G. Austin (Eds.), *The psychology of intergroup relations* (pp.33–48). Chicago: Nelson-Hall.

Taylor, S. E., & Brown, J. D. (1988). Illusion and well-being: A social psychological perspective on mental health. *Psychological Bulletin, 103,* 193–210

Taylor, S. E., Kemeny, M. E., Aspinwall, L. G., Schneider, S. G., Rodriquez, R., & Herber, M. (1992). Optimism, coping, psychological distress, and high-risk sexual behavior among men at risk for acquired immunodeficiency syndrome (AIDS). *Journal of Personality and Social Psychology, 63,* 460–473.

Tesser, A. (1988). Toward a self-evaluation maintenance model of social behavior. In L. Berkowitz (Ed.), *Advances in experimental social psychology, 21,* 181–227.

Veenstra, G. J., & Scott, C. G. (1993). A model for using time out as an intervention technique with families. *Journal of Family Violence, 8,* 71–87.

de Waal, F. B. M. (1986). The brutal elimination of a rival among captive male chimpanzees. *Ethology and Sociobiology, 7,* 237–251.

Williams, K. D. (1993, June). *Social ostracism.* Presented at the International Nags Head Conference on Groups, Networks, and Organizations. Boca Raton, FL.

Williams, K. D., & Karau, S. J. (1991). Social loafing and social compensation: The effects of expectations of coworker performance. *Journal of Personality and Social Psychology, 61,* 570–581.

Williams, K. D., Sherman-Williams, B., & Faulkner, S. (1996). [A survey of a representative U.S. sample on the incidence of using the silent treatment.] Unpublished raw data.

Williams, K. D., & Sommer, K. L. (in press). Social ostracism by one's coworkers: Does rejection lead to loafing or compensation? *Personality and Social Psychology Bulletin.*

Wortman, C. B., & Brehm, J. W. (1975). Responses to uncontrollable outcomes: An integration of reactance theory and the learned helplessness model. In L. Berkowitz (Ed.), *Advances in experimental social psychology, 8,* 277–336.

Zippelius, R. (1986). Exclusion and shunning as legal and social sanctions. *Ethology and Sociobiology, 7,* 159–166.

CHAPTER 8

CIRCUITOUS HARM

DETERMINANTS AND CONSEQUENCES OF NONDIRECT AGGRESSION

DEBORAH R. RICHARDSON AND LAURA R. GREEN

When we think of someone causing harm to another person, we usually think of that harm being delivered directly. Many of our experiences as either perpetrators or targets of aggression are likely to have involved direct confrontation; someone says something hurtful or rude to another person or someone hits or throws something at another person. However, much of the harm people experience in day-to-day life is likely to be delivered through some less direct, more circuitous route. In fact, there may be some contexts, such as the workplace (Baron & Neuman, 1996), in which nondirect aggression may be the preferred response to conflict.

Nondirect aggression can take many forms. For example, one might tell stories about another person in order to get them in trouble; one might attempt to exclude another person from a social group. These are, indeed, aversive interpersonal behaviors. Some would argue that such nondirect aggression might even be more aversive than direct harm—because such circuitous harm can be difficult to identify as aggression and, therefore, may be more difficult to respond to in a constructive or retaliative fashion.

DEBORAH R. RICHARDSON AND LAURA R. GREEN • Department of Psychology, Florida Atlantic University, Boca Raton, Florida 33431. deborah@socpsy.sci.fau.edu

Aversive Interpersonal Behaviors, edited by Kowalski
Plenum Press, New York, 1997

In this chapter, we will review the nature of nondirect aggression by considering *what* it is and *why* someone might choose to use it. We will take a rather inclusive approach, reviewing literature on rejection and gossip as well as material more directly identified as relating to nondirect aggression. In examining the determinants and consequences of nondirect aggression, we will focus on our own research program on indirect aggression while simultaneously considering how that program of research fits within the larger scheme of research on interpersonal aggression.

WHAT IS NONDIRECT AGGRESSION?

Aggression is a behavior intended to cause harm to another living being (Baron & Richardson, 1994). We specify that aggression is a **behavior** in order to distinguish it from internal processes, such as emotions (e.g., anger) and cognitions (e.g., hostility), which often are associated with harmful actions. Our definition also requires that the harmful behavior be **intended**; that is, the person engaging in the behavior must be *trying* to cause harm to the target. Accidental harm (e.g., tripping and knocking another person off the sidewalk) or altruistic pain-inducing action (e.g., a flu shot from your physician) would not qualify as aggression according to this definition. The behavior must be directed to **another living being** in order to be considered aggressive. So, beating on a car with a sledgehammer after paying for the privilege by making a contribution to some charity at a fair would not be considered aggressive action; beating on a neighbor's car with a sledgehammer because he continued to park it on your lawn would be an aggressive act—because your intention is to cause harm to your neighbor. Finally, and most importantly for this chapter, there are a variety of kinds of **harm** that might be directed toward the target. In this section, we will review many of those and especially consider how aggression might be delivered in a nondirect manner.

Although most of the empirical research on aggressive behavior has focused on direct, and mostly physical, aggression, there have been several attempts to examine other types of aggressive action. Buss (1961) was among the first to distinguish clearly among different forms of aggression. He proposed three categories for defining aggression: physical-verbal, passive-active, and direct-indirect. Physical aggression involves causing harm to another person by using physical means—hitting, punching, kicking, stabbing; verbal aggression involves employing words to deliver harm, perhaps by screaming or cursing. Whereas the most obvious aggressive acts are active, involving some action on the part of the aggressor, passive aggression involves causing harm by *not* doing something (e.g., a graduate student who is angry with his professor "forgets" to finish the analyses for an important paper they are writing). Direct aggression involves direct confrontation between the aggressor and the target, indirect aggression involves administering harm to other people without confronting them directly (e.g., telling stories about them to other people). The nondirect aggression which is the focus of this chapter involves primarily indirect and sometimes passive aggressive strategies.

Buss (1961) referred to **indirect aggression** specifically as a mode of aggression that avoids counterattack. It could be delivered verbally (spreading nasty gossip) or physically (setting fire to a neighbor's home). "Gossip is indirect in that the victim is not present, and the noxious stimuli are delivered via the negative reactions of others; the victim gets into trouble at the end of a chain of mediating events and people. Damaging a person's possessions is indirect in that the victim is not hurt or injured, but objects associated with and valued by him are destroyed" (p. 8). The Buss-Durkee Hostility Inventory (1957) included the following behaviors on the indirect aggression subscale: spreading gossip, breaking or throwing things, temper tantrum, slamming doors, sulking, banging on the table, pouting, playing practical jokes. Those items suggest a much broader definition of indirect aggression, and Buss (1961, p. 169) argues that indirect aggression in fact includes both "roundabout" ("hated person is not attacked directly, but by devious means") and "undirected" ("discharge of negative affect against no one in particular") aggression. According to the important intentional component of our definition of aggression, Buss' notion of undirected aggression would not qualify as a truly aggressive action. Rather, it might be considered simply emotional expression. This is an important distinction that may be critical for interpreting results of studies of so-called indirect aggression.

Feshbach (1969), in observations of children's aggression, identified **indirect aggression** as "responses which result in pain to a stimulus person through rejecting and excluding him" (p. 250). The following behaviors were considered indicators of indirect aggression: ignoring (paying no attention to an approach), avoiding (moving away when approached), refusals (denying requests for help or play), and excluding (active rejection). Crick and Grotpeter (1995) define **relational aggression** as "harming others through purposeful manipulation and damage of their peer relationships" (p. 711). Items in their peer nomination inventory include behaviors such as: "When mad, gets even by keeping the person from being in their group of friends"; "Tells friends they will stop liking them unless friends do what they say"; "When mad at a person, ignores them or stops talking to them"; "Tries to keep certain people from being in their group during activity or play time." Note that both Feshbach's conception of indirect aggression and Crick and Grotpeter's conception of relational aggression involve behaviors that directly confront the target (e.g., denying requests for help, saying they will stop liking them) as well as some that avoid confrontation. Cairns, Cairns, Neckerman, Ferguson, and Gariépy (1989) developed a measure of **social aggression** that is more consistent with Buss' notion of indirect aggression as avoiding confrontation. They coded evidence of active rejection from a group, "slander and defamation of reputation by gossip," and "alienation of affection" as indicators of social aggression in girls' and boys' responses to structured interviews that inquired about their experience with conflict.

Lagerspetz, Björkqvist, and Peltonen (1988) included the following items in a peer rating form designed to measure **indirect aggression**: tells untruth behind back; starts being somebody else's friend in revenge; abuses; says to others, "Let's not be with him/her"; argues; sulks; tries to put the other to his/her side; acts as if didn't know. They argue that these are behaviors that "exploit social relations among peers in order to harm the person at whom the anger is directed" (p. 409). Note that they include both Buss' "roundabout" and "undirected" actions in their measure of indirect aggression.

In a later study, Österman et al. (1994) measured **social manipulation** with the following items: shuts the other out of the group; becomes friends with another as revenge; ignores; gossips; tells bad or false stories; plans secretly to bother the other; says bad things behind the back; says to others, "Let's not be with him/her"; tells the other one's secrets to a third person; writes notes in which the other is criticized; criticizes the other one's hair or clothing; tries to get others to dislike the person. Björkqvist, Österman, and Lagerspetz (1994) measured social manipulation among university employees with the following items: insulting comments about one's private life, insinuative negative glances, backbiting, spreading of false rumors, insinuations without direct accusation, not being spoken to, "do-not-speak-to-me" behavior. In sum, the form of nondirect aggression studied by these researchers involves primarily verbal aggression that causes harm by disrupting relationships with other people.

For our own program of research on indirect aggression, we have developed a measure based on a conceptual definition consistent with Buss' (1961) original view of indirect aggression. We define **indirect aggression** as behavior intended to harm another living being without direct confrontation, thereby allowing for the possibility that the aggressor might remain unidentified. The Richardson Conflict Response Questionnaire appears in Table 1. Items intended to measure indirect aggression included some derived from Björkqvist, Österman, and Kaukiainen's (1992) measure and some that we developed ourselves. Direct aggression and filler

TABLE 1 *Richardson Conflict Response Questionnaire* (Green, Richardson, & Lago, 1996)

Here is a list of things you might do when angry with someone. How often do you make each of these responses when angry or upset with someone? Use the following code:

1 = Never 2 = Seldom 3 = Sometimes 4 = Often 5 = Very Often

Direct Aggression Items

(1) Yelled or screamed at them.
(3) Threatened to hit or throw something at them.
(6) Cursed at them.
(7) Threw something at them.
(11) Hit (or tried to hit) them with something hard.
(12) Insulted them or called them names to their face.
(16) Kicked (or tried to kick) the other person.
(19) Hit (or tried to hit) the other person but not with anything.
(21) Pushed, grabbed, or shoved them.
(26) Threw something (but not at the other) or smashed something.

Indirect Aggression Items

(4) Made up stories to get them in trouble.
(10) Made negative comments about their appearance to someone else.
(14) Spread rumors about them.
(18) Took something that belonged to them.
(20) Gossiped behind their back.
(22) Called them names behind their back
(23) Told others not to associate with them.
(25) Told others about the matter.
(27) Destroyed or damaged something that belonged to them.
(28) Gathered other friends to my side.

Filler Items

(2) Did things to irritate them.
(5) Didn't show that I was angry.
(8) Tried to make them look stupid
(9) Stomped out of the room.
(13) Talked the matter over.
(15) Sulked and refused to talk about it.
(17) Dropped the matter entirely.
(24) Waited until I calmed down and then discussed the problem.

Scoring:

Add items 1, 3, 6, 7, 11, 12, 16, 19, 21, and 26 to get a *direct aggression* score.
Add items 4, 10, 14, 18, 20, 22, 23, 25, 27, and 28 to get an *indirect aggression* score.

items derived primarily from Straus' (1979) Conflict Tactics Scale. We included measures of both direct and indirect aggression in the same scale because we wanted to investigate indirect aggression within the context of the variety of responses one might make when angry.

We have now administered this scale to over 1,000 people ranging in age from 12 to 90 who have participated in eight different investigations. The individual scales show strong evidence of internal consistency, with alphas of .77–.90 for the direct aggression scale and .80–.83 for the indirect aggression scale. Correlations between the measures of direct and indirect aggression also suggest that the two measures, though they share some variance as we would expect, are relatively independent. The correlations between direct and indirect aggression range from .07 (for a group of 44 college students) to .61 (for a group of 74 seventh graders), with the remaining correlations ranging between .34 and .57 (average correlation across all studies = .42).

As is clear from this discussion of the variety of approaches to the measurement of this "different" form of aggression, what we are calling **nondirect aggression** includes elements of indirect aggression primarily, with bits of passive aggression and a strong component of verbal aggression. In addition, most of these forms of aggression involve some intention to disrupt the target's relationship with others and sometimes with oneself. What these different approaches clearly share is what they *don't* measure: they do not measure direct, physical aggression. In view of the fact that, historically, research on aggressive behavior has focused on direct, physical action, this chapter will summarize research on a type of aversive interpersonal behavior that did not receive much research attention until the last decade. Although the specific definition of nondirect aggression may differ, as you will see, the findings from the different programs of research are quite consistent.

WHY DELIVER HARM CIRCUITOUSLY?

A person is likely to deliver harm in a circuitous fashion in order to avoid danger. Most of the nondirect strategies we have described allow the aggressor to remain unidentified or, if the person who engaged in the action *can* be identified, then the intention behind the action might not be clear to the target. The nondirect aggressor might be able to deny that he or she meant to cause harm: "It wasn't gossip; I was just concerned about you"; or "I had no idea that Nancy would make such a big deal of it when I told her you had gone out with her boyfriend"; or "I didn't mean to upset you; I wasn't really ignoring you, I was just lost in thought."

Björkqvist and colleagues (Björkqvist et al., 1994; Österman et al., 1994) propose an **effect/danger ratio** whereby the aggressor assesses the danger involved in any type of aggressive action relative to the likely effectiveness of the action. The goal of the aggressor is to maximize the effect while exposing himself or herself to as little danger as possible. Thus, nondirect strategies might be attractive because they have the potential to cause considerable harm to the target while protecting the aggressor from identification and therefore retaliation.

DETERMINANTS

Although there is some variety in the determinants of nondirect aggression (i.e., the situations and personal characteristics that seem most likely to lead to nondirect aggressive responding) selected by researchers for their investigations, most of them relate in some way to gender differences. Indeed, much of the controversy in this field arises because of the suggestion that females may use nondirect aggression more than males. But, before we examine the research literature that focuses on gender issues, we will consider how the aggressor's style of information processing might influence the probability of nondirect aggression.

Social Information Processing

There is solid evidence that overtly aggressive children are biased social information processors. Such children attribute malicious intent to peer provocations more often than do nonaggressive children, particularly if the situation is ambiguous (Crick & Dodge, 1994). These hostile attributions play an important causal role in children's aggressive behavior; they increase the likelihood that a child will behave more aggressively (Crick & Dodge, 1994).

Such a hostile attribution bias also is apparent among nondirectly aggressive children. Crick (1995) found that relationally aggressive children express feelings of jealousy in relationship conflicts and get more upset in relationship conflicts than nonrelationally aggressive children, suggesting that provocation events involving relationship conflicts are more salient and problematic than other types of provocation for relationally aggressive children. Relationally aggressive children were more likely than nonrelationally aggressive children to interpret ambiguous circumstances of social exclusion or social manipulation as intentionally motivated hostile acts. They did not show this bias for nonrelational provocations (e.g., someone breaks something that belongs to you). Thus, children who have a hostile attributional bias when it comes to relationship provocations, may retaliate with nondirect aggression.

GENDER

Folklore and common perceptions of females' behavior suggest that females are more nondirectly aggressive than males. The concept of the "catty" or backbiting female is certainly widespread. Hines and Fry (1994), for example, found that people believe that women are more likely than men to use nondirect aggression. Both males and females endorsed the idea that women are more likely than men to gossip about others and to exclude someone from a social event.

Researchers seem to share this perception. Several have suggested that the emphasis on studying direct, physical aggression has led us to conclude falsely that males are more aggressive than females. The notion is that women, being physically weaker and/or having different interpersonal goals, may simply exhibit "unique" forms of aggression, such as nondirect aggression. Björkqvist (1994) explains possible gender differences in aggressive strategies by considering how physical weakness might play a role in choice of strategy. He argues that, because females are typically physically weaker than males, "they simply have to develop other means than physical ones in order to reach successful results" (p. 178). Indeed, physical weakness would certainly enhance the probability of injury in any physically aggressive encounter; fighting with words or by enlisting the social group might be less risky.

Crick and Grotpeter (1995) suggest that people attempt to harm others in ways that best thwart the target's valued goals. As males' interpersonal goals are likely to include themes of instrumentality and physical dominance, they may use direct aggression, which is consistent with such concerns. Females' interpersonal goals are more likely to focus on relational issues. Thus, they may attempt to harm others through damaging their relationships, and some form of nondirect aggression may allow them to achieve this goal.

So, do these differential weaknesses and goals lead males and females to behave differently in conflict situations? The answer to that question is a clear, "it depends." The evidence that females engage in more nondirect aggression than males is fairly unambiguous when the subjects of investigation are adolescents. For example, Cairns et. al. (1989) found social aggression themes to be more frequent in descriptions of conflicts by 12 to 13-year-old girls than by 12 to 13-year-old boys. Björkqvist, Lagerspetz and their colleagues also have found consistent gender differences in indirect aggression among adolescents; they report that 11 to 12-year-old and 14 to 15-year-old girls are rated by their peers as being more indirectly aggressive than boys of the same age (Björkqvist, Lagerspetz, & Kaukiainen, 1992; Lagerspetz & Björkqvist, 1994; Lagerspetz et al., 1988).

The evidence concerning gender differences in indirect aggression among younger children is less consistent. For example, Österman et al. (1994) did not find a gender difference in indirect aggression in an 8-year-old sample, whereas Brodzinsky, Messer, and Tew (1979) found a marginal gender difference ($p < .1$) in peer ratings of indirect aggression in 10-year-old children. Crick and Grotpeter (1995) also found significant gender differences on their peer-nomination measure of relational aggression in a sample of 8 to 12-year-olds; girls were perceived to be more relationally aggressive than boys. However, when assessed with self reports, boys reported more overt *and* relational aggression than girls did.

Cairns et al.'s (1989) longitudinal study of aggression in children provides evidence of age-related changes in nondirect aggression. This study revealed that girls reported more social aggression themes in early adolescence than they did in childhood. By the seventh grade, over one-third of same-gender conflicts among girls involved social aggression, compared to 10% in the fourth grade. Boys always reported very low levels of social aggression.

Björkqvist, Österman, and Kaukiainen (1992) suggest that these age and gender differences may be due to developmental trends in choice of aggressive strategies. As indirect aggression demands relatively well-developed verbal and social skills, neither gender has the requisite skills to carry out indirect aggression before adolescence. However, in adolescence, as females mature faster than males, their better-developed social and verbal skills may allow them to make greater use of nondirect aggressive strategies. Kaukiainen, Björkqvist, Österman, Lagerspetz and Niskanen's (1994) finding that 12-year-old girls scored higher on social intelligence and engaged in more indirect aggression than did 10-year-old girls provides some indirect support for this proposition.

What about adults? There is little evidence concerning gender differences in indirect aggression in adulthood, and what does exist is contradictory. Lagerspetz and Björkqvist (1994) found that 18 to 19-year-old females rated themselves and were rated by their peers as performing more indirectly aggressive acts than males. Björkqvist et. al. (1994), in a study of harassment in the work setting, found that adult (mean age = 40) victims of social manipulation reported that the perpetrators of social manipulation were more often females than males. Leaper and Holliday (1995) found that among young adults (mean age = 19), negative gossip was more likely to occur and be encouraged in female dyads than in male or mixed-gender dyads. Hines and Fry (1994) also found that women (mean age = 23) reported more indirect aggression than men did. Thus, there is considerable evidence of gender differences in nondirect aggressive strategies among young adults. However, some studies have failed to find such differences. For example, Björkqvist et al. (1994) found no gender differences in indirect aggression among a group of 23-year-olds.

A study from our own lab (Green, Richardson, & Lago, 1996) was designed to examine gender differences in indirect aggression among young adults and to consider how differences in social network density might account for such differences. The rationale for this study was based on Lagerspetz et al.'s (1988) hypothesis that dense or tight networks may lead to the exhibition of more indirect aggression because that form of aggression may be more effective in these social networks. As dense networks are networks in which the members have many ties among themselves, these networks can be used in a number of ways to harm people (i.e. by gossiping about them with members of the network, by trying to disrupt their relationships with other members of the network). People with less dense networks, on the other hand, should have fewer opportunities to use indirect aggression. We administered the Richardson Conflict Response Questionnaire and a social network measure to male and female college students (mean age = 21) and found, as we expected, that network density was associated with aggressive responding. However, the nature of that association was not exactly what we had expected. First, our hypothesis of a relationship between density and indirect aggression was supported only for *male* research participants. That is, males with high-density networks reported more indirect aggression than those with low density networks; they also reported more indirect aggression than direct aggression. Females' aggressive behavior was unrelated to network density. With regard to gender differences, we found that, as is typical in most other investigations, males reported more direct aggression than females did. However, there were no gender differences in reports of indirect aggression although females did report using indirectly aggressive strategies more frequently than directly aggressive strategies. Males in high-density networks responded much like the females (regardless of network density) in reporting more indirect than direct aggression. Indeed, this pattern of results may reflect other differences related to gender. Males in high-density networks may have social skills equivalent to those of most females of their age. The research participants might be considered either late adolescents or young adults; thus, these young men may be just catching up with their female counterparts in developing social and verbal skills that allow them to form relationships with a connected network of others and that allow them to engage in indirect aggression. Those who have not yet "caught up" may not be using indirect aggressive strategies because they do not yet have the necessary skills.

In sum, the relationship between gender and indirect aggression in adulthood is still somewhat ambiguous. Although more research is needed to clarify this relationship, the explanation may lie in the verbal/social skills hypothesis. That is, indirect aggression requires relatively sophisticated verbal and social skills. Whereas younger males may be less able than their more socially skilled female peers to engage in indirect aggression, that difference may disappear in later adolescence or adulthood when males have acquired the verbal and social skills needed for indirect aggression.

Target Characteristics

Most of the research on gender differences in nondirect aggression has focused on same-sex interaction. Thus, the design of the studies confounds gender of aggressor with gender of target. Perhaps apparent differences between males and females in their form of aggression might be explained in terms of differences in response to male and female targets. That is, females may be more likely to be targets of indirect aggression, whether that aggression is delivered by a male or by a female. The design of gender studies has not allowed us to determine which might be the case.

Cairns et al. (1989) considered both sex of aggressor and sex of target in their investigation of physical aggression and social aggression among fourth through ninth graders. Although fourth-grade boys and girls reported little use of social manipulation strategies in conflict, girls evidenced a major increase in the use of such strategies in early adolescence, and most of that increase involved conflicts with other females. The overall picture in this study is one in which males engage in physical aggression with other males and females engage in social aggression with other females.

We examined the role of target gender in a study (Green & Richardson, 1995) in which male and female research participants responded to our questionnaire indicating how frequently in the past month they had engaged in the listed behaviors when angry with an opposite-sex (not romantic partner) and a same-sex person. Although both males and females reported delivering equal amounts of indirect aggression to males and females, males reported using direct aggression in interactions with males more than in interactions with females. In addition, females demonstrated a general preference for indirect aggression over direct aggression, regardless of the gender of the target.

However, in natural interaction, gender of target is likely to be confounded with relationship to the target. In fact, it was just that consideration that led us to exclude romantic partner from the responses for the previous study. So, we conducted another study in which we could consider the nature of the relationship with the same or opposite gender (Richardson, 1996). In this study, we collected both peer and self-ratings of a subject's aggressive responding. That is, in addition to filling out the questionnaire for themselves, participants gave a similar questionnaire to someone who knew them well, with whom they had experienced conflict. The person to whom the participant gave the questionnaire completed it with reference to the behavior of the subject. We received 115 peer reports. Because the gender of the peer as well as the relationship to the participant were included in the background information we collected, we were able to examine effects of gender of target and effects of relationship to target. Much to our surprise, our analyses revealed no effects of gender of target or aggressor on *direct* aggression. However, both self and peer ratings revealed that females directed more *indirect* aggression to females than to males, and that females directed more indirect aggression to females than males did. Indeed, it appears that the female-female dyad is a likely context for indirect aggression to take place. Note that these differences do not replicate the findings of the previous study in which we had excluded romantic partner as a target. Our analysis of relationship effects helps to explain the apparent discrepancy.

So, who are these male and female targets? Our analysis of the effect of relationship type revealed that romantic partners received less indirect aggression than anyone else and more direct than indirect aggression, siblings received more direct aggression than anyone else, and friends received more indirect than direct aggression. Indeed, the gender effects in the previous analysis, in which females were found to report relatively high levels of indirect aggression in interaction with females are likely to be accounted for by the nature of the relationship. Who is a better target for indirect aggression than one who is part of the social network and likely to be well connected with other people to whom one can gossip?

The association between type of relationship and type of aggression might be interpreted in terms of the effect/danger ratio mentioned earlier. With regard to *effectiveness*, indirect aggression might work particularly well with friends because those friends are part of a social network, so there are opportunities for rumors or stories to be spread through the group. However, indirect strategies might not be so effective with a romantic partner because the romantic partner is not likely to be so well integrated in the network. In fact, direct confrontation is likely to be more effective in romantic relationships; problems are not likely to be solved by talking behind the partner's back or by spreading rumors. With regard to *danger*, the risk associated with direct and indirect aggression may vary with type of relationship. Gender differences in the ability to cause physical injury to another person may make women more likely to employ indirect than direct strategies. However, those strategies have the potential to backfire if used in response to conflict with a romantic partner; that is, spreading rumors about one's romantic partner might eventually cause harm to oneself (i.e., friends might think badly of the partner).

In sum, these studies reveal that the nature of the relationship with the target may be more important than the gender of the target when studying nondirect aggressive strategies. Perhaps this is less likely to be an issue in research with children because most of their aggressive interactions are likely to involve same-gender friends or acquaintances and the measurement technique defines their aggression as taking place within the peer group (i.e., peer nomination or peer ratings). However, when considering aggression of adults, who have opportunities for conflict with people in a variety of different roles, relationship may be more important than gender as a determinant of type and strength of aggressive response.

CONSEQUENCES

Because nondirect aggression tends to be indirect and hidden from the target, the consequences may be difficult to locate. It is the intention of the aggressor to remain unidentified, to avoid any untoward consequences, such as retaliation. Indeed, the most favorable consequence from the perspective of the aggressor would be for the target to be harmed but for that target to be unable to retaliate. There is, in fact, relatively little research on the consequences of nondirect aggression (perhaps because such aggression is relatively hidden). The research that has been reported focuses on negative consequences for the aggressor.

Social Isolation

Studies on the consequences of nondirect aggression have been conducted primarily with children and have revealed consequences similar to those that arise from direct aggression. Engagement in nondirect aggression is related to negative well-being and rejection by the peer group; the nondirectly aggressive child is likely to be socially isolated.

Children who use nondirect aggression are at risk for social maladjustment. Children who are frequently nominated as relationally aggressive by their peers report higher levels of depression and perceive themselves to be more poorly accepted by their peers than those who are nominated less frequently for that category. Relationally aggressive girls are also more lonely and report more isolation than their nonrelationally aggressive counterparts (Crick & Grotpeter, 1995).

Nondirectly aggressive children also are at risk for social rejection. Crick and Grotpeter (1995) found that third to sixth grade relationally aggressive children were significantly more disliked by their peers than their nonrelationally aggressive counterparts. Vaughn and her colleagues have found similar results. In a study of third and fourth graders in which five subtypes of aggressive behavior (i.e., provoked physical, outburst, verbal, indirect, and unprovoked aggression) were assessed, Lancelotta and Vaughn (1989) found that indirect aggression was more strongly correlated with low peer acceptance ratings for both boys and girls than were the other types of aggressive behavior. Spetter, La Greca, Hogan, and Vaughn (1992) found that engagement in indirect aggression distinguished between aggressive-rejected boys and aggressive-nonrejected boys. Boys who were aggressive and also rejected by their peers engaged in more indirect aggression (e.g., doing something sneaky in retaliation) than boys who were aggressive but not rejected.

These results suggest that, although engaging in most types of aggression has negative consequences, nondirect aggression is the least tolerated and accepted by peers. However, it is important to note that the majority of these studies are correlational in nature, and cannot address causation. We know that indirect aggression is related to rejection and negative well-being, but we do not know if the indirect aggression causes the rejection and negative well-being, or if rejected, unhappy children use indirect aggression because they choose to avoid confrontation of any type.

Retaliation

Exclusion is one of the most frequently mentioned forms of nondirect aggression, and it is a form that is likely to put the aggressor at risk for retaliation. That is, there is some chance that the target may discover the identity of the initiator of the exclusion. Thompson and Richardson (1983) investigated retaliative responses of a person who had been excluded from a group. Male research participants found themselves being excluded by a pair of other purported research participants who generally interacted only with one another and ignored the male participant. One of the members of the dyad that excluded the participant initiated the rejection by interrupting a conversation the other person was having with the research participant and by asking the experimenter if they (the confederates of the experimenter) could work together. In this study, one of the central questions involved the extent to which the person who was excluded (i.e., the target of nondirect aggression) would direct retaliation to the initiator or to the follower of the exclusion.

We were particularly concerned with examining how the gender of the initiator and follower would influence retaliative responding. Although initiators should receive higher levels of retaliation than followers, male initiators should be particularly vulnerable to retaliation and this would be especially the case when they were paired with a female follower. Thus the researchers were testing the "rooster effect," which involves male competition for female appreciation (Eskilson & Wiley, 1976). The results of the study revealed an important consequence of nondirect aggression—retaliation. The research participants directed more retaliative aggression (i.e., electric shocks) to the initiator than to the follower, and the initiator was particularly vulnerable to retaliation when he had encouraged a female to join him in excluding the research participant from their interaction.

In sum, the consequences of nondirect aggression that have been the focus of study are not ones that a person would be likely to seek. To be isolated from one's peer group or to become vulnerable to retaliation are not desirable outcomes. However, we can consider possible positive consequences of nondirect aggression as well. For example, as we suggested earlier, the circuitous nature of nondirect aggression may allow the aggressor to cause harm to another person without acknowledging his or her aggressiveness. In fact, the nondirect aggressor may find it easy to deny, to himself or herself as well as to others, that the behavior was aggressive.

CONCLUSION

Nondirect aggression is clearly an aversive interpersonal behavior. It has negative consequences for the victim, and it is even likely to have negative consequences for the perpetrator. Our conclusions about nondirect aggression are based on limited research so they are quite speculative and might be more appropriately considered suggestions for future research.

First, what do we know? It is probably safe to say that female adolescents engage in more nondirect aggression than do male adolescents. Whether those gender differences are maintained in adulthood is still open to question. Among adults, the nature of one's relationship with the target may be more important than gender in determining aggression strategies. It also seems to be reasonably clear that nondirect aggression is associated with negative social experiences such as rejection by or isolation from the peer group; at least that is the case among adolescents. However, one might speculate that the consequences for adult aggressors might not be as bad. That is, if nondirect aggression is associated with good social and verbal skills in adults, we might expect that adult nondirect aggressors would experience more positive social outcomes than their less skilled peers—as long as they don't get caught. If their aggression is detected by the victim, then retaliation may be the outcome.

This reasoning reveals an apparent contradiction which is worthy of attention. That is, several researchers have made an argument that indirect aggression requires relatively advanced social skills. On the other hand, children who engage in nondirect aggression are likely to be socially maladjusted and rejected by their peers. It seems unlikely that such socially skilled individuals would also face rejection from the peer group. Perhaps the problem is our rather global conception of social skills. In fact, there are a variety of different social skills that may play a role in the individual's choice of aggressive strategies. For example, people who have good assertiveness skills might not employ indirect aggressive strategies because they are able to, and effective at, confronting interpersonal problems directly and constructively. Individuals who are skilled at influencing members of the social group might have more opportunity for indirect aggression, and those who are particularly agreeable or extraverted might develop stronger social networks which will also provide more opportunity for indirect aggression. Thus, researchers might examine the relationship of *specific* social skills to nondirect aggression.

Another issue that deserves the attention of researchers involves how nondirect aggression is measured. Most of the studies reviewed here employed peer nomination, peer ratings, or self-report techniques. The differences in measurement strategies make interpretation of the literature as a whole fairly difficult, for one cannot determine if differences in findings are attributable to methodological or substantive differences. Each of the approaches to measurement of nondirect aggression has advantages and disadvantages. Self-report allows one to collect information from the person who should know best. And, in the case of nondirect strategies in which the behavior may be hidden and the aggressor is attempting to remain unidentified, peers may not have an accurate view of the behavior of the person they are evaluating—unless they have been a victim of the nondirect aggression *and* they were aware of the source of their negative outcomes. Cairns et al. (1989) note that "such hidden assaults are superior to direct confrontations on several counts, not the least of which is the inability of a victim to identify the antagonist and to reciprocate. And what is hidden to the victim may also be hidden to the researcher" (p. 329). On the other hand, such self-report techniques are vulnerable to social desirability and social presentation concerns as well as possible denial, even to the self, of aggressive intentions. Thus, many researchers prefer peer reports because they avoid such biases, and they offer the advantage of increased reliability from multiple measures (i.e., reports from many peers).

Whatever the determinants and consequences of the behavior might be, it is important to recognize that nondirect aggression can be quite effective and quite traumatic to the victim. If, indeed, humans have a basic need to belong (Baumeister & Leary, 1995), then these nondirect strategies that attempt to disrupt the individual's personal relationships attack a very vulnerable spot. Nondirect aggression can be destructive to the victim's position in his or her social world. It can also disrupt the social world of the aggressor if, indeed, one effect of perpetrating such aggression is to face rejection by the peer group.

REFERENCES

Baron, R. A., & Neuman, J. H. (1996). Workplace violence and workplace aggression: Evidence on their relative frequency and potential causes. *Aggressive Behavior, 22,* 161–173.

Baron, R. A., & Richardson, D. R. (1994). *Human aggression.* New York: Plenum.

Baumeister, R & Leary, M. (1995). The need to belong: Desire for interpersonal attachments as a fundamental human motivation. *Psychological Bulletin,* 497–529

Björkqvist, K. (1994). Sex differences in physical, verbal, and indirect aggression: A review of recent research. *Sex Roles, 30,* 177–188.

Björkqvist, K., Lagerspetz, K., & Kaukiainen, A. (1992). Do girls manipulate and boys fight? Developmental trends in regard to direct and indirect aggression. *Aggressive Behavior, 18,* 117–127.

Björkqvist, K., Österman, K., & Kaukiainen, A. (1992). The development of direct and indirect aggressive strategies in males and females. In K. Björkqvist & P. Niemela (Eds.), *Of mice and women: Aspects of female aggression.* San Diego: Academic Press.

Björkqvist, K., Österman, K., & Lagerspetz, K. (1994). Sex differences in covert aggression among adults. *Aggressive Behavior, 20,* 27–34.

Brodzinsky, D., Messer, S., & Tew, J. (1979). Sex differences in children's expression and control of fantasy and overt aggression. *Child Development, 50,* 372–379.

Buss, A. H. (1961). *The psychology of aggression.* New York: John Wiley and Sons.

Buss, A.H., & Durkee, A. (1957). An inventory for assessing different kinds of hostility. *Journal of Consulting Psychology, 22,* 196–302.

Cairns, R., Cairns, B., Neckerman, H., Ferguson, L., & Gariépy, J. (1989). Growth and aggression: 1. Childhood to early adolescence. *Developmental Psychology, 25,* 320–330.

Crick, N. (1995). Relational aggression: The role of intent attributions, feelings of distress, and provocation type. *Development and Psychopathology, 7,* 313–322.

Crick, N., & Dodge, K. (1994). A review and reformulation of social information-processing mechanisms in children's social adjustment. *Psychological Bulletin, 115,* 74–101.

Crick, N., & Grotpeter, J. (1995). Relational aggression, gender and social-psychological adjustment. *Child Development, 66,* 710–722.

Eskilson, A., & Wiley, M.G. (1976). Sex composition and leadership in small groups. *Sociometry, 39,* 183–194.

Feshbach, N. (1969). Sex differences in children's modes of aggressive responses to outsiders. *Merrill-Palmer Quarterly, 15,* 249–258.

Green, L., & Richardson, D. (1995, July). *Gender relates to direct, but not indirect, aggression.* Paper presented at the meeting of the American Psychological Society, New York.

Green, L., Richardson, D., & Lago, T. (1996). How do friendship, indirect, and direct aggression relate? *Aggressive Behavior, 22,* 81–86.

Hines, N., & Fry, D. (1994). Indirect modes of aggression among women of Buenos Aires, Argentina. *Sex Roles, 30,* 215–236.

Kaukiainen, A., Björkqvist, K., Österman, K., Lagerspetz, K., & Niskanen, L. (1994). *Social intelligence and the use of indirect aggression.* Paper presented at the 11th World Meeting of the International Society for Research on Aggression, Delray Beach, Florida.

Lagerspetz, K., & Björkqvist, K. (1994). Indirect aggression in boys and girls. In L.R. Huesmann (Ed.), *Aggressive behavior: Current perspectives* (pp. 131–150). New York: Plenum.

Lagerspetz, K., Björkqvist, K., & Peltonen, T. (1988). Is indirect aggression typical of females? Gender differences in aggressiveness in 11- to 12- year-old children. *Aggressive Behavior, 14,* 403–414.

Lancelotta, G., & Vaughn, S. (1989). Relation between types of aggression and sociometric status: Peer and teacher perceptions. *Journal of Educational Psychology, 81,* 86–90.

Leaper, C., & Holliday, H. (1995). Gossip in same-gender and cross-gender friends' conversations. *Personal Relationships, 2,* 237–246.

Österman, K., Björkqvist, K., Lagerspetz, K., Kaukiainen, Huesmann, L., & Fraczek, A. (1994). Peer and self-estimated aggression and victimization in 8-year-old children from five ethnic groups. *Aggressive Behavior, 20,* 411–428.

Richardson, D.R. (1996, May). *The effects of gender and relationship on direct and indirect aggression*. Paper presented at the annual Nags Head Conference, Highland Beach, Florida.

Spetter, D., La Greca, A., Hogan, A., & Vaughn, S. (1992). Subgroups of rejected boys: Aggressive responses to peer conflict situations. *Journal of Clinical Child Psychology, 21,* 20–26.

Straus, M. A. (1979). Measuring intrafamily conflict and violence: The Conflict Tactics (CT) Scales. *Journal of Marriage and the Family, 41,* 75–88.

Thompson, H.L. & Richardson, D. (1983). The Rooster Effect: Same-sex rivalry and inequity as factors in retaliative aggression. *Personality and Social Psychology Bulletin, 9,* 415–425.

CHAPTER 9

SOCIAL ALLERGENS AND THE REACTIONS THAT THEY PRODUCE

ESCALATION OF ANNOYANCE AND DISGUST IN LOVE AND WORK

MICHAEL R. CUNNINGHAM, ANITA P. BARBEE, AND PERRI B. DRUEN

Much of the research in our laboratory has focused on the positive aspects of human interaction, such as attraction (Cunningham, Roberts, Barbee, & Druen, 1995), partner selection strategies (Druen, 1995), helpfulness (Cunningham, Shaffer, Barbee, Wolfe, & Kelley, 1990), honesty (Cunningham, Wong, & Barbee, 1994), and socially supportive cheering-up behaviors (Barbee & Cunningham, 1995). Yet, there may be limits to what can be learned about relationship dynamics by focusing solely on the determinants of prosocial actions.

Studies of relationship maintenance behaviors (Argyle & Henderson, 1985; Baxter & Dindia, 1990; Bell, Daly, & Gonzalez, 1987; Lund, 1985; Shea & Pearson, 1986; Stafford & Canary, 1991; Tolhuizen, 1989), for example,

---

MICHAEL R. CUNNINGHAM, ANITA P. BARBEE, AND PERRI B. DRUEN • Department of Psychology, University of Louisville, Louisville, Kentucky 40223. mrcunn01@ulkyvm.louisville.edu.

Aversive Interpersonal Behaviors, edited by Kowalski
Plenum Press, New York, 1997

concentrate on dimensions such as positive acts (giving gifts, building self-esteem), assurances (emphasizing commitment), sharing (helping with tasks, doing favors), and network activities (spending time with the partner's friends and family). Whereas the performance of such behaviors undoubtedly contributes to relationship quality, it is not clear that the absence of such positive acts leads to strong negative reactions. The following account illustrates a situation that is common in relationships:

> Kim described her college roommate, Sally, as really nice to people and capable of being supportive. On the other hand, Sally and Kim's friendship of 15 months was not going smoothly. Over time, Kim learned that Sally was often nice to others in person, but that she would say negative things behind their backs. Kim also noted that Sally did not seem to be grateful for favors, that Sally's side of their room was always messy, and that she smelled badly, especially after exercising. Finally, Kim reported that she often felt disgusted by and angry toward Sally, although Sally probably did not know it. Instead, Kim believed that Sally thought of her as her best friend.

The roommate's negative emotions toward Sally did not stem from an absence of positive behaviors from her, nor to unresolved major conflicts, as such issues traditionally have been studied. The friendship was not characterized by dominance or physical abuse, by lies or betrayal, or by a failure to fulfill role expectations for providing time, energy, or material support. Sally was not abhorrent, but her roommate had begun to avoid her as much as possible.

DESCRIPTION OF THE SOCIAL ALLERGEN-ALLERGY PROCESS

Without minimizing the impact of major problems and conflict, we suggest there is also a process of gradual abrasive erosion that can be just as destructive to personal well-being and relationships. This response has many similarities to the physical response of people who are allergic to ragweed, cat dander, shellfish, poison ivy, or other substances.

We believe that relatively minor, but nonetheless obnoxious behaviors, such as intrusiveness, annoying habits, or insensitivity, may affect a person psychologically the same way that physical allergens function immunologically. The first experience with a physical allergen such as grass pollen, or with an obnoxious behavior such as being cut off by another driver at a highway exit ramp, is likely to produce little reaction. With repetition, however, the physical response to poison ivy and the emotional response to being cut off while driving, tend to escalate.

We refer to the objectively minor but emotionally major experiences of social life that grate on people's nerves or make them emotionally "sick," as social allergens. A **social allergen** is defined as a behavior or situation created by another person that may be seen as unpleasant, but not as strongly aversive, to objective observers.

Through repeated exposure at periodic intervals or through prolonged initial contact, a social allergen may produce a social allergy in an individual. A **social allergy** is defined as a reaction of hypersensitive disgust or annoyance to a social allergen. Contempt is a mixture of pronounced anger and disgust (Ekman & Friesen, 1986; Rozin, 1994). The initial feeling of disdain and aversion evident in a social allergy can be distinguished from contempt, although contempt may be experienced after such feelings have accumulated and escalated over multiple experiences with a social allergen.

Social allergies are also distinct from conditioned emotional reactions. Differences lie in both the initial valence of the stimulus and the profile of the emotional reaction over time. A conditioned emotional reaction begins with a neutral stimulus, and comes to elicit negative affect through repeated association with an unconditioned, inherently aversive stimulus. The conditioned stimulus seldom matches the unconditioned stimulus in the amount of emotion that it elicits, and it tends to elicit lessened affect over time.

A social allergy, by contrast, is stimulated by a social allergen that is either inherently aversive, such as the smell of a person who has not bathed, or by a conditioned aversive stimulus, such as the statement by a partner that: "you're a slob; you really need to dress more stylishly." In addition, repetition of the social allergen causes increased sensitivity and escalation of the intensity of the emotional reaction. Colloquial descriptions of emotional reactions to continuing interpersonal problems suggest that repeated experiences cause negative emotions to accumulate and to escalate. Some examples of these colloquial descriptions are:

- It's starting to grate on my nerves.
- It's getting under my skin.
- That's beginning to rub me the wrong way.
- It's becoming a pet peeve of mine.
- I'm really getting tired of this.
- That's starting to drive me crazy.
- It's getting to be a sore spot with me.
- I'm just getting fed up with it.

The basic elements of the social allergen-allergy process are outlined in Figure 1. As will be discussed below, there are four major categories of allergens, which may produce different characteristic emotional reactions.

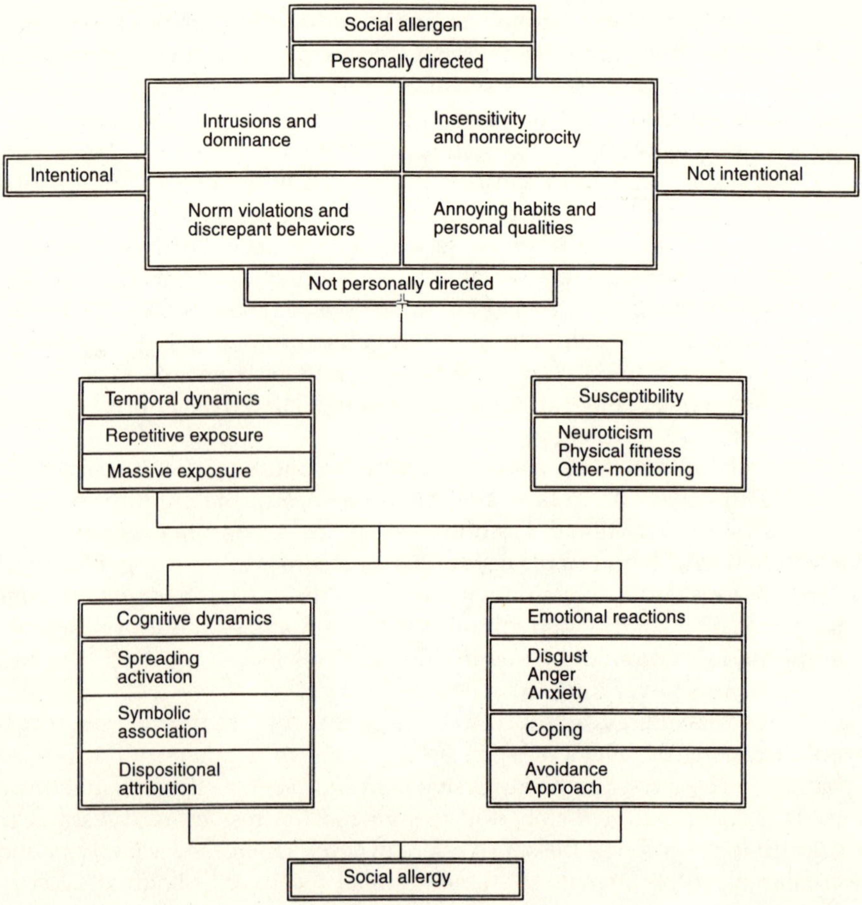

FIGURE 1. Model of social allergen-allergy dynamics.

The course or intensity of a social allergy may also be influenced by such variables as: a) the temporal course of the exposure to the allergen, b) cognitive dynamics, including the individual's attributions about the allergenic behavior, c) individual susceptibility to various allergens, and d) individual difference in coping responses.

Types of Social Allergies

We conducted two surveys of a total of 150 respondents, asking them to nominate acts that caused annoyance or disgust (Cunningham, Barbee, Druen, & Bledsoe, 1993; Cunningham, Barbee, Druen, & Pospisil, 1993;

Pospisil, Cunningham, Barbee, & Druen, 1995). Because we will be discussing the results of these surveys throughout this chapter, it is useful to clarify how the topic was introduced to the survey respondents:

> This survey is concerned with people whom you cannot stand to be around, who drive you crazy without them necessarily intending to do so. We are particularly interested in situations in which you have such strong feelings toward a person that it takes very little for the person to irritate, offend you, or cause physical symptoms.

Every respondent was able to name at least one person who got under his or her skin; the average was one relative and three non-relatives. When asked to identify the individuals who generated the strongest feelings, the nominations were about equally divided between the voluntary relationships of friends (30%) and romantic partners (18%), and the involuntary relationships of co-workers (18%), bosses and teachers (17%), and relatives (14%).

We specifically asked respondents to "please describe the characteristics or actions about the person whom you named that cause the *strongest* emotions." Dozens of social allergens were nominated by our respondents, but we found that the behaviors could be reliably classified using the two dimensions of intentionality and personalism.

The construct of intentionality was derived from Heider (1958), who originally suggested that individuals often strive to determine if an action is intentional or purposive when judging the blameworthiness of an action. In the case of a fully intentional action, such as parentally reminding a romantic partner to sit up straight at the table, the individual consciously intends to perform the action and is aware that the action may cause some negative reaction, although the importance of the partner's emotion may be minimized. In an unintentional action, the individual is not consciously aware, for example, of rooting for earwax with the little finger, nor of the disgust feelings that such actions cause in onlookers. In reality, actions may be partially intentional, such as when a cigarette smoker consciously intended to light up but did not intend to cause coughing in a sensitive bystander. From the bystander's perspective, however, if the consequences were forseeable, the action may be regarded as intentional (cf. Ferguson & Rule, 1983).

Jones and Davis (1965) introduced the dimension of personalism, which involves the extent to which an action is directed specifically toward a given individual, or is the by-product of actions directed toward other objectives. An action that is personally directed tends to produce a more polarized dispositional attribution than an action that is not personally directed. The intersection of the two dimensions of intentionality and personalism produces a fourfold typology of allergenic behaviors. The four categories of allergens that produce social allergic reactions are displayed in Figure 1.

Intrusions and Dominance (Intentional and Personal)

Mutual respect, acceptance, and appreciation are expected in most relationships. But such expectations are not always met, and partners may behave in an intrusive or controlling fashion. Davis and Schmidt (1977) observed that people's behavior is regarded as obnoxious if it implies that they are trying to impose on another person a self that the other person does not want, such as lower status or an alternate persona.

A person who boasts about accomplishments or status may implicitly challenge others to either match the braggart's asserted qualifications or acknowledge a position of lower rank (cf. Tice, Butler, Muraven, & Stillwell, 1995). Although displays of bragging and arrogance may be particularly obnoxious, there are more subtle intrusive actions that also threaten the self-esteem of the recipient.

Providing unsolicited advice or other forms of corrective feedback implies that the offender sees the target as personally deficient or inadequate. Accepting unsolicited "help" may entail acknowledging that one is less competent than the person providing the aid (Nadler & Fisher, 1986), producing a drop in self-esteem. Suggesting that unsolicited help is stimulated more by egotism than altruism, individuals who scored high on power motivation provided more unrequested help than did others (McClelland, 1975).

A variety of other manipulative actions, such as transparent flattery (Jones & Wortman, 1973), demands for a partner's accountability due to jealousy, statements designed to induce guilt (Cunningham, Steinberg, & Grev, 1980), sexual interest, greed, dependency, or other motives all may stimulate negative emotions in the target, and, possibly, social allergies. Attesting to the aversiveness of this form of social allergen, intrusions were disproportionately represented among the reported behaviors that caused strong feelings. Thirty-four percent of the behaviors that were reported as causing the most problems were classified as intrusions. Among the acts of obnoxious intrusiveness, dominance, and put-downs that we observed were comments about another person who:

- Gives commands (without having legitimate authority)
- Engages in unwarranted boasting
- Is frequently critical
- Gives unwanted suggestions
- Implies the partner is of lower status
- Acts jealously possessive and controlling

Insensitivity and Nonreciprocity (Unintentional and Personal)

Our research on interactive coping in close relationships indicated that partners are expected to be attentive to the verbal and nonverbal behaviors of their associates, and to reciprocate courtesies and help (Barbee, Gulley, & Cunningham, 1990). If an individual has had a bad day and expects cheering up, for example, but the partner does not provide the expected nurturance, then the individual may feel hurt, disgusted, or angry. When other conflict exists in the relationship, the current insensitivity or nonreciprocity may accrue added negativity by suggesting a lack of dedication and commitment. In the worst case, a minor insensitive behavior, such as interrupting in conversation, can begin to seem intentional rather than impulsive (cf. West, 1979).

Recipients of emotional support also can induce social allergies. Defensive pessimists may express low expectations for success, in part as a means of harnessing their anxiety. Because defensive pessimists seem to prefer a negative focus in conversations (Showers, 1992), they may resist the suggestions of people who try to cheer them up. Indeed, if a friend tries to motivate a defensive pessimist by mentioning reasons to be confident, the pep talk may actually reduce the pessimist's performance (Norem & Cantor, 1986). Listening to the defensive pessimist's consistently gloomy complaining, however, may lower the mood of a conversational partner (Showers, 1992). Over time, the defensive pessimist may cause a social allergy.

Another form of insensitivity involves unintentional threats to another person's self-esteem. When one person is outperformed by another on a noncompetitive but personally relevant task, the less successful person tends to react with defensiveness, by perceiving less similarity with the more successful one, expressing less willingness to work with the other again, and by sitting further away (Tesser, 1988). To avoid stimulating such social comparison envy, people may learn to minimize the quality of their performance, or the relevance of that performance to the other person's self-evaluation. Those who do not minimize their positive outcomes may stimulate social allergies in the less fortunate.

Insensitivity ranked second as the cause of problems (30% of nominations), but once such a behavior became allergenic, it produced the most rapid allergic reaction. Among the insensitive behaviors that we sampled were:

- Ignores nonverbal cues
- Is inattentive in conversations
- Engages in monologues or interrupts
- Asks inappropriate personal questions
- Complains, ignores advice, and complains again

Annoying Habits and Personal Qualities (Unintentional and Not Personal)

Conscientious parents teach manners and good grooming to their children so that their habits and other personal characteristics do not intrude on other people and cause them irritation. Those who do not closely monitor themselves, or ask for feedback, may be unaware of possessing aversive mannerisms, such as the habit of sighing loudly and rolling the eyes whenever slightly displeased. Other habits, such as picking one's nose, are performed with some awareness but the negative effect on other people is unintentional. Some habits, such as standing too close during a conversation (Fisher & Byrne, 1975), and personal qualities, such as emitting unpleasant odors (Todrank, Byrnes, Wrzesniewski, & Rozin, 1995), have been documented as irritants.

Unpleasant habits also may be annoying if the partner's behavior reflects negatively on the self through association. The desire to cast off reflected failure has been documented (Cialdini, 1989) and may be extended to the desire to avoid being associated with stigmatizing personal qualities. A date who belches loudly and then pats his stomach with pleasure may raise embarrassing doubts about the partner's taste. The habit may be particularly annoying if one has controlled it oneself. It is widely believed that no one is more zealous against smoking than an ex-smoker.

Annoying habits were the least frequently mentioned cause of problems (14%), but were the cause of the strongest disgust reactions (5.0 vs 4.0 for other types of allergens on a 7 point scale). Among the allergenic habits and personal qualities that we sampled were the following:

- Conveys physically unpleasant sounds, odors, or appearance
- Frequently expresses negative emotions
- Consistently stands too close
- Is careless with property
- The person is incompetent in performing tasks

Sally, who was mentioned at the beginning of this chapter as a nuisance to her roommate, displayed a number of these annoying habits, probably without being aware of them.

Norm Violations and Discrepant Behaviors (Intentional and Not Personal)

People whose behavior and values are dissimilar to one's own may seem intriguing and novel for awhile, but later may just seem irritating (cf. Rosenbaum, 1986; Smeaton, Byrne, & Murnen, 1989). Felmlee (1995) found that the same unique qualities that drew people to romantic partners often were later recognized as extreme or unacceptable violations of social norms. Thus, a relaxed attitude was later seen as laziness, cleverness was later seen as lying, devotion was seen as possessiveness, and ambition was later seen as workaholism.

Negative reactions to norm violations are not limited to romantic relations. People who violate rules on the job may create more work for their coworkers; friends who violate norms may create friction with other friends; those who violate laws may expose others to a variety of risks. Aside from such practical responses to norm violations, moral outrage could arise. An adult who violates social norms threatens conventional understandings of what is good and proper, and risks contempt and ostracism.

Norm violations were mentioned by 23% of respondents. Among the allergenic behaviors that we recorded that seemed discrepant from social norms were:

- Avoids work
- Expresses envy of other people
- Takes risks when driving
- Cheats or tells lies to other people
- Gossips

It should be noted that norm violations, like all social allergens, are very much in the mind of the beholder. Depending on their own subjective norms, some people may be relatively indifferent to the indolence, recklessness, or gossip of their associates, and, therefore, unlikely to develop allergies to them.

TEMPORAL DYNAMICS

The social allergy model suggests that allergies may develop as a result of repeated exposure to allergens. Experimental support for the relation of cumulative experiences to the intensity of emotional reaction can be derived from literature on the mere exposure effect. Repeated exposures to a stimulus, such as pictures of faces or tracks of music, may cause attraction (Zajonc, 1968), but repeated exposure also can cause boredom (Brickman & D'Amato, 1975). Repeated exposure to a stimulus that has become boring or obnoxious produces polarization and increased negativity (Tesser, 1978; Zajonc, Markus, & Wilson, 1974).

Repeated exposure to people to whom one has become emotionally sensitized can cause escalation of the negative emotion. The repetition-sensitization-escalation process was evident in research by Coyne (1976a, 1976b), and others, on reactions to depressed roommates. Although people were initially sympathetic to their depressed roommates, they generally rejected and avoided such roommates after a few months.

In our research, respondents interacted with the person who they felt displayed allergenic behavior a median of 5 times per week, with a median exposure of between 4 and 5 hours. Respondents stated that they could spend about one hour with the person who displayed allergenic behavior without negative emotions, but, after the allergic emotions were elicited, the feelings took nearly 3 hours to subside.

Respondents knew the person for a median time of one year before developing negative feelings, and it took a year and a half for the negative feelings to develop to their strongest. The more positive feelings that the respondent had toward the other person, the longer it took for the negative feelings to develop. The longer that it took for the allergic reaction to develop originally, the longer the emotion lasted after contact with the person manifesting allergenic behavior. Such outcomes suggest that those who do not address allergenic stimuli early in a relationship may suffer more from it later.

Although intermittent exposure to an allergen may cause social allergies, continuous exposure may exacerbate allergy development. The combination of unrelenting doses of the allergen with physical fatigue may wear down both problem-focused and emotion-focused coping resources (Lazarus, 1991) and increase the emotional impact of the allergen. Continuous exposure to an allergen is not uncommon. Sixty percent of our respondents indicated that there was a time when they were constantly in the presence of the person who caused them strong emotions. Of these, 52% had continuous exposure during travel for work, school, or vacation. Another 33% had constant exposure as a result of an involuntary relationship, such as at work, as roommates, or as siblings.

Constant contact with a person may entail not only a massive quantity of the allergenic behavior, but also the feeling of inescapability. If a social allergen, such as a coworker's bad habit of loud gum-chewing or the intrusive behavior of relentless criticism, seems likely to continue inescapably for the foreseeable future, the sufferer may experience the additional aversiveness of learned helplessness. We found that the more that our respondents perceived an allergenic behavior to be long-lasting, the more disgust ($r=.38$), discomfort ($r=.41$), and annoyance ($r = .38$, all $ps < .05$), that they reported.

COGNITIVE DYNAMICS IN SOCIAL ALLERGIES

Once the physical immune system has been sensitized to a pathogen, the system retains a "memory" of the pathogen to insure rapid and effective response to future disease assaults. A physical allergy occurs when the immune system "remembers" and provides massive retaliation against a relatively benign challenge, such as pollen.

Cognitive network dynamics may be involved in social allergies. Unlike the types of allergens, temporal dynamics, and feelings of disgust and annoyance mentioned earlier, we have not yet investigated cognitive dynamics in depth. The results of other investigators, however, provide provocative leads. Mood-dependent memory is a complex area (Eich, 1995), but it seems clear that emotional arousal tends to cue up material with a similar level of arousal stored in memory (Clark, Milberg & Erber, 1988). Thus, a portion of the aversiveness of social allergens may stem from their associations with recalled thoughts, feelings, and experiences, including unresolved issues in the relationship.

Consider the example of a relationship partner who has some bad habits involving personal neatness. When the partner's undergarments were left to dry in the shower the night before, and fall on the individual's dim eyes as the shower is turned on the next morning, the sufferer may become irritated. That irritating episode may then remind the sufferer of numerous other frustrating incidents, including broken promises by the partner to be more considerate and better organized.

A social allergy may become stronger each time that the allergen is repeated, because each new event may stimulate the recall of N+1 accumulated incidents and emotions. A small annoyance may eventually cause the individual to be overwhelmed by a flood of automatically remembered negative experiences, causing a disproportionate emotional reaction. Rumination about the event may cause the feelings to polarize even further (Tesser, 1978). The strong emotions may affect judgments, and cause an excessively negative evaluation, both of the provocative act and of the person who performed it (Erber, 1991; Forgas, 1995). Over time, the social allergen may be incorporated into a highly accessible mental schema or script (Huesmann, 1988), through which new events are interpreted (or misinterpreted).

SYMBOLIC ASSOCIATIONS IN SOCIAL ALLERGEN-ALLERGY RELATIONSHIPS

Symbolic associations, in the form of linkages with deep values and needs, may be involved in some social allergies. In the Aron, Aron, Tudor, and Nelson (1991) analysis, love involves the incorporation of the other person within the self. Yet, what happens if the other person possesses some bad habits that one does not wish to be a part of oneself? The desire to completely accept the other person may be in conflict with prejudice against some aspect of the person's behavior, and that tension may increase the strength of the allergy. The motive to exclude an undesired behavior of another person from oneself may produce the same facial disgust and anger reaction of raising the nose and rolling the eyes as does a piece of spoiled food (Rozin & Fallong, 1987).

In a second manifestation of symbolic associations, people often seem to act like amateur psychoanalysts by inferring hidden motivations in the actions of other people. For example, it was suggested that "Love is patient, love is kind. It does not envy, it does not boast, it is not proud. It is not rude, it is not self-seeking, it is not easily angered" (1 Corinthians 13:4–8). If a person has absorbed that definition and then perceives that the partner's behavior is not patient and sensitive, then the person may question whether it is really love. Each instance of insensitivity may raise more disquieting questions, and such suspicions may be as pivotal as the insensitive behavior in the development of the social allergy.

The tendency for symbolic linkages to accelerate the development of social allergies may not be limited to romantic relationships. If a coworker both engages in frequent flirtations with sales prospects and also generates more commissions, envy may cause the flirtatious behavior to be seen as an extreme norm violation, and increase feelings of disgust and resentment. If a boss has the bad habit of nose-picking in public, the behavior may be seen as unworthy of a supervisor. But because the position of subordinate does not allow challenging the boss' behavior, the combination of reactance with contempt may accelerate the development of a social allergy.

Loss and Anxiety about Bigger Issues

A person who performs an intrusive, insensitive, proscribed, or vulgar behavior not only introduces a negative element into a relationship but suggests the lack, or the loss, of expected positive elements (Barbee, Cunningham, Druen, & Yankeelov, 1996). The loss of positive qualities, in turn, may raise anxieties about the prospect of more serious problems occurring in the future. As Figure 2 illustrates, the dimensions of intentionality and personalism can be used to organize categories of current feelings of loss and anxieties about the future. The dimensions to be discussed below have not yet been investigated, and should be regarded as speculative.

Each kind of social allergen may be associated with a particular kind of loss. Intrusive behavior by a dating partner could cause the person to lose the feeling of being respected as an autonomous person, and may raise the prospect of physical or psychological abuse in the future. The perception of insensitivity and nonreciprocity could cause the loss of feeling

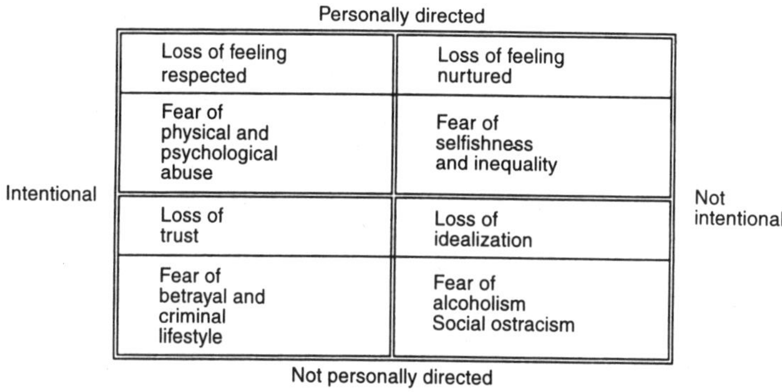

FIGURE 2. Four categories of allergen-based loss and fear of serious problems.

nurtured and deeply cared about. Such feelings could raise concerns about whether the partner might become increasingly selfish and inequitable. A person who engages in minor norm violations might cause a loss of trust, and seem like the sort of person who could engage in major forms of betrayal (Jones & Burdette, 1994), including infidelity, abandonment, or a criminal lifestyle. Finally, a person who fails to control small annoying personal habits not only may cause the loss of romantic idealization, but may suggest the absence of self-discipline in other domains, such as drinking, saving money, and maintaining friendships, which could lead to financial and social problems.

ATTRIBUTIONS IN SOCIAL ALLERGEN-ALLERGY RELATIONS

Social allergies may be like other aspects of close relationships in taking place over time, and through constantly revised understandings (Duck Rutt, Hurst, & Strejc, 1991). The first few times that an individual shows insensitivity, displays an annoying habit, or violates a norm, the action may be shrugged off as unrepresentative or irrelevant. But consistency in the occurrence of allergenic behaviors over time may create a negative dispositional attribution (Fincham & Bradbury, 1990).

Each repetition of the allergenic action may seem to confirm the negative attribution, for example, "He leaves the seat up on the toilet even though I have told him that annoys me. He really is a selfish person." Although a simple bad habit may be the proximal cause of this allergenic behavior, folk psychology suggests that bad habits can be controlled through concentration and effort. If the bad habit is not altered, the person must be viewed as the sort who does not care enough to try. Our research respondents confirmed this supposition. The more that our respondents believed that the allergenic behavior was controllable, the greater the disgust ($r=.23$) and the more discomfort ($r=.29$, both $ps < .05$) that they experienced.

A negative dispositional attribution seems particularly warranted if an allergenic behavior is seen as both intentional and personally directed (Heider, 1958; Jones & Davis, 1965). We suspect that people do not always recognize that their behavior is perceived as allergenic, perhaps because they do not intentionally perform negative behaviors or direct them personally at someone else. Whereas everyone in our sample nominated people to whom they felt allergic, only 25 percent of our respondents recognized that they caused such reactions in other people.

Consistent with our finding, Davis and Schmidt (1977) suggested that obnoxious people do not believe that they are persecuting others, even when they are. That observation was further supported by Baumeister, Stilwell, and Wotman (1990), who found that, when people were perpetrators of provocative acts, they tended to see their behavior as meaningful and justifiable. They also saw such actions as isolated events that did not have lasting implications. When the same perpetrators reported to Baumeister et al. (1990) about incidents in which they were victims, their evaluations were quite different. When describing victim experiences, they tended to see the incidents as arbitrary, gratuitous, and carrying lasting implications for continuing harm and loss. Victims may respond with anger to an accumulated series of provocations, but perpetrators may see the anger as unjustified. Believing that a person who performs an allergenic behavior will not accept responsibility for it may inhibit allergic people from expressing their concerns.

INDIVIDUAL DIFFERENCES IN SUSCEPTIBILITY TO SOCIAL ALLERGIES

Individuals may vary in their susceptibility to developing social allergies, and such differences may entail physical as well as psychological variables. The heritable personality dimension of neuroticism entails heightened sensitivity to negative emotions (Eysenck & Eysenck, 1968). Individual differences in sensitivity to seven types of disgust elicitors (food, animals, body products, sex, body envelope violations, death, and hygiene) were correlated with neuroticism (Haidt, McCauley, & Rozin, 1994). As might be expected, those who were high in neuroticism in our study also had stronger social allergy reactions than those low in neuroticism, including greater disgust ($r=.30$) and anger ($r=.26$).

Yet, while emotional sensitivity may stem in part from a biologically based temperament, it may also be related to how the biological system is used and maintained. Dienstbier (1989; 1991) suggested that those who are high in "physiological toughness" respond to challenges and stress through arousal of the sympathetic-adrenal-medullary system, which results in the secretion of catecholamines such as adrenaline. Those low in physiological toughness respond to challenges and stress through arousal of the pituitary-adrenal-cortical system, which stimulates the secretion of corticosteroids such as cortisol. Compared to adrenaline, cortisol is less efficient in that it is slower to produce maximum arousal. But the effects of cortisol persist much longer than those of adrenaline, making it more difficult for the person to relax and calm down after stress. Cortisol arousal is also associated with defensiveness, poor performance on physical tasks, and reduced immunocompetence.

Physiological toughness, including the differential secretion of adrenaline rather than cortisol, may be acquired through intermittently repeated experiences with challenges, including intensive physical exercise. Because physiological toughness may be associated with physical fitness, we assessed physical fitness in terms of respondents' body mass, based on their height and weight. The body mass index was not a direct predictor of the intensity of allergic emotions in our study, but body mass index was correlated with neuroticism ($r=.29$), which was correlated with the intensity of social allergies. Thus, those low in physical fitness may be less physiologically tough and more emotionally sensitive, and those who are more emotionally sensitive may be more likely to develop intense social allergies.

Other personality dimensions that are linked to emotion also may be related to social allergies. Individuals with the Type A behavior pattern were found to differ from Type Bs in the intensity of two of their facial expressions of emotion, glare and disgust. Glare and disgust also correlated with a number of speech components, most notably hostility, which is often associated with coronary heart disease (Chesney, Ekman, Friesen, & Black, 1990). Because disgust and annoyance are major emotional components of social allergies, the Type A pattern may play a role in social allergies.

An allergic person may be aware that an emotional reaction is excessive but may still feel like the allergenic event was "the straw that broke the camel's back." Individual differences in memory organization that influence spreading activation of emotional memories may play a role in responses to social allergens. Individuals who are more forgetful, such as Alzheimer's victims, and those who compartmentalize events in a more complex and differentiated fashion (cf. Linville, 1985), might be less vulnerable to the escalation of social allergy emotions than individuals with average levels of memory organization.

Another personality dimension that may be associated with social allergies is other-monitoring (Rowatt & Cunningham, 1995). An other-monitor notices and attempts to influence the personal impression created by partners. The prototypical other-monitor is an approval-seeking parent who maintains a stance of hypervigilance in the vain hope of deterring the child from saying or doing anything inappropriate in public. But other-monitoring is not limited to parents, or to others with supervisory authority such as managers, ministers, and teachers. Friends, dates, and spouses may be concerned about the appropriateness of their partner's behavior, due to both altruistic concern for the partner's social standing and to egoistic concern about how the partner reflects on him- or herself.

Because of their stronger motivation, other-monitors may be more likely than other people to develop social allergies if their partner's behaviors do not meet their expectations. Such individual differences may be most evident with those social allergens that are not personally directed, including bad personal habits and norm violations, which say a great deal about the partner without being focused on the self.

Not only may other-monitors suffer social allergies as a result of the gaffes and indiscretions of their partners, but they also may serve as social allergens to those partners. Despite the best of intentions, the parental scrutiny, running commentary, and stage management of the other-monitor may be seen as intrusive by the partner, causing reactance and resentment.

ADAPTIVE FUNCTIONS OF SOCIAL ALLERGIES

Social allergies may be an unfortunate by-product of normal emotion, memory, and attribution responses, the same way that physical allergies are a maladaptive by-product of normal immunological responses. Yet, before considering how to cope with social allergies, it is useful to consider the possibility that social allergies actually may have an adaptive function.

Baumeister and Leary (1995) noted that relationships are relatively easy to form but difficult to break. Even if a partner is irritating, it is difficult to put at risk the time, effort, and resources that have been invested in a job or relationship (Rusbult, Verette, Whitney, Slovik, & Lipkus, 1991). Part of the cause may be the practical problems associated with disentangling habitual interdependent behaviors; disruption of a relationship may alter role allocations that were effective (Berscheid, Snyder, & Omato, 1989), despite the fact that the relationship had dysfunctional components. It may be difficult to terminate even a destructive relationship because an attachment has been formed, the other has been incorporated into the self, and termination may be experienced as an amputation (cf. Weber & Harvey, 1994).

The costs of disrupting or terminating an aversive relationship tend to be large and immediate, whereas the costs of continuing an aversive relationship tend to be moderate and spread out over time. To overcome such barriers, and to motivate the individual to make a change, the repetition-sensitization-escalation mechanism may have evolved. Thus, it might be adaptive to ignore one or ten or one hundred acts of insensitivity, but, after the thousandth or ten-thousandth such act, it might be appropriate for a spouse to seek marital counseling, a worker to seek a new company, or Sally's roommate Kim to look for new lodgings.

There is some empirical evidence to support the notion that individuals who respond to the repetition of small aversive events with increasing emotional intensity may experience the negative reinforcement incentive necessary to make difficult but adaptive choices (Gottman & Krokoff, 1989). Krokoff (1991) reported that a conflict-avoidant wife's feelings of disgust/contempt were found to predict improvements in her marital satisfaction over three years, suggesting that strong negative emotions motivated some positive change.

Finally, an individual's sensitization to the allergenic behavior that is displayed by one associate likely influences emotional responses to similar behaviors displayed by other people. Such stimulus generalization can be highly adaptive, as when an individual who developed an allergy to one insensitive relationship partner effectively avoids insensitive people thereafter. Indeed, an inability to develop social allergies, or to act on them in a timely fashion, may restrict personal development.

Coping with Social Allergies through Avoidance

Social allergies need not cause relationship dissolution. Rosenblatt and his collaborators investigated the dialectics of togetherness and apartness and the strategies that couples use to reduce relationship tension. Their working hypothesis was that each relationship has an optimal level of togetherness time, and that, if a particular couple exceeded their optimal level, they would experience increased friction and diminished relationship satisfaction.

Rosenblatt and his associates demonstrated the negative impact of too much togetherness in a number of studies. They showed that families who travelled across the country on family vacations often experienced excessive levels of togetherness and increased tension (Rosenblatt & Russell, 1975). Similarly, when high school teachers stayed at home during the summer months, rather than taking a summer job, their marriages declined more from April to August compared to those who had less daily contact with their spouses (Rosenblatt, Titus, Nevaldine, & Cunningham, 1979). The negative impact of increased togetherness was most apparent for those with a personality style of disrespect or perfectionism (Rosenblatt, Titus, & Cunningham, 1979), which entails intrusive behaviors.

Rosenblatt found that people often used avoidance strategies to cope with excessive amounts of togetherness. Such strategies included television watching, joining volunteer organizations, and escaping to a private space in the house to avoid their families (Rosenblatt & Cunningham, 1976). Perhaps those with higher levels of emotional intelligence (Mayer, Salovey, Gomberg-Kaufman, & Blainey 1991) use additional strategies to decompress from social allergens.

Coping with Allergies by Voicing Concerns

There may be a limit to how much intrusiveness people are willing to take. Brehm and Brehm (1981) observed that, when people feel that their freedom is threatened, they may experience psychological reactance, and actively take steps to restore their freedom. Whereas Rosenblatt's studies of togetherness and apartness emphasized avoidance behaviors, Rusbult (1987) noted that, in a distressed relationship, individuals could choose to engage in passive behaviors such as loyalty or neglect, or active behaviors such as voice and exit. The behaviors of voice and loyalty were further classified as constructive, whereas the behaviors of neglect and exit were classified as destructive.

Our respondents were asked to indicate the order in which they engaged in a series of behaviors when faced with a social allergen. The reported rank order of problem solving, and the interpretation based on Rusbult's categories were as follows: tried to ignore the problem (passive/constructive: loyalty); tried to avoid the person (passive/destructive: neglect); told person what was bothering respondent (active/constructive: voice); tried to get the person to change (active/constructive: voice); tried to change own reaction (active/constructive: loyalty); told the person to leave the subject alone (active/destructive: exit). These results suggest that respondents tended to move from the passive to the active, and from the constructive to the destructive: from loyalty to neglect to voice to exit.

It is interesting to note that 81% of our respondents said that the reported destructive situation had not been resolved. That may have been due to the fact that voice was given only an intermediate emphasis. Social allergy sufferers did not discuss with the other people the extent to which their behavior had been allergenic.

Interpersonal Resolution of Social Allergies

An individual who suffers from a social allergy may have several reasons for being ambivalent about trying to resolve the problem by discussing the matter with the person who displays the allergenic behavior. First, disgusting or annoying behaviors may cause the offending person to be seen as morally tainted (cf. Rozin, Markwith, & McCauley, 1994) and make the allergic person uncertain whether the person will respond in a socially predictable fashion. For example, most people would want to know if they were being offensive so that they could quickly stop it. But a person who repeatedly engages in intrusive, insensitive, proscribed, or vulgar behavior might disdain any such feedback. Asking the person to change could make the allergic person feel like a spurned helper (Rosen, Mickler, & Collins, 1987).

Second, because a social allergy is a subjective phenomenon, there are grounds for self-doubt. A behavior that is experienced as obnoxious by an allergic person may be extremely banal, and pass unnoticed by most other people. If the allergic person seeks social comparison information (Wills, 1983), the feedback may be unhelpful or even dismissive because the other people do not feel the same degree of negativity, having not experienced the same number of repetitions. Indeed, allergic people may risk becoming allergens to their friends, by repeatedly raising unpleasant topics and complaining about other people. Further, in an attempt to make others understand, the allergic person may try to enumerate as many instances of the allergenic behaviors as possible. This could have the unexpected effect of spreading the allergy to a person who may not have even met the allergenic person.

Finally, the allergic person may wonder if he or she is simply oversensitive or lacking in toughness. The allergic person may worry that the person who performs the allergenic behavior will regard a complaint as unwarranted whining, and say just that if confronted (Fincham & Bradbury, 1992; Rusbult et al., 1991). What was a moderate frustration could be escalated into an extremely unpleasant open conflict.

Rather than discussing allergenic behavior as a legitimate complaint (Kowalski, 1996), the allergic person might consider framing the issue as a personal adjustment problem and raising the topic as a request for a favor. After all, the person performing the allergenic behavior is being asked to exert attention and effort to modify a behavior simply to benefit the emotional well-being of the allergic person. Even with a norm violation, the person performing an allergenic behavior is under no obligation to change.

If the person performing the allergenic behavior has made investments in the relationship, has derived satisfaction from it, and wants it to continue harmoniously, then that person likely will make an effort to accommodate the request (Rusbult et al., 1991). If the favor is rebuffed, then the social allergy can help to motivate the allergic person's exit.

Although escaping from an allergenic stimulus can be adaptive, the capacity of people to develop social allergies can be used for interpersonal manipulation. That is, an individual who wishes another person to modify or leave the relationship might deliberately engage in allergenic behaviors to provoke the other person. We know of one case in which a wife had very traditional religious beliefs that deterred her from expressing the fact that she was very unhappy in her marriage. Instead, she engaged in such actions as putting starch in her husband's underwear and cooking lima beans four times a week, which he detested. When her husband confronted her about the annoyances, she acknowledged that her actions were occasionally insensitive but claimed that they were unintentional, and that her husband was petty and impatient. Although she rejected counseling, the wife seemed to derive a great deal of moral superiority from the fact that it was her husband who filed for divorce eight months later.

EXPLORATION OF SOCIAL ALLERGENS IN OTHER DOMAINS

We have focused on social allergies in close relationships, but such reactions also may occur in other contexts. Increased specialization in the workplace, from bureaucratic offices to medical facilities, may cause people to function with the same coworkers, and work with others who have the same kind of needs, for long periods of time. For example, instead of having a ward with a variety of different kinds of illnesses, medical specialization may cause some nurses to work every day with the same type of highly challenging cases. Repeated exposures may cause social allergies toward the patients, as well as burnout about the job (Bromley & Emerson, 1995; Palsson & Norberg, 1995).

The social allergy pattern of allergen repetition, heightened sensitivity, and escalating emotion may seem reminiscent of the Freudian hydraulic theory or the overcontrolled aggressive personality (Megargee, 1970). The cognitive mechanisms proposed for social allergies are very different from those in earlier models, but a question might be raised whether social allergies are related to violent behavior. Cases of overstressed or disgruntled employees or city dwellers who turn violent have some similarities with accounts of social allergies, but confirmation of the congruities must await future research.

Emotional dynamics, such as clinical depression, can have an impact on the immune system, including the reduction of immunocompetence (Herbert & Cohen, 1993; Weisse, 1992). The reverse also may be the case. Researchers have reported that individuals with physical allergies have cholinergic hyperresponsiveness and beta-adrenergic hyporesponsiveness in the autonomic nervous system, and that physical allergies may be associated with endogenous depression (Marshall, 1993). The relationship of social allergies to these processes remains to be determined.

It may not be necessary to meet a person to develop a social allergy. Overexposure through the news media to the wealth, power, beauty, or talent of politicians, royalty, athletes, or entertainers may be experienced as intrusive, and cause annoyance. Excessively repeated media exposure of the personal weaknesses of such celebrities may cause disgust. It is reasonable that social allergies would cause the desire to expel allergenic public figures from awareness, but the public figures may be legitimately dismayed at how rapidly the public becomes destructive toward them. The irony is that the actual number of public appearances or offensive behaviors made by the public figure may have been low. The frequency of his or her media exposures may have been determined by people who were unconcerned about protecting his or her popularity. Aside from the waste of prematurely truncated careers, a social problem arises in that the citizenry may become sick of a politician yet retain the need to delegate authority for governance, which then is unsatisfied.

We have outlined our conception of social allergies and allergens, have described some initial findings on how and why they occur, and suggested some possible remedies. Clearly, much work is needed to comprehend this intriguing and troublesome phenomenon fully. We do not know how many exposures to an allergen, of how much intensity, over what period of time, produces the strongest social allergies. The social impact theory's (Latané, 1981) power function linking strength, immediacy, and number of stimuli, however, may provide some predictions.

After a few bad relationship experiences, some people may be disgusted and annoyed by all women or all men, but we do not know the determinants of such stimulus generalizations. Nor do we fully understand the mechanisms that allow people to become desensitized to allergens over time. A conscious decision to accept a partner's foibles and refrain from unflattering dispositional attributions may reduce some, but not necessarily all, of socially allergic emotions. We have known couples who seemed allergic to one another, who chose to separate for a time, and lost much of their hypersensitivity. Unfortunately, after a brief second honeymoon, some of those couples found that their allergies returned.

Additional forms of emotional allergies also remain to be explored, including the possibility of escalating annoyance and disgust toward jobs, cars, houses, or ideas. If researchers can avoid becoming sick of the topic of social allergies, we may gain a great deal of insight into the complexity of human emotions!

REFERENCES

Argyle, M., & Henderson, M. (1985). *The anatomy of relationships*. London: Heinemann.

Aron, A., Aron, E. N., Tudor, M., & Nelson, G. (1991). Close relationships as including other in the self. *Journal of Personality and Social Psychology, 60*, 241–253.

Barbee, A. P., & Cunningham, M. R. (1995). An experimental approach to social support: Interactive coping in close relationships. In B. Burleson (Ed.), *Communications yearbook* (Vol 18, pp. 381–413). Thousand Oaks, CA: Sage.

Barbee, A. P., Cunningham, M. R., Druen, P. B., & Yankeelov, P. A. (1996). Loss of passion, intimacy and commitment: A conceptual framework for relationship researchers. *Journal of Personal and Interpersonal Loss, 1*, 93–108.

Barbee, A. P., Gulley, M. R., & Cunningham, M. R. (1990). Support seeking in close relationships. *Journal of Social and Personal Relationships, 7*, 531–540.

Baumeister, R. F., & Leary, M. R. (1995). The need to belong: Desire for interpersonal attachments as a fundamental human motivation. *Psychological Bulletin, 117*, 497–529.

Baumeister, R. F., Stilwell, A., & Wotman, S. R. (1990). Victim and perpetrator accounts of interpersonal conflict: Autobiographical accounts about anger. *Journal of Personality and Social Psychology, 59*, 994–1005.

Baxter, L. A., & Dindia, K. (1990). Marital partners' perceptions of marital maintenance strategies. *Journal of Social and Personal Relationships, 7*, 187–209.

Bell, R. A., Daly, J. A., & Gonzalez, C. (1987). Affinity-maintenance in marriage and its relationship to women's marital satisfaction. *Journal of Marriage and the Family, 49*, 445–54.

Berscheid, E., Snyder, M., & Omato, A. M. (1989). The relationship closeness inventory: Assessing the closeness of interpersonal relationships. *Journal of Personality and Social Psychology, 57*, 792–807.

Brehm, S., & Brehm, J. W. (1981). *Psychological reactance: A theory of freedom and control*. New York: Academic Press.

Brickman, P., & D'Amato, B. (1975). Exposure effects in a free-choice situation. *Journal of Personality and Social Psychology, 32*, 415–420.

Bromley, J., & Emerson, E. (1995). Beliefs and emotional reactions of care staff working with people with challenging behaviour. *Journal of Intellectual Disability Research, 39*, 341–352.

Chesney, M. A., Ekman, P., Friesen, W. V., & Black, G. W. (1990). Type A behavior pattern: Facial behavior and speech components. *Psychosomatic Medicine, 52*, 307–319.

Cialdini, R. B. (1989). Indirect tactics of image management: Beyond basking. In R. A. Giacalone & P. Rosenfeld (Eds.), *Impression management in the organization* (pp 45–56). Hillsdale, NJ: Lawrence Erlbaum Associates.

Clark, M. S., Milberg, S., & Erber, R. (1988). Arousal-state-dependent memory: Evidence and implications for understanding social judgments and social behaviors. In K. Fiedler & J. Forgas (Eds.), *Affect, cognition and social behavior* (pp. 63–83). Toronto: Hogrefe.

Coyne, J. C. (1976a). Depression and the response of others. *Journal of Abnormal Psychology, 85*, 186–193.

Coyne, J. C. (1976b). Toward an interactional description of depression. *Psychiatry, 39*, 28–40.

Cunningham, M. R., Barbee, A. P., Druen, P. B., Bledsoe, L. K. (June,1993). *Social allergies: The development of negative emotions in close relationships*. Paper presented at the meeting of the American Psychological Society, Chicago, IL.

Cunningham, M. R., Barbee, A. P., Druen, A. P., & Pospisil, J. (October, 1993). *Social allergies: The development of annoyance and disgust in close relationships*. Paper presented at the meeting of the Southeastern Social Psychologists Conference, Gatlinburg, TN.

Cunningham, M. R., Roberts, R., Barbee, A. P., & Druen, P. B. (1995). "Their ideas of beauty are, on the whole, the same as ours": Consistency and variability in the cross-cultural perception of female physical attractiveness. *Journal of Personality and Social Psychology, 68*, 261–279.

Cunningham, M. R., Shaffer, D. R., Barbee, A. P., Wolfe, P. L., & Kelley, D. J. (1990). Separate processes in the relationship of elation and depression to altruism: Social versus personal concerns. *Journal of Experimental Social Psychology, 26*, 13–33.

Cunningham, M. R., Steinberg, J., & Grev, R. (1980). Wanting to and having to help: Separate motivations for positive mood and guilt induced helping. *Journal of Personality and Social Psychology, 38*, 181–192.

Cunningham, M. R., Wong, D. T., & Barbee, A. P. (1994) Self-presentation dynamics on preemployment integrity tests: Experimental studies of the Reid Report Inventory. *Journal of Applied Psychology, 79*, 643–658.

Davis, M. S., & Schmidt, C. J. (1977). The obnoxious and the nice: Some sociological consequences of two psychological types. *Sociometry, 40*, 201–213.

Dienstbier, R. A. (1989). Arousal and physiological toughness: Implications for mental and physical health. *Psychological Review, 96*, 84–100

Dienstbier, R. A. (1991). Behavioral correlates of sympathoadrenal reactivity: The toughness model. *Medicine and Science in Sports and Exercise, 23*, 846–852.

Druen, P. B. (1995). *Cumulative relationship experience and partner selection strategies: Associations and implications for relationship quality*. Unpublished doctoral dissertation. University of Louisville.

Duck, S., Rutt, D. S., Hurst, M. H., & Strejc, H. (1991). Some evident truth about conversation in everyday relationships: All communications are not created equal. *Human Communication Research, 18*, 228–267.

Eich, E. (1995). Searching for mood dependent memory. *Psychological Science, 6*, 67–75.

Ekman, P., & Friesen, W. V. (1986). A new pan-cultural facial expression of emotion. *Motivation and Emotion, 10*, 159–168

Erber, R. (1991). Affective and semantic priming: Effects of mood on category accessibility and inference. *Journal of Experimental Social Psychology, 27*, 480–498.

Eysenck, H. J., & Eysenck, S. B. G. (1968). *Manual for the Eysenck Personality Inventory*. San Diego: Educational and Industrial Testing Service.

Felmlee, D. (1995). Fatal attractions: Affection and disaffection in intimate relationships. *Journal of Social and Personal Relationships, 12*, 295–311.

Ferguson, T. J. & Rule, B.G. (1983). An attributional perspective on anger and aggression. In R. G. Geen & E. Donnerstein (Eds.), Aggression: *Theoretical and empirical reviews* (Vol 1: Theoretical and methodological issues, pp.41–74). New York: Academic Press.

Fincham, F. D., & Bradbury, T. N. (1990). *The psychology of marriage: Basic issues and applications*. New York: Guilford Press.

Fincham, F. D & Bradbury, T. N. (1992). Assessing attributions in marriage: The relationship attribution measure. *Journal of Personality and Social Psychology, 62*, 457–468.

Fisher, J. D., & Byrne, D. (1975). Too close for comfort: Sex differences in response to invasions of personal space. *Journal of Personality and Social Psychology, 32*, 15–21.

Forgas, J. P. (1995). Mood and judgment: The affect infusion model (AIM). *Psychological Bulletin, 117*, 39–66.

Gottman, J. M., & Krokoff, L. J. (1989). The relationship between marital interaction and marital satisfaction: A longitudinal view. *Journal of Consulting and Clinical Psychology, 57*, 47–52.

Haidt, J., McCauley, C., & Rozin, P. (1994). Individual differences in sensitivity to disgust: A scale sampling seven domains of disgust elicitors. *Personality and Individual Differences, 16*, 701–713.

Herbert, T. B., & Cohen, S. (1993). Depression and immunity: A meta-analytic review. *Psychological Bulletin, 113,* 472–486.

Heider, F. (1958). *The psychology of interpersonal relations.* New York: John Wiley & Sons.

Huesmann, L. R. (1988). An information processing model for the development of aggression. *Aggressive Behavior, 14,* 13–24.

Jones, E. E., & Davis, K.E. (1965). From acts to dispositions: The attribution process in person perception. In L. Berkowitz (Ed.), *Advances in experimental social psychology* (Vol. 2, pp. 219–266). New York: Academic Press.

Jones, E. E., & Wortman, C. (1973). *Ingratiation: An attributional approach.* Morristown, NJ: General Learning Press.

Jones, W. H., & Burdette, M. P. (1994). Betrayal in relationships. In A.L. Weber & J. H. Harvey (Eds.), *Perspectives on close relationships,*(pp. 243–262). Boston: Allyn and Bacon.

Kowalski, R. M. (1996). Complaints and complaining: Functions, antecedents and consequences. *Psychological Bulletin, 119,* 179–196.

Krokoff, L. J. (1991). Communication orientation as a moderator between strong negative affect and marital satisfaction. *Behavioral Assessment, 13,* 51–65.

Latané, B. (1981). The psychology of social impact. *American Psychologist, 36,* 343–356.

Lazarus, R.S. (1991). *Emotion and adaptation.* New York: Oxford University Press.

Linville, P. (1985). Self-complexity as a cognitive buffer against stress-related depression and illness. *Journal of Personality and Social Psychology, 42,* 193–211.

Lund, M. (1985). The development of investment and commitment: Scales for predicting continuity of personal relationships. *Journal of Social and Personal Relationships, 2,* 3–24.

Marshall, P. S. (1993). Allergy and depression: A neurochemical threshold model of the relation between the illnesses. *Psychological Bulletin, 113,* 23–43.

Mayer, J. D., Salovey, P., Gomberg-Kaufman, S., & Blainey, K. (1991). A broader conception of mood experience. *Journal of Personality and Social Psychology, 60,* 100–111.

McClelland, D. C. (1975). *Power: The inner experience.* New York: Irvington.

Megargee, E. I. (1970). Undercontrolled and overcontrolled personality types in extreme antisocial aggression. In E.I. Megargee & J.E. Hokanson (Eds.), *The dynamics of aggression* (pp. 108–120) New York: Harper & Row.

Nadler, A., & Fisher, J.D. (1986). The role of threat to self-esteem and perceived control in recipient reactions to help: Theory development and empirical validation. In L. Berkowitz (Ed.), *Advances in experimental social psychology* (Vol. 19, pp. 81–122) San Diego, CA: Academic Press.

Norem, J. K., & Cantor, N. (1986). Defensive pessimism: Harnessing anxiety as motivation. *Journal of Personality and Social Psychology, 51,* 1208–1217.

Palsson, M. B., & Norberg, A. (1995). District nurses' stories of difficult care episodes narrated during systematic clinical supervision sessions. *Scandinavian Journal of Caring Sciences, 9,* 17–27.

Pospisil, J., Cunningham, M. R., Barbee, A. P. & Druen, P. B. (1995, June). *Getting sick of other people: Personality and physical fitness in the development of social allergies.* Paper presented at the International Network of Personal Relationships, Williamsburg, VA.

Rosen, S., Mickler, S. E., & Collins, J. E. (1987). Reactions of would-be helpers whose offer of help is spurned. *Journal of Personality and Social Psychology, 53,* 288–297

Rosenbaum, M. E. (1986). The repulsion hypothesis. On the nondevelopment of relationships. *Journal of Personality and Social Psychology, 51,* 1156–1166.

Rosenblatt, P. C., & Cunningham, M. R. (1976). Television watching and family tension. *Journal of Marriage and the Family, 18,* 105–111.

Rosenblatt, P. C., & Russell, M. G. (1975). The social psychology of potential problems in family vacation travel. *Family Coordinator, 24,* 209–215.

Rosenblatt, P. C., Titus, S. L., & Cunningham, M. R. (1979). Disrespect, tension, and togetherness-apartness in marriage. *Journal of Marital and Family Therapy, 5*, 47–51.

Rosenblatt, P. C ., Titus, S. L., Nevaldine, A., & Cunningham, M. R. (1979). Marital system differences and summer-long vacations: Togetherness-apartness and tension. *American Journal of Family Therapy, 7*, 77–84.

Rowatt, W., & Cunningham, M. R. (1995, June). *Managing the impression of significant others: Other-monitoring theory and scale development*. Paper presented at the International Network of Personal Relationships, Williamsburg, VA.

Rozin, P. (1994). Varieties of disgust faces and the structure of disgust. *Journal of Personality and Social Psychology, 66*, 870–881.

Rozin, P., & Fallong, A. E. (1987). A perspective on disgust. *Psychological Review, 94*, 23–41.

Rozin, P., Markwith, M., & McCauley, C. (1994). Sensitivity to indirect contacts with other persons: AIDS aversion as a composite of aversion to strangers, infection, moral taint, and misfortune. *Journal of Abnormal Psychology, 103*, 495–505.

Rusbult, C. E. (1987). Responses to dissatisfaction in close relationships: The exit-voice-loyalty-neglect model. In D. Perlman & S. W. Duck (Eds.), *Intimate relationships* (pp. 209–237). London: Sage.

Rusbult, C. E., Verette, J., Whitney, G. A., Slovik, L. F., & Lipkus, I. (1991). Accommodation processes in close relationships: Theory and preliminary empirical evidence. *Journal of Personality and Social Psychology, 60*, 53–78.

Shea, B. C., & Pearson, J. C. (1986). The effects of relationship type, partner intent, and gender on the selection of relationship maintenance strategies. *Communication Monographs, 3*, 354–364.

Showers, C. (1992). The motivational and emotional consequences of considering positive or negative possibilities for an upcoming event. *Journal of Personality and Social Psychology, 63*, 474–485.

Smeaton, G., Byrne, D., & Murnen, S. K. (1989). The repulsion hypothesis revisited: Similarity irrelevance or dissimilarity bias? *Journal of Personality and Social Psychology, 56*, 70–80.

Stafford, L., & Canary, D. J. (1991). Maintenance strategies and romantic relationship type, gender and relational characteristics. *Journal of Social and Personal Relationships, 8*, 217–242.

Tesser, A. (1978). Self-generated attitude change. In L. Berkowitz (Ed.), *Advances in experimental social psychology* (Vol 11, pp. 296–338). New York: Academic Press.

Tesser, A. (1988). Toward a self-evaluation maintenance model of social behavior. In L. Berkowitz (Ed.), *Advances in experimental social psychology* (Vol 21, pp. 181–227). San Diego, CA: Academic Press.

Tice, D. M., Butler, J. L., Muraven, M. B., & Stillwell, A. M. (1995). When modesty prevails: Differential favorability of self-presentation to friends and strangers. *Journal of Personality and Social Psychology, 69*, 1120–1138.

Todrank, J., Byrnes, D., Wrzesniewski, A., & Rozin, P., (1995). Odors can change preferences for people in photographs: A cross-modal evaluative conditioning study with olfactory USs and visual CSs. *Learning and Motivation, 26*, 116–140.

Tolhuizen, J. H. (1989). Communication strategies for intensifying dating relationships: Identification, use and structure. *Journal of Social and Personal Relationships, 6*, 413–34.

Weber, A. L., & Harvey, J. H. (1994). Accounts in coping with relationship loss. In A. L. Weber & J. H. Harvey (Eds.), *Perspectives on close relationships* (pp. 285–306). Boston: Allyn and Bacon.

Weisse, C. S. (1992). Depression and immunocompetence: A review of the literature. *Psychological Bulletin, 111*, 475–489.

West, C. (1979). Against our will: Male interruptions of females in cross-sex conversation. *Annals of the New York Academy of Sciences, 327*, 81–97.

Wills, T. A. (1983). Social comparison in coping and help-seeking, In B.M. DePaulo, A. Nadler, & J.D. Fisher (Eds.), *New directions in helping: Help-seeking* (Vol 2, pp. 109–114). New York: Academic Press.

Zajonc, R. B. (1968) Attitudinal effects of mere exposure. *Journal of Personality and Social Psychology Monograph, 9*, (2, Part 2) 1–27.

Zajonc, R. B., Markus, H., & Wilson, W. R. (1974). Exposure effects and associative learning. *Journal of Experimental Social Psychology, 10*, 248–263.

CHAPTER 10

AVERSIVE INTERPERSONAL BEHAVIORS

AN OVERARCHING FRAMEWORK

ROBIN M. KOWALSKI

In 1993, James Redfield published the *Celestine Prophecy*, an intriguing book describing the nine insights of life as revealed in a fictitious Peruvian manuscript. As individuals uncover each of the insights in sequence, they learn that the physical world is a huge system of energy. However, because people do not know how to harvest that energy, they compete with other individuals for the energy that they can acquire directly from them. Thus, throughout history, human conflict has stemmed from competition for the energy that flows between individuals. By controlling another person, people can increase their own energy by "stealing" some of the other individual's energy. The method that people use to gather another's energy is referred to as a control drama and reflects patterns of behavior that were learned in childhood. Thus, some people control others by making them feel guilty. Others direct people by monopolizing conversations. Still others control people by ostracizing them and depriving them of valued interpersonal resources. So, aversive interpersonal behaviors, at least in part, reflect people's control dramas or the methods that they invoke to gather energy from others (Redfield, 1993).

ROBIN M. KOWALSKI • Department of Psychology, Western Carolina University, Cullowhee, North Carolina 28723. kowalski@wcuvax1.wcu.edu

Aversive Interpersonal Behaviors, edited by Kowalski
Plenum Press, New York, 1997

Although behavioral scientists might not agree with the metaphysical principles adopted by Redfield, few would disagree that (a) people frequently use aversive interpersonal behaviors to influence or control the behavior of others and that (b) they often feel empowered or "energized" as a function of having done so. Although the specific behavior adopted to influence a friend or relationship partner may vary across individuals or situations, all of the behaviors share elements in common.

WHAT MAKES BEHAVIORS AVERSIVE?

Most traditional discussions of aversiveness have focused on stimuli such as shock or food deprivation. The aversive behaviors discussed in this book, however, focus on symbolically mediated aversiveness. As with physically aversive stimuli, social behaviors are determined to be aversive when they either deprive people of valued outcomes or impose undesired outcomes. As will be discussed in the section that follows, aversive interpersonal behaviors interfere with basic psychological needs, such as people's need to belong. In addition, they set up social confrontation episodes that most people find disquieting. The social inappropriateness and ambiguity of many of the behaviors also renders them undesirable, at least from the perspective of the target of the behaviors.

INTERFERENCE WITH BASIC PSYCHOLOGICAL NEEDS

All of the aversive behaviors that have been discussed in this book interfere with certain basic psychological needs, including the need to belong, the need for control, and the need to maintain or enhance one's self-esteem.

Need to Belong

Virtually all of the aversive behaviors covered in this book (as well as many that were not specifically discussed such as teasing and bullying) threaten a person's need to belong. Baumeister and Leary (1995; see also Baumeister, 1991) suggested that the need to belong is a fundamental motivation underlying human behavior. According to their belongingness theory, individuals who are deprived of a sense of belongingness with others will experience a number of negative effects, including, in some instances, manifestations of psychopathology. However, the ill effects produced by threats to one's inclusionary status should motivate behavioral changes to reestablish desired social contacts.

To the degree that people's need to be included is a motivation behind human behavior, anything that interferes with the satisfaction of this need would clearly be aversive. The extent to which any particular behavior threatens an individual's need to belong depends not only on individual differences in people's need to be included but also on the behavior itself. Specifically, whereas some behaviors lead to complete exclusion by a group (i.e., ostracism, Williams, this volume), other aversive interpersonal behaviors result in only temporary or symbolic exclusion as when people feel left out of an inside joke being made at their expense (Leary, 1990). Indeed, even within a particular behavioral category, such as ostracism, different manifestations of the behavior have different levels of perceived aversiveness. For example, social and physical ostracism differ in their perceived aversiveness. As Williams (this volume) noted, "during social ostracism, one is continually reminded of being ignored."

Similarly, Leary, Bednarski, Hammon, and Duncan (this volume) suggested that one reason some individuals find egotism aversive is because their own social relationships seem to suffer by comparison. Sommer and Baumeister (this volume) included anxiety over social exclusion as one of the two affective roots of guilt. "Guilt may alert individuals to the potential exclusion by others with whom they have formed strong, emotional bonds."

Ironically, in spite of the fact that aversive interpersonal behaviors threaten the target's sense of belongingness, the perpetrator may actually be performing the behavior to enhance the belongingness between the individuals. "A major reason for inducing guilt is to cause one's partner to exert himself or herself more to maintain the interpersonal relationship....Many episodes of guilt can thus be understood as responses to disturbances or threats to interpersonal attachments" (Baumeister & Leary, 1995, p. 507; see also Vangelisti, Daly, & Rudnick, 1991). If threats to belongingness motivate people to change their behavior, then the relationship stands to benefit from the occasional use of aversive behaviors.

Aversive interpersonal behaviors not only threaten people's need to be included by others but, as an outcome of that, generate negative emotions in the target of the aversive behavior. Any number of different negative emotions may be precipitated, including anxiety, depression (including social depression), jealousy, loneliness, hostility, contempt, disgust, and boredom (Baumeister & Leary, 1995; Leary, 1990). According to Sommer and Baumeister (this volume), "even if guilt does not directly cause these other affective states, it should activate the possibility of these emotions in the event that the relationship is not restored to its previous status."

The relationship between aversive interpersonal behaviors and people's need to belong illustrates why people can so readily hurt the ones they love (Miller, this volume). The implications of exclusion by strangers are typically less serious than exclusion by friends and romantic partners. People have a vested interest in maintaining social contacts with those close to them. Knowing this, perpetrators of aversive interpersonal behaviors can wield a significant amount of power over another individual by potentially threatening the interaction partner's inclusionary status.

Need for Control

Aversive interpersonal behaviors also rob people of a sense of control over their social interactions and desired outcomes (Thompson, 1981; Williams, this volume). In general, people are fairly optimistic about what they can expect from others and from life. People's unrealistic optimism, however, often leads them to believe that they are less likely than most other people to experience adverse life circumstances or unpleasant interpersonal relationships (Taylor & Brown, 1988). When such circumstances do arise, then, people frequently react more negatively than had they adopted a more realistic perspective. For example, people expect certain things from relationships, including the smooth functioning of those relationships. When these expectations are violated as when someone disrupts the smooth flow of interactions, the other's behaviors are considered to be aversive. In other words, behaviors that are considered interpersonally aversive set in motion a series of disrupted interpersonal exchanges (Leary et al., this volume; Sharkey, this volume). Normal interactions become sidetracked and the target of the aversive interpersonal behavior is made to focus on saving face or altering the behavior that has been called into question. Interactions like these are labeled as problematic and defined as situations in which "interaction is disrupted, identities are threatened [and] people have intentions that run counter to others' wishes" (Stokes & Hewitt, 1976, p. 842; see also Newell & Stutman, 1991).

Need for Self-Esteem

Many of the behaviors in which people engage are performed with the intent of maintaining or enhancing self-esteem. Because of the salience of the self-esteem motive, people become apprehensive at the real or imagined possibility of receiving evaluations from others that threaten self-esteem, and they behave in ways that allow them to protect their self-esteem (Markus, 1980).

Aversive interpersonal behaviors are aversive, in part, because they threaten an individual's self-evaluation. When other people complain about our behavior, make us look worse by inflating their own presentations of themselves, or exclude us from valued social groups or activities, they challenge our view of ourselves as basically good, well-liked individuals.

Obviously, individual differences in one's level of self-esteem would moderate the degree to which people are distressed by others' negative evaluations of them. Targets of aversive interpersonal behaviors are being told that something about themselves is not good and should be changed. People who have high self-esteem will be more likely than those with low self-esteem to (a) perceive the information constructively without viewing it as a negative reflection on the self and (b) react in a manner that reflects the adaptive encoding of the aversive behavior (Campbell & Lavallee, 1993; Shrauger, 1975). While reacting less defensively to the aversive behavior, high self-esteem people might also be less inclined than low self-esteem people to alter the undesired behavior. Part of this reluctance may stem from the failure of high self-esteem people to recognize any problems with their behavior or from their self-serving attributional style that leads them to attribute any untoward behavior on their part to a momentary situational variable.

The degree to which any of the behaviors detailed in this volume would adversely influence self-esteem also depends on the salience of the behavior to the self (Tesser, 1988). For example, people who are egotistical on dimensions that are either irrelevant or unimportant to our own sense of self will pose little threat to our self-esteem. On the other hand, someone boasting about their accomplishments or virtues on dimensions that are highly relevant to the self will clearly have a more adverse effect on one's self-esteem.

SOCIAL CONFRONTATION

Many of the aversive interpersonal behaviors that have been discussed in this volume are aversive in part because they involve social confrontation and, thus, represent social confrontation episodes (Newell & Stutman, 1988; 1991). As defined by Newell and Stutman (1991), social confrontation episodes involve initiation, development, and closing. One individual confronts another over a behavior that he or she perceives to be problematic. Because most people would choose to avoid confrontations with other people, particularly ones that portray the self in a negative or undesired light, behaviors that initiate such encounters are perceived negatively.

Although any of a number of different methods may be used by a confronter to initiate the social confrontation episode, "in general, most initiating acts of social confrontation can be classified as complaints, as they express, directly or indirectly, dissatisfaction with the confrontee's behavior" (Newell & Stutman, 1991, p. 273). The response of the confrontee determines how the social confrontation episode will develop. If the individual being confronted about his or her behavior acknowledges that a transgression was made and the confronter accepts this, the confrontation episode closes. In many instances, however, the episode may continue as the person confronted either denies wrongdoing or the confronter fails to accept the response offered by the confrontee.

One aversive interpersonal behavior, ostracism, seemingly fails to fit the social confrontation model. As noted by Williams (this volume), "unlike other forms of aversive behaviors, ostracism involves a unilateral stance by one person (or group) over another. There is no give and take." However, social confrontation episodes involving ostracism are simply defined as "episodically incomplete" because closure never occurs, at least for the person being ostracized.

Inappropriateness

As described in the Planned Strategic Embarrassment Model (see Sharkey, this volume), behavioral plans of action revolve around efficiency and social appropriateness. Efficiency involves an individual's assessment of the time and effort involved in achieving a desired goal. Sometimes, however, the most efficient behavior may not be the most socially appropriate, introducing costs or dangers into the interpersonal equation. Any one of the aversive interpersonal behaviors discussed within this volume may be classified along the dimensions of efficiency and social appropriateness. The aversiveness of certain behaviors emerges from their social inappropriateness. For example, teasing and intentional embarrassment at a roast are expected and, therefore, contextually appropriate. Similar behaviors at a funeral would be considered very inappropriate.

An evaluation of the social appropriateness of any behavior will be determined by characteristics of both the interactants as well as the situation. "In the end what is considered an aversive form of interpersonal behavior will be implicitly and explicitly negotiated, within a specific context, between those involved in a relationship" (Sharkey, this volume).

Ambiguity

Many, if not most, aversive behaviors are ambiguous. From the target's perspective, the intentions and motivations underlying the behaviors are frequently unclear. From the perpetrator's viewpoint, creating an ambiguous presentation may be the safest mechanism to use in relaying negative feedback to the target or in pursuing other goals (Goffman, 1955; Taylor & Brown, 1988).

Ambiguous presentations are more important for some of the interpersonal behaviors than others. For example, ambiguity is a cornerstone of indirect aggression. Indeed, one reason that people elect to use indirect as opposed to direct aggression in confronting others is because indirect aggression has a higher probability of allowing the perpetrator to remain anonymous (Richardson & Green, this volume). Even when the perpetrator's identity is revealed, the intentions behind the behavior remain unclear. Similarly, "a key feature of ostracism is that it is inherently ambiguous...often not clear to the victim if it is occurring or why it is occurring" (Williams, this volume).

One of the features influencing the ambiguity of aversive interpersonal behaviors centers around the construal of the situation by the individuals involved. People approach interpersonal interactions with expectations regarding the other individuals and the course that the interaction will likely take. These expectations are influenced by individuals' prior histories with the other individuals present or with similar interpersonal encounters in the past. Particularly when there is a shared relationship history, each person will approach their interaction partner with a readiness to perceive certain behaviors from their partner—what Holmes and Murray (1996) refer to as a recognition threshold. In other words, people who expect undesired behaviors from their interaction partner will likely have a lower threshold for interpreting behaviors as aversive than individuals who typically expect favorable behaviors from others. Because of the differences in recognition thresholds of the interaction partners, "the given structure of situations may be much more ambiguous than is often assumed, permitting considerable license in individuals' construals of situational features" (Holmes & Murray, 1996, p. 628).

SUMMARY

Aversive interpersonal behaviors interfere with people's intrapsychic and interpersonal needs and goals. Specifically, they interfere with people's needs for belongingness, control, and self-esteem maintenance. Above and beyond this, however, behaviors are considered aversive when they create disruptive, awkward social interactions. Few people enjoy confrontational episodes, particularly when they are the confrontee. Not only do such confrontations impede smooth interpersonal interactions, but they create ambiguity in the confrontee's mind regarding the motivations of the perpetrator as well as how he or she should respond.

FUNCTIONS OF AVERSIVE BEHAVIORS

Given the risks associated with enacting the aversive interpersonal behaviors discussed in this book, clearly there must be some substantial rewards to be gained from them. From the perpetrator's perspective, aversive interpersonal behaviors may enhance the relationship, allow for increased control, enhance his or her self-esteem, provide a means of discrediting an interaction partner, or influence the perceptions of others.

Relationship Enhancement

Aversive interpersonal behaviors would be expected to produce only undesired social and relational consequences. What possible benefit could intentionally embarrassing another, ostracizing someone, or constantly griping about a friend to his or her face possibly have? Although no one could deny that people sometimes engage in aversive interpersonal behaviors with the full intention of hurting another person, sometimes these behaviors are performed to bring about positive changes in relationships. For example, in their discussion of jealousy, Leary and Miller (1986, p. 99) noted that "the fact that anyone would try to induce jealousy suggests that the experience of jealousy does not necessarily damage a relationship; because partners can 'prove their love' by becoming jealous, people sometimes find jealousy desirable" (see also Pines & Aronson, 1983). In this sense, any of the aversive social behaviors discussed could be viewed as social influence strategies.

Specifically, aversive interpersonal behaviors may be used to illustrate relationship solidarity. There are three ways in which behaviors may be used to accomplish this goal. First, as noted throughout this volume, aversive interpersonal behaviors may trigger excitement in the relationship and serve as a type of "relational play." As will be discussed later in this chapter, however, the degree to which behaviors, particularly aversive interpersonal behaviors, may be invoked and perceived as relational play varies with the nature of the relationship. Among people who perceive themselves to be close, teasing and intentional embarrassment may be perceived good-naturedly (Baxter, 1992). Indeed, Lutz (1982, cited in Baxter, 1992) found a positive correlation between playfulness in marriage and the level of reported intimacy between the partners.

Second, aversive interpersonal behaviors, such as teasing or intentional embarrassment, may be used to socialize people into the group. For example, among adolescent males, there is a male culture of teasing. Relative to girls, boys are far more likely to engage in merciless teasing of one another. When asked about this, most men will simply report that it is just a part of male socialization.

Third, for aversive behaviors to have their desired effects (whatever those effects might be), the target of the behavior must have some interest in maintaining a relationship with the partner. For example, few people would feel guilty despite another's best efforts if they care nothing for the other person or their relationship with that person. Thus, one way in which people can assess the commitment of their relationship partner is by engaging in aversive behaviors.

CONTROL

People frequently enact aversive interpersonal behaviors as a means of controlling or changing the annoying behaviors of another. By enacting an aversive interpersonal behavior such as guilt-induction, one is conveying to another dissatisfaction with his or her behavior. Assuming that the partner has some interest in maintaining the relationship, he or she will alter the offensive behavior or perform reparative behaviors as compensation for the annoyance.

By initiating an aversive interpersonal behavior, such as guilt-induction, people also gain considerable control over the ensuing interactional episode (Newell & Stutman, 1991). As the initiator of the interaction, the confronter automatically limits the behavioral response options of the individual confronted. The confrontee can either deny any wrongdoing, discount the legitimacy of the confronter's complaints, or engage in reparative behaviors. The confronter can then choose a counterresponse that best allows him or her to achieve desired outcomes. For example, he or she could refuse any reparative attempts by the individual confronted, thereby forcing that individual to continue in his or her attempts to save face. In this way, the confronter ultimately controls the behavior of his or her interaction partner and, therefore, regulates the entire interpersonal exchange.

DISCREDITING ANOTHER

One of the most salient features of all of the aversive interpersonal behaviors discussed is their relationship-enhancing function. Generally, people perform these behaviors with the intent of modifying the annoying behavior of another. However, there are also instances in which people enact aversive interpersonal behaviors with the intent of discrediting another person and making that individual feel bad. Because of feelings of anger or hurt, people may opt for aversive behaviors that will induce negative emotions in the interaction partner, thereby "redistributing emotional distress within the relationship" (Sommer & Baumeister, this volume).

Relatedly, aversive interpersonal behaviors may be used, perhaps more rarely, to get rid of undesired others. Although this is the express purpose of ostracism, other interpersonal behaviors may be enacted with this as the ultimate goal. The withdrawal of the target may be self-initiated or indirectly suggested by the behavior of others. Specifically, because of the undesired affective feelings often generated from being confronted, targets of aversive interpersonal behaviors may withdraw from social interactions that are continuously aversive. Similarly, many of us have encountered instances where we no longer wished another person to be around us, but felt compelled not to say anything untoward to that person. As opposed to stating our wishes directly, we behaved in ways that, while perhaps more hurtful, conveyed to the individual our desires for them to leave. As noted by Cunningham, Barbee, and Druen (this volume), "the capacity of people to develop social allergies can be used for interpersonal manipulation. That is, an individual who wishes another person to modify or leave the relationship might deliberately engage in allergenic behaviors to provoke the other person."

Self-Esteem Enhancement

The influence of aversive interpersonal behaviors on the target's self-esteem was discussed earlier. However, the self-esteem motive is also involved in the enactment of aversive interpersonal behaviors. Particularly among people who are insecure or who have experienced some recent blow to their self-esteem, making other people feel bad through the enactment of aversive interpersonal behaviors may be one way of bolstering a damaged self-concept (Amabile & Glazebrook, 1982; Hogg & Sunderland, 1991). In their discussion of defensive egotism, Leary et al. (this volume) note that in some instances egotism may be "a compensation or defense against a negative or fragile self-concept." Similarly, complaining about another's behavior, poking fun at another's attributes through intentional embarrassment, or inducing guilt in a friend are all ways in which a person could conceivably make themselves look or feel better by comparison with others (Wills, 1991).

Influencing the Perceptions of Others

Aversive interpersonal behaviors may be used to influence others' perceptions of the target in either a positive or a negative way. On the positive side, behaviors such as teasing and intentional embarrassment may be used to convey to others that the target of the tease is a friend and that he or she has a good sense of humor. The downside, however, is that the exact same behaviors may be used to convey to others that the target is incompetent, irresponsible, and annoying. In those instances where the perpetrator's goal was to exclude the individual from a group, influencing the perceptions of other group members would be important to goal attainment. Indeed, Richardson and Green (this volume) point out that indirect aggression is more effective with friends than relationship partners simply because of the social networks of which friends are a part. Specifically, rumors and gossip are more likely to spread through a group. In addition, rumors and gossip about one's relationship partner may ultimately backfire and reflect negatively on oneself.

Cost-Benefit Analysis

Despite their advantages, aversive interpersonal behaviors also carry various risks. Because of these risks, people who initiate behaviors that others might regard as interpersonally aversive often do a cost-benefit analysis or an assessment of the effect-danger ratio (Björkqvist, Österman, & Lagerspetz, 1994). In other words, people evaluate the rewards and costs (i.e., dangers) associated with each particular behavior. For example, to induce guilt in someone may provide valuable rewards in the form of changing the other person's behavior and, ultimately, improve the quality of the relationship. However, such benefits come at a cost. By inducing guilt in another, one risks hurting the other individual's feelings, setting up a defensive posture in the other person, or damaging the relationship. Thus, the effective use of any of the aversive interpersonal behaviors requires an ability on the part of the actor or perpetrator to forecast the probable reaction of another person to the behavior. As we will see later in the chapter, perceptions of the aversiveness of certain behaviors by perpetrators differs markedly from that of targets of the behavior.

In emotionally charged interpersonal encounters, the cost-benefit analysis stage is frequently bypassed. Strong emotion often overrides the cognitions, leading to aversive behaviors that are ultimately detrimental to the relationship.

VARIATIONS IN PERCEPTIONS

As discussed in Cunningham et al.'s chapter on social allergens, people have different tolerances for the seemingly annoying behaviors of others. What one person views as annoying another may perceive to be endearing. Differences in perceptions of the aversiveness of interpersonal behaviors can be examined in terms of relationship variations, cross-cultural variations, individual differences, and the perceptual differences of victims and perpetrators.

Relationship Variations

Relationships obviously vary along a number of dimensions. At minimum, relationships can be differentiated from one another based on the degree of closeness or intimacy that characterizes the relationship. The closeness that characterizes a relationship influences the degree to which people engage in the behaviors discussed in this book, the motivations underlying the behaviors, and the emotional impact of the behaviors on the target as well as the perpetrator. Thus, people are more likely to engage in aversive interpersonal behaviors with those that they have known for an extended period of time and to whom they are close (i.e., good friend, romantic partner). For example, because of our increased knowledge base, it is much easier to embarrass or tease people that we know well as compared to those we know little about (Sharkey, this volume), a phenomenon referred to by Miller (this volume) as access to weaponry. Similarly, one's effectiveness at inducing guilt is dependent largely on one's relationship with the target. The closer one's relationship with the target, the more guilt the target is likely to feel (Sommer & Baumeister, this volume).

According to Berscheid's (1983) theory of emotion in interpersonal relationships, it is this degree of closeness that determines the extent to which others influence our emotional state. Specifically, Berscheid argued that people's behavior typically proceeds according to action sequences. The closer one is to another person, the more enmeshed the individuals' action sequences will be, suggesting that each person has increasing power to interrupt the action sequence of the other. Interruptions in one' s action sequences trigger physiological arousal that instigates searches for the cause of the arousal. Interruptions that interfere with an individual's action plan will be viewed negatively and stimulate negative emotions. Interruptions that undo previous interruptions or over which one has control tend to elicit positive emotions (Clark & Bennett, 1992). All of this would contribute to our understanding of why we hurt the ones we love (Miller, this volume).

The influence of aversive interpersonal behaviors on a relationship and, indeed, the perception of the behaviors as aversive at all, varies as a function of the current affective state of the relationship (Cunningham et al., this volume). Because of the ambiguity inherent in aversive interpersonal behaviors, they can be coded by the target as either positively or negatively valenced. Individuals in distressed relationships will be less likely than partners in harmonious relationships to give their relational partner the benefit of the doubt. Thus, they will be more inclined to encode the behavior as negatively valenced.

In addition to the overall affective evaluation of another's behavior, the affective state of the relationship may also influence the attributions that are made for others' behavior. This would apply to both the victim and the perpetrator. People's attributions for their partner's behavior are one distinguishing characteristic of distressed and nondistressed couples

(Bradbury & Fincham, 1990). Specifically, partners in distressed couples attribute positive behaviors of their spouse to specific, unstable, and uncontrollable factors (Clark & Bennett, 1992; Fincham, 1985; Fincham & O'Leary, 1983; Holmes & Murray, 1996). Positive behaviors are viewed as influenced by ulterior motives. For example, a positive gesture by one spouse might be interpreted by the other as an attempt to induce guilt or to get some desired outcome. Satisfied couples, on the other hand, give each other credit for positive behaviors and excuse negative behaviors (Leary & Miller, 1986).

Cross-Cultural Variations

Cultures can be differentiated into those that are predominantly individualistic and those that are primarily collectivist. Collectivist cultures emphasize unity and interdependence whereas individualistic cultures focus on the individual and his or her independence from others. Many of the relationships of which people are a part in collectivist cultures are dictated by family and, thus, permanent (Phinney & Cobb, 1996). The majority of relationships in individualistic cultures, however, persist only as long as they are mutually satisfying to the people involved. Thus, relationships are more tenuous and vulnerable to dissolution in individualistic cultures relative to collectivist cultures. Members of individualistic cultures view the self as distinct from and better than others. On the other hand, individuals from collectivist cultures perceive themselves more modestly (Triandis, 1994).

The nature of relationships also differs between the two types of cultures. For example, people in collectivist cultures have difficulty establishing friendships and relationships initially but, once established, those relationships are characterized by considerable intimacy. By contrast, relationships among people in individualistic cultures are formed easily, but often exist at only a superficial level. Perhaps because of this different relationship focus, members of collectivist cultures more readily engage in mutual face-saving than people in individualistic cultures (Sharkey, this volume). Because of this, they should be less likely to engage in aversive interpersonal behaviors and more likely to help the target of such behaviors save face in the event that they did invoke such aversive exchanges (Triandis, 1994).

The role of cultural type on the enactment of aversive interpersonal behaviors was discussed by Leary et al. (this volume). Exaggerated self-presentations, while consistent with individualistic cultures, would be unlikely to be tolerated in collectivist cultures. Similarly, in a comparison of collectivist and individualistic cultures, Triandis (1994) noted that, whereas a major calamity for people living in individualistic cultures is dependence on others, a similarly harmful calamity in collectivist cultures is ostracism. In general, then, aversive behaviors as discussed in this volume would be less likely in collectivist cultures than individualistic cultures. Because of the partially self-serving nature of aversive interpersonal behaviors, they are more likely to match the needs and goals of individual's living in independent as opposed to interdependent cultures.

INDIVIDUAL DIFFERENCES

People differ in their perceptions of the aversiveness of particular interpersonal behaviors. Part of this individual variation may stem from differences in susceptibility to the development of social allergens (Cunningham et al., this volume). In other words, just as some people are more likely to develop physical allergies, so some individuals have little tolerance for the development of social allergies.

Individual variation in perceptions of behavioral aversiveness may stem from individual differences in the attributions that people make for others' behavior (Layden, 1982). People who have a tendency to attribute others' behavior to characterological features of that person will likely perceive behaviors as more aversive than people who typically give others the benefit of the doubt.

The self-relevant implications of a behavior should also influence perceptions of its aversiveness. Behaviors that challenge central aspects of the self-concept or that jeopardize valued relationships should be evaluated more negatively than those that focus on behaviors or attributes that are not central to the self. As noted by Duck (1994, p. 18), "items from others' behavior which are likely to be interpreted and treated as significant are those that have personal meaning to the perceiver, or have meaning to the person within the relationship."

Finally, basic personality differences between people will account for some of the variation observed in people's perceptions of behavior. Although it is beyond the point of this chapter to discuss every individual difference variable thought to influence the perception of behaviors as aversive, two deserve mention. Sommer and Baumeister (this volume) list empathy as one of the affective roots of guilt. Thus, people who are higher in empathy should be more likely to view guilt-induction as aversive relative to those who are low in empathy. As a result, people high in empathy may be less inclined to enact behaviors that hurt or distress others.

Individuals who are higher in negative affectivity will also be more likely to perceive ostracism, complaining, guilt-induction, or any of the other behaviors as aversive. Many of the negative mood states experienced as a result of the experience of aversive interpersonal behaviors are commonly experienced by individuals high in negative affectivity. In addition, people with a dispositional tendency to experience negative affect impute more negative meaning to ambiguous stimuli than people low in negative affectivity and demonstrate a higher tendency to perceive themselves as victims (Clark & Watson, 1991; Crocker, Alloy, & Kayne, 1988).

People who are high in negative affectivity not surprisingly generate many aversive interpersonal behaviors of their own. Therefore, they are likely targets to be ostracized, complained about, or intentionally embarrassed. Unlike people low in negative affectivity, high negative affect individuals will be less likely to recognize their own role in precipitating aversive interpersonal behaviors from others. They will also be less willing to recognize the adaptive intentions of others who are trying to modify their behavior.

Victims and Perpetrators

To hear victims describe an incident in which they were wronged by the perpetrator, one would think that a truly horrible event had transpired. To watch the expression of the perpetrator during this same telling suggests that he or she does not even recognize the incident as the one that transpired with the victim. As implied by their label, victims feel victimized. They feel as if they or their rights have somehow been violated. They typically perceive the event as much more severe than the perpetrator. Perpetrators, on the other hand, are frequently unaware that they have done anything wrong, and they will often react defensively at the very suggestion that they have done something untoward.

Because of the interactive nature of interpersonal exchanges, who is the victim and who is the perpetrator in an interaction is sometimes difficult to identify and is determined, in part, by the method of social confrontation initiation selected by the confronter. According to Newell and Stutman (1991), confronters may elect to focus on either the problematic behavior or their own emotional reaction to the behavior. In those instances in which the confronter focuses on the behavior, he or she would typically be perceived as the perpetrator of the aversive confrontation and the confrontee would be assigned the role of the victim. However, should the confronter decide to focus on his or her emotional reaction to the confrontee's behavior, then the confronter himself or herself assumes the role of the victim and the confrontee the role of the transgressor or wrongdoer.

Regardless of who assumes which role (i.e., victim or transgressor), differences in the perceptions of victims and perpetrators reflect clear actor/observer biases (Nisbett, Caputo, Legant, & Maracek, 1973). People who are the targets or victims of aversive interpersonal behaviors are much more likely than the behavioral perpetrators to perceive that the aversive behavior was intentional and motivated by some self-serving characterological attribute of the perpetrator (Sharkey, this volume). Perpetrators, on the other hand, view their behavior more positively. When questioned about their motives, they report justifiable attempts to sanction the target's behavior with the ultimate goal of improving the quality of the relationship (Baumeister, Stillwell, & Wotman, 1990).

Illustrating these points, Baumeister et al.(1990) examined autobiographical accounts of episodes in which people were angered (i.e., victim) or in which they angered another (i.e., perpetrator). They found marked differences in the narratives as a function of the writer's status as a victim or a perpetrator. Specifically, perpetrators saw the behavior as meaningful whereas victims found the behavior meaningless and incomprehensible. Relative to perpetrators who perceived the angry episode as an isolated event that was atypical for his or her behavior, victims perceived the behavior as having a longer time frame and as part of an ongoing pattern of behavior

Of course, in the grand scheme of things, what is most important in terms of the long-term functioning of the relationship is how the behavior is perceived by the target when examined in the context of the entire relationship (Holmes & Murray, 1996). As noted by Sharkey (this volume) in his discussion of the reactions of victims and perpetrators to intentional embarrassment, "It is not the embarrassor's positive or negative perception or intention of their goals that lead to various consequences for targets but the targets' perceptions of the embarrassor's goals."

Although people may make negative attributions about another on the basis of a single enactment of an aversive interpersonal behavior, the negativity and confidence of their attributions will increase with repeated episodes of the behavior (Cunningham et al., this volume). However, the attributions made by the victim and the perpetrator make this situation very problematic. Unlike the victim, the perpetrator is unaware of the aversiveness of his or her own behavior because he or she is, typically, not intentionally performing the aversive behavior or, at the very least, not performing the behavior with malevolent intentions. Thus, he or she will likely repeat the aversive behavior unwittingly.

CONCLUSIONS

Based on the interactional schema and inclinations of an individual, any behavior, whether performed by a friend or a romantic partner, could be considered an aversive interpersonal behavior. As a function of situational and dispositional variables, good-natured teasing could be perceived as intentional malice (Feinberg, 1996; Pawluk, 1989). Hateful remarks intended to hurt a romantic partner may be interpreted by that partner as humorous sarcasm.

As people approach interactions with others, particularly close others, they bring to those interpersonal exchanges their own expectations, relational baggage, and unmet needs. To the degree that another person's behaviors measure up to one's expectations, rarely remind one of previously annoying behaviors of other interaction partners, and satisfy one's needs, those behaviors will seldom be perceived as aversive. Because interaction partners are not mind readers, however, it is likely that, with repeated interactions, another person's behaviors will start to grate on the nerves. People's expectations are typically too high for most others to reach all of the time. Others are often not privy to the relational baggage that people bring to relationships and, therefore, are unaware of what may set another person off. Finally, no one person can meet all of the needs of another.

Although seldom investigated, changes in people's perceptions of an interactional partner's behavior over time merit research attention. Behaviors that were initially perceived to be neutral or even endearing gradually erode away at one's patience and may, with time, precipitate the development of social allergies. Where people once gave the benefit of the doubt to their partner when he or she behaved inappropriately, now they consistently make dispositional attributions for any misstep on the part of the other.

As pointed out throughout this book, however, the picture of aversive interpersonal behaviors that has been painted is not entirely dark. Rather, people may choose to engage in aversive interpersonal behaviors as a means of stopping another's annoying behaviors and improving relationship solidarity. Taking into account both the positive and negative motivations that may underlie these behaviors, the favorable and unfavorable ways in which these behaviors may be perceived, and the contextual features that influence both motivation and perception, perhaps the best way to view aversive interpersonal behaviors is along a constructive-destructive continuum. Used appropriately, aversive interpersonal behaviors have the potential to improve relationships. Like anything used too frequently or inappropriately, aversive interpersonal behaviors can easily become destructive to relationship functioning.

REFERENCES

Amabile, T. M., & Glazebrook, A. H. (1982). A negativity bias in interpersonal evaluation. *Journal of Experimental Social Psychology, 18,* 1–22.

Baumeister, R. F. (1991). *Meanings of life*. New York: Guilford.

Baumeister, R. F., & Leary, M. R. (1995). The need to belong: Desire for interpersonal attachments as a fundamental human motivation. *Psychological Bulletin, 117*, 497–529.

Baumeister, R. F., Stillwell, A., & Wotman, S. R. (1990). Victim and perpetrator accounts of interpersonal conflict: Autobiographical narratives about anger. *Journal of Personality and Social Psychology, 59*, 994–1005.

Baxter, L. A. (1992). Forms and functions of intimate play in personal relationships. *Human Communication Research, 18*, 336–363.

Berscheid, E. (1983). Emotion. In H. H. Kelley, E. Berscheid, A. Christensen, J. H. Harvey, T. L. Huston, G. Levinger, E. McClintock, L. A. Peplau, & D. R. Peterson (Eds.), *Close relationships* (pp. 110–168). New York: Freeman.

Björkqvist, K., Österman, K., & Lagerspetz, K. (1994). Sex differences in covert aggression among adults. *Aggressive Behavior, 20*, 27–34.

Bradbury, R. N., & Fincham, F. D. (1990). Attributions in marriage: Review and critique. *Psychological Bulletin, 107*, 3–33.

Campbell, J. D., & Lavallee, L. F. (1993). Who am I? The role of self-concept confusion in understanding the behavior of people with low self-esteem. In R. F. Baumeister (Ed.), *Self-esteem: The puzzle of low self-regard* (pp. 3–20). New York: Plenum.

Clark, L. A., & Watson, D. (1991). General affective dispositions in physical and psychological health. In C. R. Snyder & D. R. Forsyth (Eds.), *Handbook of social and clinical psychology* (pp. 221–245). New York: Pergamon.

Clark, M. S., & Bennett, M. E. (1992). Research on relationships: Implications for mental health. In D. N. Ruble, P. R. Costanzo, & Oliveri, M. E. (Eds.), *The social psychology of mental health* (pp. 166–198). New York: Guilford.

Crocker, J., Alloy, L. B., & Kayne, N. T. (1988). Attributional style, depression, and perceptions of consensus for events. *Journal of Personality and Social Psychology, 54*, 840–846.

Duck, S. (1994). Shades of darkness in interpersonal relations. In W. R. Cupach & B. H. Spitzberg (Eds.), *The dark side of interpersonal communication* (pp. 3–24). Hillsdale, NJ: Lawrence Erlbaum.

Feinberg, L. S. (1996). *Teasing: Innocent fun or sadistic malice?* Far Hills, NJ: New Horizon Press.

Fincham, F. D. (1985). Attribution processes in distressed and nondistressed couples: 2. Responsibility for marital problems. *Journal of Abnormal Psychology, 94*, 183–190.

Fincham, F. D., & O'Leary, K. D. (1983). Causal inferences for spouse behavior in maritally distressed and nondistressed couples. *Journal of Social and Clinical Psychology, 1*, 42–57.

Goffman, E. (1955). On face-work: An analysis of ritual elements in social interaction. *Psychiatry: Journal for the Study of Interpersonal Processes, 18*, 213–231.

Hogg, M. A., & Sunderland, J. (1991). Self-esteem and intergroup discrimination in the minimal group paradigm. *British Journal of Social Psychology, 30*, 51–62.

Holmes, J. G., & Murray, S. L. (1996). Conflict in close relationships. In E. T. Higgins & A. W. Kruglanski (Eds.), *Social psychology: Handbook of basic principles* (pp. 622–654). New York: Guilford.

Layden, M. A. (1982). Attributional style therapy. In C. Antaki & C. Brewin (Eds.), *Attributions and psychological change: Applications of attributional theories to clinical and educational practice* (pp. 63–82). New York: Academic Press.

Leary, M. R. (1990). Responses to social exclusion: Social anxiety, jealousy, loneliness, depression, and low self-esteem. *Journal of Social and Clinical Psychology, 9*, 221–229.

Leary, M. R., & Miller, R. S. (1986). *Social psychology and dysfunctional behavior*. New York: Springer-Verlag.

Markus, H. (1980). The self in thought and memory. In D. M. Wegner & R. R. Vallacher (Eds.), *The self in social psychology*. New York: Oxford University Press.

Newell, S. E., & Stutman, R. K. (1988). The social confrontation episode. *Communication Monographs, 55,* 266–285.

Newell, S. E., & Stutman, R. K. (1991). The episodic nature of social confrontation. In J. A. Anderson (Ed.), *Communication Yearbook 14* (pp. 359–392). Newbury Park, CA: Sage.

Nisbett, R. E., Caputo, C., Legant, P., & Maracek, J. (1973). Behavior as seen by the actor and as seen by the observer. *Journal of Personality and Social Psychology, 27,* 154–165.

Pawluk, J. (1989). Social construction of teasing. *Journal for the Theory of Social Behavior, 19,* 145–167.

Phinney, J., & Cobb, N. (1996). Reasoning about intergroup relations among Hispanic and Euro-American adolescents. *Journal of Adolescent Research, 11,*306–324.

Pines, A., & Aronson, E. (1983). Antecedents, correlates, and consequences of sexual jealousy. *Journal of Personality, 51,* 108–136.

Redfield, J. (1993). *The celestine prophecy.* New York: Warner Books.

Shrauger, J. S. (1975). Responses to evaluation as a function of initial self-perceptions. *Psychological Bulletin, 82,* 581–596.

Stokes, R., & Hewitt, J. P. (1976). Aligning actions. *American Sociological Review, 41,* 838–849.

Taylor, S. E., & Brown, J. D. (1988). Illusion and well-being: A social psychological perspective on mental health. *Psychological Bulletin, 103,* 193–210.

Tesser, A. (1988). Toward a self-evaluation maintenance model of social behavior. *Advances in Experimental Social Psychology, 21,* 181–227.

Thompson, S. C. (1981). Will it hurt less if I can control it? A complex answer to a simple question. *Psychological Bulletin, 90,* 89–101.

Triandis, H. C. (1994). *Culture and social behavior.* New York: McGraw-Hill.

Vangelisti, A. L., Daly, J. A., & Rudnick, J. R. (1991). Making people feel guilty in conversations: Techniques and correlates. *Human Communication Research, 18,* 3–39.

Wills, T. A. (1991). Social comparison processes in coping and health. In C. R. Snyder & D. R. Forsyth (Eds.), *Handbook of social and clinical psychology* (pp. 376–394). New York: Pergamon.

AUTHOR INDEX

SUBJECT INDEX